Christmas 1986.

To Jacqui
& all my ♡

Ian

# Pick of PUNCH

*"No – stupid boy! Exclamation mark! Doesn't that pratt
Bairnswater teach you anything?"*

# Pick of
# PU

*"God knows where your father is – still playing with that new four-wheel drive thing of his, I expect."*

# Edited by ALAN COREN

**A PUNCH BOOK**

Published in association with

**GRAFTON BOOKS**

A Division of the Collins Publishing Group

LONDON GLASGOW
TORONTO SYDNEY AUCKLAND

*"Actually, this place is too big for me. I'm moving into an individual mince-pie next week."*

Grafton Books
A Division of the Collins Publishing Group
8 Grafton Street, London W1X 3LA

Published by Grafton Books 1986

*British Library Cataloguing in Publication Data*

Pick of Punch.
1. English wit and humour
I. Coren, Alan   II. Punch
827′.914′08     PN6175

ISBN 0-246-13056-3

Printed in Great Britain by
William Collins Sons & Co. Ltd, Glasgow

# CONTENTS

# Alan Coren

# MAN-EATING BATSMEN OF DEATH-RAY ISLAND

*A Full Length Yuletide Yarn*

"**N**ative war canoes coming this way?" cried Flight Sergeant "Footy" Boote VC, two-fisted ginger-mopped Headmaster of The School That Would Not Die. "Are you sure?"

In answer, Beaky Finkel, madcap tailor of the Remove, whipped out the hundred-inch refracting telescope he had made just that morning from two old cocoa-tins and a broken ping-pong bat, and put it to his eye.

"Yes, skipper, it's a dusky band all right," he retorted, shinning rapidly down the yucca tree again, "and what's more, they've got Johnny Dodds on clarinet! Of course, it might just be a devilish Hun trick!"

His plucky Headmaster considered this for a moment, cocking an ear for the insistent beat of distant drums echoing across The Lagoon They Could Not Smell.

"*King Porter Stomp*," he mused aloud. "Do you know, Beaky, I think you may be spot on. I happen to know that Obersturmbanngruppenführer Hermann "Spotty" Knackwurst, the Nazi That Time Forgot, went missing not twenty miles from here while trying to snare The Giant Squid Of Atlantis, which his fiendish bosses back in Berlin planned to clone in the laboratories of kindly old Professor Mondieu, whose lovely young daughter was being held to ransom by The Panzers Of The Damned. Tall and blonde, too, I hasten to add."

"Hum! Sho' sound like dat ole Nazi up to his tricks again! Only one name fo' a man messin' aroun' wid a tall blonde squid!"

The speaker was none other than Prince Nbing Nbong, known as Shine to his chums in the Remedial Shell, who had hurtled faithfully up on his trusty monocycle at the first inkling of trouble, and was now wrinkling his dusky brow,

as was his native wont. How they all chuckled! Footy Boote clapped him on the back so smartly that the multi-millionaire paramount chief's enormous eyes rolled around in his gleaming ebony head like marbles in a saucer!

"God bless my soul, Shine," he cried, "what a jolly old black scallywag you are! It was the *daughter* who was tall and blonde, ha-ha-ha!"

"Ha-ha-ha!" shrieked The School That Would Not Die dutifully, rolling around among the coconuts, and trying to imagine how jolly rotten it must be to be a tall blonde daughter with your skirt ripped to the thigh and buttons bursting off your blouse while beastly Boche tank commanders tried to get you to play doctors and nurses with them.

"The Giant Squid, on the other hand," continued Footy Boote, drawing reflectively on The Trusty Briar From Outer Space, "was an extremely unsavoury cove – Johnny Hun planned to make a thousand of them, you know, and parachute them all over the Home Counties, prior to the invasion. Can you imagine what havoc they would have wrought, and not just on the County Cricket Championship?" His bright carrot-red hair grew serious for a moment. "Can any of us say for sure how he would have reacted if he had found a Giant Squid doing things to his sister?"

"I should have run the pair of them through!" cried Corky Lino, The Centre Half With The Dynamite Studs.

"Well said, Corky!" bellowed his trusty Head. "Best be on the safe side, eh?"

The chaps all nodded. Sage old Footy Boote VC! He had his head screwed on all right, for a beak. It was common sense like his that had seen

them through all the hair-raising escapades that had befallen them ever since the ship taking them to New Zealand for their annual rugger fixture had been torpedoed by the devilish Japs and they had been luckily plucked out of the ocean by albatrosses and deposited here on The Island From One Million BC, miles from the trade routes, where dinosaurs, because of a unique medicinal fern, still roamed, laying the eggs with which The School That Would Not Die was able to supplement the diet of roots and berries they had been able to identify from *Ye Booke of South Sea Rootes and Berrys* that Buggy Bolsover had found mysteriously wrapped in a yellow oilskin pouch inside the hollow tree he had been using to practise ventriloquism in case cannibals turned up and needed to be scared off by talking shrubs.

It was Buggy who stood up now, as the drums throbbed ever closer.

"Do you think I should get inside the tree, skipper?" he enquired. "We ought to be ready when the war canoes hit the beach!"

In answer, Footy slapped him on the shoulder with such force that Buggy's startled exclamation appeared to come from a boulder two hundred yards away, fortunately thwarting a column of giant ants who had, unbeknownst to the chaps, been bearing down on them with a view to stripping their bones bare in seconds!

"Lord bless you, no, Buggy!" cried the cheery Head. "I have no intention of letting our chum Johnny Man-Eater ever reach the beach! I intend borrowing Desmond d'Arcy's monocle and focussing the sun's rays on the canoes so that the tinder-dry animal skins catch fire and sink, precipitating our dusky adversaries into the shark-infested waters!"

"But isn't that just what they'll be expecting, sir?" enquired Lawrence "Tiny" Featherstonehaugh, The Fat Boy With Surprising Agility For One So Large.

"That's a chance we'll just have to take!" riposted Flight Sergeant Boote, raising his aquiline nose and sniffing expertly. "Fortunately, the wind has just changed in our favour!"

The chaps all nodded. Sage old Footy Boote VC! He had his beak screwed on all right, for a head.

Desmond d'Arcy, however, took leave to demur.

"It'll take more than my old monocle, sir," opined that worthy. "Those canoes must be two miles off. I rather doubt that we can focus the sun's rays effectively over that distance."

Beaky Finkel, madcap tailor of the Remove, who had been sketching some rapid equations in the dust with a sharp stick, now looked up.

"It's perfectly possible, chaps," he said, quietly. "It's all a question of physics."

The School That Would Not Die gazed at him in admiration.

"Go on, Beaky," muttered Footy, through clenched teeth.

"Basically," explained the wily Levantine, "I shall need sixty-three cocoa-tins."

"Then there's no time to be lost!" roared the Head. "Scour the island, you chaps!"

As one man, the plucky lads leapt up and plunged into the scrub, heedless of the poisonous giant thorns stabbing at their sinewy limbs, which – thanks to an antidote made from giant jellyfish that "Stinks" Cholmondeley-Cholmondeley, The Masked Chemist Who Rode With The Quorn, had accidentally stumbled upon while diving for The Lost Hoard Of Captain Blood – were now not only immune to the deadly barbs, but incredibly strengthened, enabling all of them to run the hundred yards in under five seconds, a skill which, regular readers will recall, had stood them in particularly good stead The Night The Saucer Landed.

Nevertheless, a good ten minutes had passed before they reassembled, dropping their gathered cocoa-tins at the feet of Beaky Finkel.

"Well done!" cried Footy Boote VC. "I'd been rather dreading the news that they had all been trampled by dinosaurs. He's a delicate thing, your Johnny Cocoa-Tin!"

"Right first time, skipper!" retorted Corky Lino. "We *did* find that a number *had* been flattened, but, as luck would have it, Shine here stumbled into an old disused elephant trap, and what do you suppose was at the bottom of it?"

"Shine, at a guess!" cried Footy Boote, quick as a flash.

How they all chortled, not least the big darkie, despite the two broken legs, which, in a white man, might have been very serious, but which, because of the many years of dancing, were in Prince Nbing Nbong's case so strongly reinforced by muscle that he felt no more pain than if he had fallen on his massively boned head.

"Yassum, baas, dat sho' true, ah *was* at de bottom ob de hole," laughed the latter, "but dat weren't de only ting down dere. What ah foun' wuz de remains of a Fust Worl' War zeppelin, shot down by curare-tipped pyggermy arrows

while ferryin' a cargo o' tinned cocoa to a German climbin' team trapped by lava unexpectedly whizzin' f'om de mouf o' De Volcano Dat Nobody Noo!"

"Good work, Shine!" cried Footy Boote VC. "Now, off you go, and wrap some incredibly restorative gully-gully leaves around those legs of yours, you'll be going in third wicket down after we've seen your coon cousins off, and if there's no fancy work off the front foot, I shall be down on you like the proverbial ton of bricks!"

Thus congratulated by the fellow he loved most in all the world, the sheepishly grinning giant loped happily away, while the rest of the chaps gathered around Beaky Finkel, whose dextrous ring-spanners, cunningly fashioned from a triceratops rib-cage, were already flashing among the cocoa-tins, faster than the eye could follow!

Five minutes and some pretty swift hammering later, the madcap tailor's masterpiece stood revealed. A great gasp went up from the assembled chums!

"I say, Beaky, old sport," cried Corky Lino, voicing everyone's unspoken thoughts, "what on earth *is* that extraordinary contraption?"

It was Beaky's turn to chuckle.

"It may be just an extraordinary contraption to you," he said, "but to me it's sixty-three cocoa-tins with d'Arcy's monocle wedged in the end."

Footy Boote pursed his lips and let out a low whistle.

"I call it," said Beaky, "my Death Ray!"

In the ensuing silence, you could have heard the proverbial pin drop!

"Wow!" called Prince Nbing Nbong, from his little compound, "Man hab bin lookin' fo' de secret ob de Def Ray since de beginnin' ob time."

"But it took Beaky here to find it!" exclaimed the Head. "What a dashed clever race they are, albeit a trifle short in the slow left-arm spin department. What say we take it down to the beach, chaps, and give our visitors the shock of their jolly old lives?"

The boys needed no second bidding. With great whoops, they sped through the scrub on sturdy limbs, bearing the precious death ray on their tanned shoulders, and did not stop until their pounding feet met the bone-white sand.

Where they suddenly fetched up, their eyes on stalks, their mouths agape!

"Curses!" cried Footy Boote. "There's one thing we reckoned without!"

"You mean——?" muttered an anguished Corky.

"Exactly!" retorted the plucky Head, smiting himself on the brow and silently cursing himself for a fool. "The Tidal Wave That Came From Nowhere!"

For, while they had been busy at their various tasks, they had not realised quite how rapidly the native canoes had sped shorewards! Even now, the howling Hottentots were hurtling up the beach towards them, shrunken skulls rattling at their skimpily clad waists, their sinewy hands brandishing the murderous cricket bats retrieved from the wreck of HMS Spofforth after that fine ship had struck a Japanese mine

while bound for Guadalcanal with The Team That Would Go Anywhere For A Game!

"I'm afraid my death ray is no use at this range, skipper!" cried Beaky Finkel.

"And even if it were," muttered Footy Boote, knotting his muscles and preparing to sell himself dearly with several clean uppercuts of his own design, "I fear it would be no match for honest British willow!"

Whereupon, setting jaws and gritting teeth, The School That Would Not Die formed, as their plucky ancestors had done, a square, and got ready to go down fighting!

And then, suddenly, without any warning, the sky became absolutely pitch-black! As one animal, the gleaming savages came to a confused stop, muttering and mumbling, until all that the brave lads could see in the inky gloom was eyeballs and teeth!

"What the——?" hissed Corky Lino.

"Just hold on!" hissed Flight Sergeant Footy Boote VC. "For, unless I am very much mistaken——"

He was not. A split-second later, the queer tropical darkness was suddenly lit by eerie flashes of light that hissed and crackled in the very air above the beach, to be followed by what seemed to be glowing footballs bouncing astonishingly from tree to tree!

"Just as I thought!" thundered Footy Boote. "It is a combination of a total eclipse of the sun with an unprecedented display of St. Elmo's Fire! I knew, of course, that such a coincidence occurs roughly every eighteen thousand years, but it had quite slipped my mind that today was the day!"

His words had risen to a bellow to make them audible above the penetrating shrieks of the terrified savages! For those fellows were certainly not staying around, succulent white dinner or no succulent white dinner! By the time the eclipse had passed, their panic-stricken canoes were no more than paddling dots on the brightening horizon!

"Gosh," exclaimed Beaky, "that was a pretty close shave, eh, sir?"

Footy Boote plucked a still glowing ember from a lightning-struck tree, and lit his pipe with a steady hand.

"A great Englishman once had a word for it, Beaky," he murmured, blowing a smoke ring and calmly watching it dissolve in the clear afternoon air. "He, unlesss I am very much mistaken, would have described it as a damned close-run thing!" ❧

"We've always been butchers in my family."

"I assure you we use only French additives."

# ADDITIVE INTERESTS

## Michael Heath

"I think we may have to put in an additive called meat."

"He's the best there is – he was trained at ICI, Switzerland."

"My compliments to the chemist."

"It's gone off."

# COUNTRY LIFE

£5 is the sum paid for each clipping used in "Country Life".
Cuttings should cover some item of news which never made it
to the national press, and should be sent to:
Country Life column, Punch, 23 Tudor Street, London EC4Y 0HR.

**THREE** fieldmice are alive and well in Cambridgeshire today thanks to firemen who revived them with oxygen after a grass fire.

E. Kent *(Hull Daily Mail)*

---

Bargain apartments, popular resorts, sea, shops, pool, sleeping 6-7, fights arranged.

R. Tallon *(Exchange & Mart)*

---

The owner told The Herald: "I came to work on Tuesday and found my windows smashed. There was a perfect hole right in the middle and the glass had fallen out all around."

A. Box *(Hemel Hempstead Herald)*

---

**Divorce may end marriage**

C. Goodges *(Rugby Advertiser)*

---

A man who spent the last eight years working with Franciscan monks, punched a woman and hit another when they refused to kiss him on an Edinburgh-Glasgow train.

T. McCormick *(Glasgow Evening Times)*

---

## INTERNATIONAL SECTION

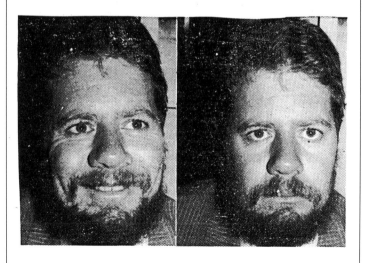

The manager of the Sunninghill shopping centre, Mr David Hack, before the robbery (left). . . and after.

P. Terry *(Midrand Reporter, South Africa)*

---

**Rabbits on Stamps**
by Bunny Kaplan
Assisted by Frances Hare

R. Sternberg *(Topical Times stamp magazine, USA)*

---

Kelly Tarlton's Underwater World, on Tamaki Drive, should open today after minor flooding forced it to close yesterday.

E. Baylis *(New Zealand Herald)*

---

**Drunken driving efforts applauded**
P. Costello *(St Paul Pioneer Press & Dispatch, USA)*

Two Dornoch Firth fishermen test the warmth of the water from the stern of a sardine fisher.

A. Seftor *(Scottish Field)*

---

A television crew filming in Bude Bay last week was monitoring the sewage that swills along with the tides. They were collecting material for the Channel 4 programme "Wellbeing", to be transmitted at 10.30 on Friday.

M. Balston *(Cornish & Devon Post)*

---

**WHEN** times are tough and the road is long, it helps to remember what the Armenians say: "The water melon will not ripen in your armpit."

M. Miller *(Bournemouth Evening Echo)*

---

A butler was shot dead and had five bullet holes in his head, but a doctor and a police inspector thought that he had died from natural causes. A mortuary attendant noticed the wounds two days later. Mr Michael Neligan, prosecuting, said there was blood on the man's face, clothes, and the carpet and walls of his Chelsea flat. There was a bullet hole in the middle of his forehead, Mr Neligan added.

P. Coleman *(The Standard, London)*

---

**Salmon faces cartilage op**

L. Brody *(Manchester Evening News)*

---

At three months the Queen carried her youngest son Prince Edward on to the balcony of Buckingham Palace following the Trooping ceremony.

R. Sandeman *(The Scotsman)*

---

**POISON** will be launched mid-March in all the NAAFI shops for Mother's Day and Easter.

C. Parker *(British Forces Leisure Guide)*

---

## INTERNATIONAL SECTION

**Oyster empire on the rocks**
D. Moore *(Gosford Star, Australia)*

---

**MOON PLAZA HOTEL**
**presents**
**"THE WIND BREAKER BAND"**
**performing at the**
**ALADDIN RESTAURANT**
A. Topham Smith *(Gulf Daily News)*

---

**Plane too close to the ground, crash probe told**
P. Buckland *(Vancouver Sun, Canada)*

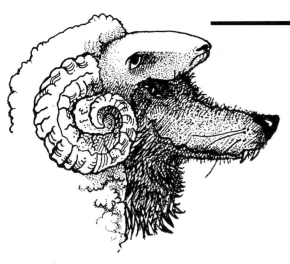

# ROGUE MALE
## JEFFREY BERNARD on women

AFTER quite a few years of being married to someone or other, it is quite a pleasant change to be on the outside and looking in. In my present role as roving dinner guest – friends are either pimping for me or I am making up the right number – I am the fly on the wall of marriage and the spy behind the net curtain.

Of course, I get to eat some very good meals this way but it really is rather depressing to listen to and watch the wheels fall off mine hosts as the evenings wear on. The dangerous game of "home truths" is usually begun with the cheese or, in the case of more down-market households, with the guttering of the candles and the circulation of After Eights. The antagonists open fire with the coffee and by the time the brandy arrives, when the verbal flak is reaching a crescendo, I find myself wondering just how the hell they've managed to stay married to each other for twenty years, never mind why on earth they got married in the first place.

Last week I went to dinner with a literary couple who had invited half the literati in London to their table. Most of the women there had written books or had novels under wraps and their husbands, even if they weren't quite in the Nobel Prize for Literature bracket, had at least appeared on *Call My Bluff* or *Start the Week*. Inevitably, the conversation got around to sex, although everybody called it "personal relationships". That started it, just like a referee calling two fighters into the middle of the ring and telling them that he wanted a good, clean fight without a chance in hell of getting one.

Then, my host suddenly said to his wife, Cynthia, "Of course, the trouble with women is that they have no imagination, which is why they've achieved so little."

Stifled screams from the ladies and our hostess counter-punched with, "Funny you should say that, darling – after all, you've achieved so much, we can't even pay the rates." Then, turning to me – and it's awful being picked out to be the middleman – she said, "D'you know, Jeffrey, marriage is so disgusting, I really wish I was dead."

I protested feebly, mumbling something about what a dreadful loss she would be to all of us, and she said, "No, I really mean it. I want to die." She took another gulp of brandy and lit a cigarette.

"Yes, I look forward to it. Just think of all that peace. Anyway, I've done everything. What's left? I've written books, had children, been in love, not for bloody years I might add," she said, looking daggers at her husband, "and I don't really see anything else to do. Yes, I'd really like to die."

There isn't a lot you can say to that, so I poured myself another drink.

"If you really wanted to die," said her husband, "then you would."

"Not just to please you, you bastard, I wouldn't." Then, turning her venomous eyes

> ## "The antagonists open fire with the coffee and by the time the brandy arrives, I find myself wondering just how the hell they've managed to stay married to each other for twenty years."

away from her husband, she said to me, "You have to admit, Jeff, that men are pretty bloody disgusting, aren't they?"

"Well, it's about fifty-fifty," I said nervously.

"Why are we so disgusting to you?" ventured an academic who had once appeared on *Down Your Way*.

"Well, for a start, you're all so bloody selfish; secondly, I loathe the way you can go to bed with someone without being in love with them, although, mind you, I bloody well could *now*," she said with another poisonous look at the husband, "and, thirdly, you're all so bloody patronising. You think women can't *do* anything."

"But of course we think you can, darling. It's just that a farmer doesn't expect much else of a chicken than that she lay eggs."

"I've laid my last bloody egg for you, you sod, and as soon as the youngest egg, as you like to call her, leaves home, then I intend to die."

"R.I.P.," he said, as she threw a piece of Camembert at him.

"Well, *I* think Cynthia's absolutely right," said a lady cellist from Hampstead. "I mean, let's face it, you are all complete and utter pigs, aren't you, Jeff?"

"If you say so."

"Oh, come on. We're kinder, more gentle, more loving and..."

"But darling..." her husband tried to interrupt.

"Shut your face, you. As I was saying, we're not called the gentle sex for nothing. Could you bring up a baby, Jeff?"

"Yes," I said, "and I have. Well, for three years or so, some time ago."

"I bet he can iron shirts, too, and cook and sweep a floor," said Cynthia's husband. I suddenly wished I had a riot shield.

"If you men are so good at cooking then," said Cynthia, "why didn't you cook dinner?"

"I thought paying for it was sufficient."

I made that forty-thirty to him. Match point and a breathless hush in the close tonight, I thought. I couldn't take a lot more and so I telephoned for a taxi. As I was leaving, Cynthia was again expressing a desire to embrace death. Her husband was detailing the defects of women. As I got into my taxi I could hear Cynthia's voice from the basement reiterating woman's war cry: "You make me sick."

In the morning I telephoned Cynthia to thank her for the dinner.

"Oh, I'm so glad you liked it," she said, "it was a lovely evening."

"And how's the old man?" I asked.

"Fine, just fine. He's just left for work. He can be so *funny* sometimes, can't he?"

After we rang off, I wondered about that. I suppose that one of the blessings of brandy after dinner is that it does make for amnesia. Had she forgotten already that the old man was disgusting and did she no longer want fervently to die? I suppose so. I can also only suppose that women like Cynthia start every new day with a clean sheet, as it were. They are addicted to these disgusting things called husbands and the doves don't turn into shrikes until the coffee is served.

Shall I get married again? I don't think it a very good idea but, should some miracle occur and I meet Miss Right yet again, then you must all come to dinner and have a cosy chat about "personal relationships".  ❧

## Le Pavement Artiste

**Monsieur:** Cette picture, sur le pavement. C'est tout votre work?

**Artiste:** Oui.

**Monsieur:** C'est très bon. Elle a une fluidité, une verve, qui est simultanément optimiste et mélancholique. Elle montre les traces d'influence de Francis Bacon, il est vrai, mais...

**Artiste:** Vous êtes un art critic, ou something?

**Monsieur:** Oui.

**Artiste:** Alors, scram! Je n'aime pas les critics. Les critics sont l'acne sur la complexion de l'art.

**Critic:** C'est un peu hard.

**Artiste:** Pas du tout. J'étais ruiné par les critics, moi!

**Critic:** Dites-moi votre triste life-story.

**Artiste:** Once upon une fois, j'étais un big name. Régulier dans le Summer Show, featuré dans les Sunday mags, même une fois interviewé par David Taylor.

**Monsieur:** Qui? Le joueur de snooker?

**Artiste:** Non, non – le bloke en *Punch*. Et puis – désastre! Une profile dans le *South Bank Show*!

**Monsieur:** C'est un disaster?

**Artiste:** Oui. Oh, M.Bragg était très aimable, but l'art world était terriblement jaloux. Sold out ... populiste ... artiste commercial ... les insultes étaient endless. Suddenly, j'étais dans le cold, une non-personne. Désillusioné, j'ai vendu mon studio et maintenant je travaille sur les pavements.

**Monsieur:** Et vous gagnez un living?

**Artiste:** Je gagne une fortune! D'abord, j'impose un voluntary admission fee de £2. Et après, les Américains achètent mon work pour millions de dollars.

**Monsieur:** Un moment, svp. Comment pouvez-vous merchandiser les paving-stones?

**Artiste:** Facilement. Je rentre avec un crow-bar dans la middle de la nuit, et je les rémouve forciblément. Mes pavement pictures sont très chic sur 5th Avenue.

**Monsieur:** Ah! Vous êtes Jack Grigsby!

**Artiste:** Oui. Comment vous savez?

**Monsieur:** Voici mon triste life-story. Once upon une fois, j'étais art critic pour un grand Sunday. J'étais le Clive James de Bond Street. Un jour, j'ai écrit un article sur vous: "Jack Grigsby, Un Grand Artiste". C'était le jour de votre *South Bank Show*. J'étais un laughing-stock. J'ai reçu le sack. J'ai travaillé un peu pour le *Daily Mirror*, puis Maxwell m'a donné le chop. Maintenant, je suis unemployable. Je suis devenu pavement critic.

**Artiste:** Pavement *critic*?

**Monsieur:** Oui. Comme vous, je travaille sur le pavement. Comme, par exemple ... Cette landscape de Dorset montre un pleasing talent pour la composition, avec overtones d'une nostalgie lyrique et une énergie plastique qui...

**Artiste:** Un moment. Voilà £2 pour vous.

**Monsieur:** Merci.

**Artiste:** Maintenant, scram!

# MALCOLM BRADBURY
# Long Vacation

UNIVERSITIES these days are cheerless places, considerably demoralised by the governmental axe which is hanging over them as the nation slides away into a new era of educational benightedness, the end-of-the-twentieth-century Dark Ages. But there is one form of cheer in academic life which, for the moment at least (though these days one counts on nothing), continues, if precariously, to survive; and that is the long vacation. Finals have ended, term is over, graduation will shortly occur, the strawberry teas will be taken with overdressed and gladdened parents on lawns that in theory at least will be sunny, and that will be that. In Cambridge now they are getting the greenfly out, the British are leaving for Spain, and the foreign language students who take over the town in the summer, falling out of punts in their Sony Walkmen, are moving in. Now is the time when the shops at last can sell those college blazers and eighteenth-century prints of traditional collegiate life. For this is the university as it should be, with no students in it at all.

Yes, the academic year has ended, at exactly the opposite time to that when the non-academic, or as some would have it, the "real" year does. Ended for some, though not the scientists, who continue to work on, much like the universe itself. But this, of course, means no ceasing of the essential academic activities. Courtyards and quads and walkways and courts still bustle, offices still function, refectories clatter; but all in a different spirit. The use of plant must be maximised, and this is the time when the refectory menus improve and the bar is at its busiest. The moment has come for the British universities to make up for that drain on resources that comes from educating the normal undergraduates for the rest of the year – and in every university in the land, life was never busier.

For what now begins is the conference and summer school season, a time when academic life indeed continues, but is conducted with somewhat different rules, decidedly different personnel, and a spirit of international confusion that everyone describes as collaboration. The new suitcases with LHR tags and the cases of claret from Berry Bros and Rudd that are coming in from the car-park are the goods and chattels of a new class of student, who does not object to salmon followed by pheasant for lunch. The tags are on all the lapels, and the conference wallets ("Please remember to get up for breakfast") are under all the arm-pits. Vice-Chancellors and College Masters offer sherry parties to welcome total strangers to their institution, and point to the traditional connection between this university and whatever the subject that has tempted this motley and polyglot crowd here should happen to be.

But who are they, all these people, holding their sherry glasses and looking bemusedly at each other's lapels? Well, those are lawyers of the sea, now gathering over there in the Moby Dick Room. These are the literary theorists now holding their reception in the Iser Room. The astro-physicists are upstairs, if not further, and the archaeologists somewhere below. Those buoyant ladies who appear to be

*"I sold my trousers to the devil."*

planning some form of collective adultery are students from the Open University; the Japanese gentleman who has tried lectures on Feminist Theatre, Medieval Jurisprudence and Diseases of the Colon is actually, with polite and stoic resignation, looking for the conference on Town Planning that he will never find.

Meanwhile the regular denizens of the institution – the dons, as university teachers used to be called, before they all took to wearing Adidas jogging shoes – are hiding somewhere, planning the conduct of their own summers. You may see them, if they are still around, sharpening their card indices and getting out notes bound with the paper-clips of last summer. If you meet them in the corridor, they talk again of The Book, that *summa* of synthesis and disciplinary innovation which will transform the way we think about, well, whatever it is: Locke, Stockhausen, or Barrault. A good book, as everyone knows, can be written only with an enormous effort of research, and if this means going to libraries in Paris, Washington or Canberra the true scholar will not stint to make the trip. Then there are academics whose task it is to work with reality itself, living with a tribe in Pago Pago or studying dysentery, frequently their own, in Africa.

Everyone, it seems, is going somewhere, perhaps to a conference or summer school rather like the one taking place round about. Here the golden rule is, however, that, as with sex, one should never summer-school or congress on one's own patch – unless one is forced by fate to be the host for others. The right thing is to go elsewhere, even if this requires the miseries of high season, top-of-the-shoulder travel. For this is the one time of year when one has the unique opportunity to catch up with the latest developments in the subject, and when scholars who have not been through a duty-free lounge all year at last have the chance to consort with their peers. If this means meeting in some disquieting distant venue where the waves crash infuriatingly on the beach and the endless clatter of ice in drinks interrupts discussion of Optative Counterfactuals in Elegaic Works, or whatever is the heated issue of this summer, then so be it; that is the kind of price that often has to be paid for keeping up with advanced scholarship.

And if all this sounds like pure pleasure, or confirms the impression that dons have curiously long holidays, then let me assure you that life is not so simple. For some years now I have been chairman of the British Council English Studies seminar held annually in Cambridge, a studious occasion, which attracts university teachers working in the field of English literature from all over the world. They come from Brazil and Japan and Finland and Rumania, their theses on Doris Lessing and John Fowles and Pinter in their pockets, hoping to meet, of course, Lessing and Fowles and Pinter, and have them read their 900 pages, and kiss them, and say they have done well. We try to oblige, bringing writers who usually refuse to see the light of day to meet them. "I love your bog," they say in delight to

*"You call this seven-thirty for eight?"*

John Fowles. "My bog?" says Fowles, ever polite. "Your excellent bog, on the whore of the French captain." "Ah, my bog," says Fowles.

"He is very good, your Fowle," they say afterwards. "Also he likes my work. May I come and discuss it with you? I can be in your house for two week. My mother also like to see English domestic praxis. I think this is very good seminar, and I can see it will be very forthcoming. Of course, you work hard, you must be very tired." "I agree with what my friend has said, and I have an excellent student who likes to come and study at your foot. Unfortunately he has no money. Perhaps you can arrange it." "Yes, also for my book to be published, I will not want a very big fee for it." "I have brought

you a book in Bulgarian that is very funny, and I hope you will get someone to translate it and read it to you. I know you will laugh."

No, it is not simple, the academic life, and you can see why from time to time we like to relax away from it, usually by going to someone else's summer school, or seminar, or conference, or congress, or colloquium. So this week it's Helsinki ("Developments in Contemporary British Writing"), and shortly it's Toronto ("Writers' Week"), and I'm writing my lectures and buying my Entero-Vioform or Arret now. In fact, this summer is already so busy with lectures and scholarship that, really, I just don't know how I'm going to be able to fit in even the smidgin of a holiday. ↻

*"Typical! Some bastard's nicked the disabled mooring."*

# RICHARD GORDON
# Political Complexions

WHILE shaving I wonder how other authors would describe me. This morning was Somerset Maugham's turn.

"The head was totally bald, apart from some unkempt strands of pure white hair. The lids still half-open gave one the chilling impression of Oriental cunning. The eyes were red, with the mottled cheeks proclaiming him no enemy of the bottle. The neck suggested the entwined trunk of some ancient yew. The overall effect was of a Seychelles Islands turtle in a bathrobe."

Luckily authors should be read and not seen.

It mystified me when the National Book League once tried promoting sales by filling shop windows with large photographs of writers, forgetting that P. G. Wodehouse had discerned, "Authors without exception look like something that would be passed over with a disdainful jerk of the beak by the least fastidious buzzard in the Gobi desert."

Too many jobs have become physically demanding. It is suicidal for politicians to appear on television just the way they look tonight. Viewers expect good casting, having long ago lost the ability of telling life from entertainment, except that the actors are more lifelike.

Mr Reagan is thus the only man in the history of the unbeatable US mortician industry to be beautifully embalmed several years before his death. I suspect that Nancy's face has been lifted so repeatedly that the fetching dimple on her chin could be her umbilicus. Mrs Thatcher must long to let her grey hair flop and her figure

## "Why should the public expect a man to leave hospital after a deadly illness wearing a baseball cap?"

go like other OAPs, but needs contemplate nip and tuck with her eyelids. One princess much resembles another, packaged by high-tech make-up and a hair-do like meringue topping, to radiate the demure sexiness of the old girls of the Rank Charm School in the 1950s.

Gladstone had it easier. Nobody got near him. A party political broadcast meant a man going purple in the face unintelligibly at the distant end of a public hall. Now everyone is so desperate to expose themselves on television, even archbishops submit to being coated with make-up for the big performance as eagerly as strippers.

As the girl powders my pate to save me dazzling the viewers, I muse how Mr Gladstone would have responded. I expect he would have loved it. Disraeli and Palmerston would. When they were getting on a bit, they rouged up every night for their dinner dates.

For all his faults, Hitler never tried to change his political complexion. He was undersized, and kept that dreadful moustache and hair-do more ludicrous than Arthur Scargill's. Probably Attila the Hun did not give a damn what he looked like, either.

Hitler suffered the painful handicap of all superpersons. They are unable to be ill. He was a difficult patient, because he refused to take his clothes off. He could not be X-rayed because it was outrageous for anyone to see through the Führer. When he needed glasses to read the map of Europe he was violating, they became a state secret.

Hitler's famous speeches were scripted by a hush-hush typewriter with huge letters. Had Nazism not been smashed in 1945, he would soon have had difficulty hiding from the world that he was haranguing it from notes like newsvendors' placards.

Contact lenses had not been invented and his oratorical style was anyway so effervescent there would be danger of their flying out of his eye-sockets like champagne corks. The top brass of the SS grovelling round the dais under the searchlights of a Nuremberg rally, the speaker waiting grumpily to resume, would have stopped the Third Reich in its tracks. Our statesmen, now having wonderful, invisible, electronic screens, can rouse their nations when as blind as kittens.

Mrs Thatcher felt obliged to show the Falklands spirit towards her varicose veins. Mr Reagan, the Davy Crockett one towards his colon. It is puzzling why the public should expect a man after an operation for a deadly illness to leave hospital wearing a baseball cap and grinning all over his face. They should know exactly how he feels. The only item the public enjoys in common with the world's rulers is a human body. The point was forcefully made by Henry V the night before Agincourt.

Mr Kinnock lets us see his warts and all at the party conference, quoting Kipling, if unhappily misquoting an American baseball poet instead.

Lord Stockton looks much as he ever did, thanks.

The proudest flourish of British democracy is the Queen prefacing her speech from the throne by tucking a pair of gig-lamps under her crown without a second thought. The Queen remains pure Queen. Public relations for the latest in a line of monarchs almost unbroken since AD 827 is as superfluous as camouflaging Windsor Castle. The Queen can impress her subjects for real. Her year is a progress of Royal spectaculars. Henry VIII popularised the idea. His production of the Field of the Cloth of Gold was a smash hit, if his launching of the *Mary Rose* a disappointment.

I once impulsively sought Somerset Maugham amid the palm-punctured courts of Raffles Hotel in Singapore. I had never met him. I explained to the pretty Chinese receptionist that he could be staying, she dispatched a white-jacketed boy through the famous bar crying, "Paging Mr Maugham! Paging Mr Somerset Maugham!"

It was fruitless, as I had expected. Maugham had been dead for twelve years. Suddenly I took fright that some squat figure might rise from his bamboo chair and Singapore Sling sundowner.

I wonder how I should have described him?

*"Melville! Your trappings."*

# DOC BRIEF

I had so many letters responding to my last article on smelling, that I decided to write this week's piece before they arrived. It's all about taste and tasting, a subject intimately bound up with smells and smelling, as you'll find to your cost if you walk past the back door of a smart restaurant. Anyway, I shall assume for the purposes of this article that you know nothing whatever of taste, which must be right otherwise you wouldn't be reading this, just my little joke, ha ha. Here goes.

That taster's got to go!

## THE MECHANISM OF TASTING

Now, how many different flavours or tastes do you think you can taste? No, you're wrong. The answer is four. You see, what's so fascinating (a bit) about tasting things is that most of what we "taste" as a "taste" is actually an internal smell (no, not that kind). By which I mean that, if you put something in your mouth and "taste" it, most of what you perceive is from the internal odour percolating up your nose.

Your tongue itself can only detect the four basic tastes, which are: salt, sour, sweet and Thousand Island. It is for this reason that a perfume that smells so sweetly on the neck of a person, comes to taste so bitter if you inadvertently nibble her or his neck while the perfume is still fresh. Or advertently, even. This is also why

your sense of taste disappears when you have a cold in the nose: without your sense of smell, you couldn't distinguish chicken chasseur from poached turbot (or "Porsche Turbot" as it's correctly pronounced) although your tongue might just tell you the difference between chocolate mousse and sauerkraut. Even in a Howard Johnson's.

What happens in tasting is that there are four basic kinds of receptors situated in different areas round the tongue linking to different parts of the brain. Thus salt receptors are in the front of the tongue and report to the area of the brain associated with potato crisps, running away to sea and kissing sailors. The "sweet" receptors are round the side of the tongue (possibly) and

feed back to the parietal hemisphere responsible for smiling, punting, playing *Chopsticks* on the piano and becoming Foreign Secretary. The "sour" receptors are in the centre of the tongue and survive long after all the other flavours have faded. They report back to a particular part of the brain devoted predominantly, according to some neurophysiologists, to Edward Heath. The other receptors on the tongue are useful for detecting various chemical impurities that leave an undefinable taste in the mouth e.g. prawn cocktail flavour, beef 'n' tomato, hives 'n' typhoid, silver nitrate and French apples. Apart from all that, most of food tasting is, as I say, due to smelling the various aromatic components of the sauces and spices, most of which are garlic.

# ROBERT BUCKMAN

## TASTE AND OTHER SENSES

Another interesting thing (fairly) about taste is how it can be "fooled". And here we are talking about ways in which the brain can be misled by other clues arriving via other sensory pathways.

For example, if someone pours you a glass of carrot juice dyed deep orange and says, "Here's your orange juice," your brain prepares you to accept several things. e.g. the taste of oranges, the oral sensation of orange flakes, and the mental thought of having to pay for orange juice. But of all the senses, the taste is most easily overruled in this way.

Thus, in an experiment in which 45 wine-tasters were given a modest Chablis, dyed a deep ruby and served from a cut-glass Captain's decanter, 14% identified it correctly, 26% thought it was Tia Maria, 31% thought it was Duckhams 20/50, 21% thought it was the Captain's urine specimen and 8% thought it was a hamburger. Even in simpler circumstances like dining out, the sensation of taste can be affected by colour, e.g. the amount of gold lettering on the menu, and the only problem is that not all senses of taste are misled as easily, particularly your wife's. In fact, although the tongue is pretty crass at actually tasting things, it is amazingly sensitive as a tactile organ. When you get the chance. It has been calculated that there are so many pressure receptors on the tongue that it could detect objects less than 0.2 mm in diameter and weighing less than 0.05 of a gramme. A typical example is grit in watercress. What is even more amazing is that cows (*see below* – particularly when walking in the country) have even more sensitive tongues, yet they seem to eat tussocks chock-full on anthracite without minding a bit. Maybe they think it's truffle.

## TASTE IN EVOLUTION

During the evolution of all animal species, taste has served two functions. Not only what other things taste of when you eat them, but also what you taste of when you are eaten. To this end, many animals have evolved a particularly foul taste so that predators will not approach them, e.g. the tarantula, the Alasatian and the armpit.

But of course, this is not much good if you are actually eaten, since by the time the eater has eaten you and learned of your foul taste it isn't going to do you much good, unless you believe in reincarnation and enjoy the metamorphosis of being puked up in the Gents. No. So, what animals did as they evolved was to indicate with their colouring that they tasted terrible and would be dangerous if swallowed. Many examples of this so-called "warning colouration" can be seen in daily life, e.g. crème de menthe. Other colours related to bad tastes include station buffet wallpaper and Joan Collins. Now all this was particularly important to Man, because at an early stage in his evolution he was "omnivorous", which is the dietary equivalent of the Church of England. An omnivore had to be particularly careful because the chance of being poisoned was so much greater. I mean, if you are a cow and you eat only grass, you'll only get food poisoning if you eat poisoned grass, and who in the animal kingdom is going to poison grass until the evolution of newer species, e.g. the Americans?

Whereas Man, by contrast, was constantly walking around nibbling this and that, and could easily be poisoned by an aberrant this or a lethal that. Thus, Man learned to avoid eating brightly coloured things, such as tigers, or volcanoes. And it is from this phase of our development that we get our love of things that are coloured dull browns or other neutral colours e.g. kippers, Manchester, and ten-pound notes.

## THE DOCTOR ANSWERS YOUR QUESTIONS

**Q:** What are these Polyps that President Reagan had?

**A:** I honestly have no idea. I thought they were people from the South Seas, but anyway they were benign so maybe they were working as domestics or something.

**Medicine Balls**, Dr Buckman's new hardback farrago, is published by David & Charles, price £4.95.

# IRMA KURTZ
## Holy Admirable

CONFESS it is true. I actually did it. I actually promised them the Promised Land. It seemed a good idea at the time. You must understand that it had been a bad, bad season in the Diaspora. My only child had been sneezing for months, and when calls from my widowed mother, who lives in a part of America where the climate is as extreme, somehow suggested it was all my fault, I heard myself telling them both: "Okay, okay, guys, get off my back! Next year, Jerusalem!"

"You promise?" my son asked.

Of course, when the time came, as so often happens, I had second thoughts.

"But you promised!" my son said.

"I hate to say it about my own daughter, but that's you all over," my mother said. "Idle promises . . ."

I ask you, what could I do? A promise is a promise.

As a relatively experienced Israeli hand, I did my best to prepare them. I warned them that Israeli cooking is an Arab plot, for example, and that local custom holds any display of courtesy to indicate a character weakness only marginally more excusable than alcoholism. My son was fascinated when I told him that the famous lost tribe of Israel had recently been discovered. It lives in Minnesota and its pilgrims to the Holy Land are instantly recognisable, thanks to the female's native costume of cerise Terylene trouser-suits and the way she chatters through

her nose, without any intonation, incessantly, about Minnesotan minutiae, even atop the citadel where Herod thought to defend himself against Cleopatra, and in the very spot of Solomon's dilemmas.

Minnesotan males, on the other hand, are drab and mute. Mother already knew about Minnesotans because it seems those who cannot afford to go as far as the Holy Land make do with Southern California, but she was fascinated to be told that women indulging in an erotic display of their elbows will not be served by shopkeepers in the religious quarter of Mea Shearim and may even be stoned, in the biblical sense of the word.

I taught my tiny band the Hebrew for "hello/goodbye", "see you again", "you've got to be kidding!", "thank you", and "excuse me", though this last is academic, heard less frequently than Aramaic. Just to show off, I also taught them the Hebrew word for "pullover" which, it so happens, is "*sveddah*". Finally, they had to know that the only acceptable topics of conversation with Israelis one meets for the first time are religion and politics.

Travelling between two generations separated by a good deal more than half a century is like being a slice of mature Cheddar between two pieces of bread (at least, in Israel. Anyplace else I would have felt like ham). Though the pieces of bread (in this case, mother and mother's pride) have much in common, they are only

together because of the big cheese.

My mother, a tiny, white-haired woman of demonic vitality, was keen to go everywhere, see everything, and pick up every stone, even pebbles David had tossed away as unworthy of his sling-shot. My son, on the other hand, turned bright red in the heat and wanted to swim all the time. My role was to bring these two together into some semblance of a sandwich: to persuade mother, for example, that it might be as well for a septuagenarian American lady of refined habits not to attempt on foot a hill that had defeated the Roman legions, while at the same time persuading my son to come out of the shade of the cable-car and have a look around the windswept mesa where his granny was already burrowing into a Zealot's cave.

Sometimes, say, high above a vast, silent desert and a faded sea, our age differences were pressed by the weight of time around us and became nothing at all. Sometimes, at Yad Vashem, for instance, the Holocaust memorial museum, we were too raw to walk together, yet even though we went separately past the dreadful testimony, we had never been closer. Other times, notably at breakfast on a kibbutz when my son was being driven mad by a longing for crisp bacon and my mother by mosquitoes and I by being held responsible for the lack of the former and the abundance of the latter, we were not what anyone could call a united Israel.

As you might expect, the generations revealed

BANX

different intellectual interests. My mother was fascinated by history, architecture, theology, and sex; my son's chief interests were swimming-pools and war. Israel is a prismatic land that offers something for everyone, everything for some. I remember one hot afternoon when, having finally persuaded Mother to take a siesta and my son not to, he and I set out on the quest for a pool, leaving our old dear curled up with a dictionary and a book of hard porn in Hebrew she had discovered at a kiosk in Tel Aviv and purchased as one of her "collector's items" (among mother's "collector's items" are two shrunken heads, the skeleton of a snake containing the skeleton of a rather smaller mouse, and a book of African recipes including one that begins: "Take eight pieces of bat . . .").

Our own hotel pool, it happens, was dry. In the evenings it served as a sunken stage for a group of religious fanatics from America possessed by what they called "the gift of tongues", though in my opinion to be understood by Jesus while utterly unintelligible to one's fellow humans must be more of a burden. Their highly entertaining performance, lit by a blaze of ancient sunset, we three used to observe from our balcony ten flights up. They seemed to be having so much fun it was all I could do to stop my son from running down to join them, and to stop Mother, a mischievous old darling, trumpeting down from on-high her personal assurance of their salvation.

Anyhow, in our search for a pool, my son and I found instead a kind of war. The big, modern hotel next door to our humble one possessed a gorgeous pool that was brimming with water. It seemed an easy thing to stroll across what appeared to be a communal garden, except that when we arrived at mid-point we found a wall of coiled barbed-wire that made as forbidding a frontier as any in that land.

"What would King Saul have done in a case like this?" I asked my son, seeing the chance for a "learning experience", so dear to the hearts of us American mothers.

"He'd cheat," the kid replied.

I wish you could have heard the way that boy of mine lied his way first past the desk-clerk in the smart hotel, and then past the unsmiling guards posted at the entrance of the pool to keep inmates of underprivileged hotels out of the swim. It gladdened a mother's heart, and so also lightened her purse, costing us something like a fiver each, though not in the local currency, quaintly called "shekels" (my son *would* call them "shackles").

When I offered a pedlar in the Old Town a handful of shekels to buy a T-shirt on which was printed "America, don't worry! Israel is behind you!", he looked at me scornfully.

"What's the matter?" he said. "You got no pounds? No dollars? No yens? No roubles, lire, drachma, zloties? You got no real money?"

"Can we come back next year?" my son asked me as our plane took off into a Mediterranean sky. "Can we? Can we? Promise?"

"We'll see," I said.

"Do say yes!" my mother said. "Say we can come back again!"

"Please, you two!" I cried. "Enough, already! How do I know what will happen next year? What do you think I am? God?"

"*. . . Arnold Pycroft, Gavin Lymhurst, Gerald Lip, Denis McCarthy, Roger Samples, Edgar Hellier, Frank Cheesewright . . .*"

# NEM KON & DIM DUK
# Weekly Gazette
## DELIVERED FREE TO 700,000 HOMES IN TIK TOK, DING DONG, PUB MUK, NIK NAK, PHUT PHUT, TOP TIT, AND SAM PIG

**No. 76...Wednesday, September 11th, 1985**

# Pol Pot Retires

## Vociferous Gathering at Banqueting Rooms

**It was roast dog with all the trimmings when Kampuchea's elite met last Tuesday evening in the spacious Ho Hum suite of Kwantong's elegant Banqueting Rooms to put their hands together for popular Pol Pot, 60, who retired after many years of faithful and cheery service as area manager of the Khmer Rouge.**

Young and old alike among the elegantly clad throng were of one accord as Nang Dok, head of personnel, handed over the coveted music centre which chirpy Pol will take with him into retirement, along with the good wishes of all. After a real three-course blow-out, including many a bumper of vino, Nim Sung, waggish Deputy Marketing Director, rose to his feet, and no slouch at the podium he!

"Since it falls to my happy lot to propose the toast of our guest of honour," began Nim, "I am reminded of the one about the bride on her wedding-night who – if the ladies will forgive me – popped between the sheets first, to await the arrival of her beloved from the downstairs bar. Well, after about two hours, and no sign of the bridegroom, she gets up, goes to the window, looks out, and there – I should have mentioned there was a full moon – there is his head, stuck on a pole in the front garden. 'Blimey,' she exclaims – pardon my French – 'blimey, if that's what he's like with his trousers off, I'm not surprised he's kipping on the lawn!'

"Friends," Nim managed to continue after the gales of laughter had finally subsided, "friends, those of us who have worked with dear old Pol Pot here know that that silly little story has a particular application in his case. For nigh on ten years now, our respected colleague has been directly responsible for tirelessly topping upwards of two hundred thousand items, frequently laying about him personally far into the night after many a lesser man had clocked off and stuck hisself in front of the telly. I have even known him come in of a Sunday when we were, as a for instance, short-handed on totting up gold inlays, and roll up his sleeves and pick up his pliers and get stuck in along with the rest of the lads. He is both a guv'nor's guv'nor and a man's man, and you cannot say fairer than that in our business!"

Much more followed in this vein, and it may safely be said that never has that famous rendezvous echoed to more bonhomous ribaldry nor more heartfelt sentiment in all its years of top-class catering. Even this jaded old reporter's ribs were aching, he can tell you, and no mistake!

When the guest of honour's turn eventually came to respond, it was clear that he, too, was overcome by the occasion. He could do no more than thank everyone for their good wishes and their generous contributions, and pass' round lucky shrunken feet to all the ladies which we are sure will grace their corsages on many a future formal occasion.

Good luck in your retirement bungalow, Pol Pot, and do not be a stranger to all your old mates at Khmer Rouge! There will always be a welcome on the mat.

All smiles before the lavish reception, as Pol Pot and Prince Sihanouk enjoy a joke in the smart Cok Tail Bar. The joke is Prince Sihanouk.

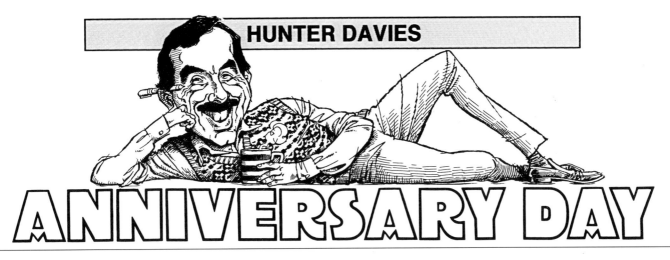

# ANNIVERSARY DAY

IT SEEMS to have been our Silver Wedding for months, as that's been the main topic in this house, but now both parties are over and we've survived the week and if only I can remember who gave us what, we can get down to writing the thank-yous, like well brung up wrinklies.

I have this terribly neat pile of silver wrapping paper, must have cost a fortune, and I've carefully unhinged the Sellotape and cut away the torn edges and it should do me for presents for decades to come, but I seem to have lost several of the little tags. This always used to happen at the children's parties, with them furiously ripping open the pressies, then leaving them lying around to get mixed up. You would have thought so-called grown-ups would have done it better.

The other thing about children's parties is that someone always gets sick or starts crying or both. We had only one such incident. A certain rather important person did become tired and emotional, but I dare not mention the name or I might get thumped.

On Tuesday we had the street party, the one for the neighbourhood friends, our extended local family as opposed to our works party for our publishing and writing family. This was on the exact anniversary, June 11, so it chose us rather than the other way round. And what bad luck it turned out.

For weeks I've been getting the garden into shape to show off its wonders, organising where all the seats and little tables would go and which neighbours I would borrow garden furniture from and how we could get lighting at the bottom of the garden by running extension leads from next door as they have an electric socket at the bottom of their garden, lucky beggars, and most important of all, I had several trial runs at working out exactly where the jazz band would play. Live music, don't you know. I always think a garden party needs that sort of thing.

We woke up early Tuesday morning and it was pouring down. Oh Gawd, what a bloody drag. Flaming June. Flaming roll on. I went out in my raincoat and climbed over various garden walls and dragged home various bits of borrowed furniture while she screamed at me not to be so stupid, stop it at once, the forecast says it's set in for the day, don't be so idiotic, nobody will be going in the garden at all. I'd even found some Christmas decoration lights and I was about to put them on the old pear tree, but I decided that would probably fuse all our electrics and kill the pears for ever.

So I came in and started helping the Old Trout. She had said originally that she would buy most dishes ready-made, just to make it easy, as catering for 50 is a big job, but in the end she had decided to do most things herself, even though it was to be a cold buffet. I was given the celery to chop up. Don't say I don't help.

I thought I was getting off lightly, as she was busy roasting eight chickens and stripping them to turn it all into this amazing American chicken salad, but we soon came to verbal blows over the celery. Get these green bits off, at once. Oh God, cut them fine, really thin slices, look, chop them into inch long bits, then slice them sideways, like this, oh what a mess, why did I ask you to do anything, come here, I'll do it.

Then I became officer in charge of the French beans, having been demoted from the celery, and that was agony. How do they top and tail them in restaurants. Must take yonkers. I tried scissors, large knives, small knives, the electric carving knife till it packed up, and even a small saw, but I'd done only about half a pound in twenty minutes, and there were still four pounds to go. Thank goodness the smoked salmon was bought. It needed noth-

ing doing to it, though Caitlin arrived later in the day from Brighton and laid it all out artistically, in the shape of a fish, with an olive for the eye. I could have done that, if only I'd got O-level Art, if only she would have let me, if only anyone would trust me to do anything except the boring physical jobs, you're all sexist in this house, yes, humping furniture around, chopping up boring vegetables, but when it's the nice easy amusing jobs, you get someone else.

I wasn't even allowed to breathe anywhere near the *Spuma Fredda Di Salmone*, which my lady person did personally. I don't even know what it means. I'll wait till Jake gets back from Italy. (He's still in Florence, and missed both parties, as this Contessa he works for as a gardening boy needed him, don't ask me what for.)

We worked solid from nine in the morning till five, just getting the food ready. Then we had to start on the house. The band would now have to play indoors, as the rotten rain was still pouring down, so I was instructed to move out furniture to make room. What screams. I probably did pounds of damage to the paintwork, forcing tables where they didn't want to go. Her room is on the ground floor, so I just dumped stuff there. I know for months ahead that we'll never find anything. In my bad temper, I just shoved everything off shelves and into her room, serve her right, Bossy Betty.

Our final panic was that we had not made the invitations clear enough. We had simply said "Celebration Party from 7.30". That was all. In talking to various people who rang up, some had not realised there would be proper food. Oh no. All this slaving away over the celery, and people might turn up having already eaten.

There is obviously a code for invitations, and not being accustomed to throwing parties we had not understood it. If you don't state there *will* be food, the implication is that there will be none, apart from dopey things on sticks or tinned pineapple on cheese, ugh, or stale water biscuits smeared with gunge, yuck, we're not doing any of that. If only we had stated there would be Supper at 8.30. Remind me, please, in another 25 years' time, when we get to our Golden.

In the end, everyone turned up on time, expecting proper food, but what was unexpected was that several people had turned up expecting to do a turn. We did have a tradition at one time of having a family party at Christmas, for neighbours and their children, in which everyone did a party piece, then dived into the lucky dip. But this was planned purely as an adult do, thank goodness, had enough of little kids these last 25 years, thank you very much, but people like Mary brought three changes of costume. She dressed up as a bride, in a bridal dress with cushions stuffed down her to look seven months pregnant, and sang some rude songs about oh, I can't remember now, but everyone thought it was very funny. Then Marion and Annabell, my twin sisters, sang *Sisters*, something that up until now only Carlisle audiences have had the pleasure of experiencing.

But the highlight of the entertainment was the jazz band. It was just a trio really, the Trogtet, organised by our neighbour, the world famous cartoonist and musician, Wally Fawkes, how kind. His bass player and his drums, like Wally, are both professionals, having played with Humphrey Lyttelton. For the night, they were joined by a fourth musician making it a quartet. This turned out to be the very talented, rather marvellous and altogether brilliant, wait for it, Flora Davies, aged 12¾.

There comes a time in every father's life in which he bursts with pride. I've experienced it with Caitlin and Jake, but with Flora it happened on Tuesday. The sight of my little petal, her left foot tapping away, playing her clarinet with real musicians, almost had me in tears. She had secretly been going to Wally's and he had rehearsed a few jazz tunes with her, which was pretty hard, as he can't read or write music and she had never heard the tunes before. She copied them from him playing, which meant she copied his mistakes as well, so he says. I got down her whole performance on tape. Oh, archive stuff.

Then we had the video show. I've been loaned this camera to try out, just for fun, and me and Flora had gone round the doorsteps last weekend interviewing people. At 10.30, by which time most guests were pretty merry, we showed the film upstairs, in our sitting-room. I fast-forwarded the very embarrassing bits, where one or two blokes could not remember how many years they had been married, or even how often, but it went down very well. There were cheers and jeers all the way through. I had also filmed a bit of the party itself, but the downstairs light was hopeless so all you could see were shadows through a snow-storm. This, too, led to cheers. Yes, some people were more than merry by this time.

They all left by two o'clock, but we didn't get to bed till three, as we decided to clear up the worst of the mess. That's the worst of doing a party yourself at home. The afterwards is hellish.

Naturally, we were thinking roll on Friday and the Groucho Club. Our works party would be like going to someone else's do, with no work for us before or afterwards. That's what you pay for. But don't ask me how much it will come to. I'm going to be hypnotised when the bill comes in.

We were both much more relaxed at the second party, particularly someone I dare not mention, and after what happened she really should be nameless for ever. But the party itself seems to have been a big success. Though of course you never can tell. People

say nice things. Personally, I would have liked both parties. The food at each was brilliant. The Groucho Club, considering how new it is, excelled itself. Everyone said.

I managed to deliver my impromptu speech at the Groucho. At the home party, no one had asked me, rotten lot. I suppose there was just so much shouting and other people performing. But this time M. Bragg, our fellow Cumbrian and man of letters, toasted us, so I had to respond, oh come on, someone had to and as *you* wouldn't speak, who else would. She is actually a v.g. speaker, while I'm not, but I'm the one always willing to have a go.

I wanted, anyway, to thank everyone for the presents. I had been slightly worried about these. When we went to a Silver Wedding two years ago, we had taken a silver birch tree, thinking how clever and original, only to find a queue of people carrying the same bloody thing. This was in the country, so at least they had a large garden to accommodate them. In our little urban patch there is hardly room to swing a tortoise, which reminds me, you don't think I electrocuted it, do you, trying out those Xmas lights. Haven't seen it all week.

Luckily, we didn't get one silver birch. We got one smaller tree, a Japanese maple, and lots of plants and flowers. But mostly it was silver, which was good. But what exactly do you do with silver? Answer, clean it.

Silver is the traditional element, if you reach 25 years, but should we have been traditional anyway?

During the week, I was talking to Malcolm Bradbury, for a radio interview, and I happened to tell him this was our Silver Wedding week. He said he had been married 26 years, but deliberately avoided any 25th anniversary party, having been to two in recent years after which both couples had split. When he makes

27 years, then he might just have a very quiet do. Is a public celebration, then, a hostage to fortune? I see it purely as a past thing, a celebration of having got this far, and the future will have to take care of itself. You have all your old friends around because what you're doing, in essence, is having a retrospective exhibition. Which brings me to another exhibition.

I was standing saying farewell to each guest, thanking them for coming, and giving out the Going Away Presents. Oh yes, we had them at both parties. Doesn't everyone? What we did was create a special mug to celebrate our Silver Wedding, 1960-1985, a mock-up of a Royal Coronation mug, in the same sort of floral designs, with the figures looking much the same as Charles and Di, though the actual physiogs turn out to be me and the Old Trout. Good idea, huh. We got two local potters to make them.

Anyway, I was giving them out and I realised I had not seen my lady person for over an hour. Where had she gone. What a hostess. A search was made, and she was eventually found, now how am I going to describe this, recovering, shall we say, in the bathroom, rather tired and quite over-emotional.

I led her outside into Dean Street and propped her up on the pavement to get some fresh air, while I rang for a cab. At that time of night, Soho is pretty busy, with quite a few T & E people propped up on the pavements. One kind woman offered to get her a cab. "You been left behind, deary?"

It's usually me who becomes the worse for wear at parties. In fact it's only the second time in 25 years I have known this to happen to her. Well, at a Silver Wedding, you're allowed, retrospectively, to make an exhibition of yourself.                                    ‎ಟ

*"Edward and I are entirely self-sufficient in cacti."*

# DAVID GALEF
## The Latest

HATE to cook? Are you the type that can't even make toast? Why, you clod! Why haven't you spoken to us about this before? Now, from Pepper-Age Firms, there's Toaste®!

Crisp, brown slices of real, white, whole wheat and rye bread, buttered and toasted to a rich, golden consistency – perfect for breakfast, snack-time, anytime. No one bakes in home-goodness like Pepper-Age Firms, and no one can infringe on our Home-Baked® image. Yes, now you can enjoy Toaste® every morning, without the fuss. Comes in cinnamon, plain, and strawberry jam. And look for our coming line of French Toaste® and Olde Tyme Waffles®.

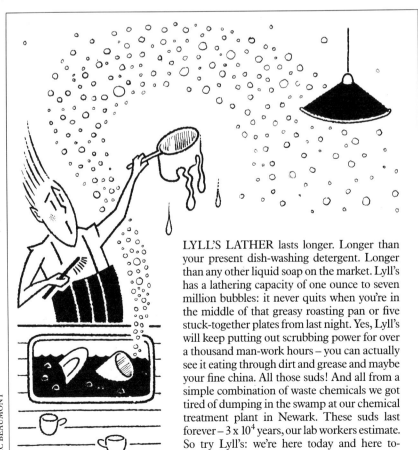

POSSIBLE, you say? A salad oil which can o make your car engine run more smoothly? ll, we guarantee it! Wackel's salad oil, made m choice grades of corn and petroleum pro-cts, makes the best dressing you ever tried – d just a half-cup in your carburretor will make ur car run better for 500 miles! Oil is oil, you ? You haven't tried Wackel's! Salad oil is

salad oil and petroleum oil is indigestible, you counter? You may have a point there, but all we have to report is a long line of satisfied consumers largely represented by phony testimonials drawn up by our promotion department.

Wackel's – for your salad, for your car. Also try new Wackel's Premium salad oil, for thicker salads and big-engine cars.

PROTOPUDDING.

What is protopudding? It's not a custard, it's not a gel. Protopudding contains none of the fattening, satanical ingredients which promote coronary infarctions and scare the hell out of consumers. Protopudding is nothing less than a biochemical miracle, a pudding so rich and creamy you could swear it was whatever you wanted to swear. But it isn't. No, it's not. Sorry, we can't reveal the true ingredients of protopudding, except to note that shares of stock in our sister company, ALGAE-PLUS, have shot up dramatically over the past year. Now you can eat all the pudding you want and not end up like one. So trust us. FDA reports should be fully in by next year. Protopudding: in convenient snak-kups or 5-gallon industrial drums.

LYLL'S LATHER lasts longer. Longer than your present dish-washing detergent. Longer than any other liquid soap on the market. Lyll's has a lathering capacity of one ounce to seven million bubbles: it never quits when you're in the middle of that greasy roasting pan or five stuck-together plates from last night. Yes, Lyll's will keep putting out scrubbing power for over a thousand man-work hours – you can actually see it eating through dirt and grease and maybe your fine china. All those suds! And all from a simple combination of waste chemicals we got tired of dumping in the swamp at our chemical treatment plant in Newark. These suds last forever – $3 \times 10^4$ years, our lab workers estimate. So try Lyll's: we're here today and here tomorrow.

KIDS, have you tried Cap'n Billy's Whiz-Bang Crunch? It's the cereal so loaded with taste, the Krunchy-Korn nuggets practically come teeming right out of the box! Tired of cereals which come in boring shapes like little rings and squiggles? Each Whiz-Bang Crunch nugget is an edible replica of an 1874 US merchant marine – look for the British destroyers mixed in (estimated density: 1 per 1,000,000) and you might win a full-sized ocean liner! See bewildering details on back of box.

ERIC BEAUMONT

# IS THERE A CHOREOGRAPHER IN THE HOUSE?

*MAHOOD brings the Ballet Rambert's repertoire up to date for their sixtieth birthday*

THE N.U.T. CRACKER Keith Joseph in the title role

SHADOW PLAY Neil Kinnock executes an *effacé*

LES PATINEURS William Whitelaw gives his usual inspired performance

BEAUTY AND THE BEAST Michael Heseltine dancing the title roles

THE LADY AND THE FOOL Margaret Thatcher and Leon Brittan perform the *pas de deux*

RITE OF SPRING Rupert Murdoch executes a *grande batterie*

SOGAT ON STRIKE

NGA OFFICAL PICKET

DON QUIXOTE Norman Tebbit does his *grand jêté dessus en tournant battu*

SWEENEY TODD David Owen helps David Steel with his *cabriole*

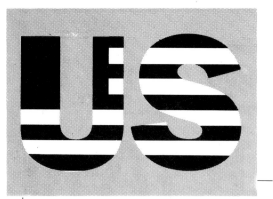

# US

We know what we think. They know what they think. But what do they think we think?

## SIMON HOGGART

reports from Washington on what he thinks they think we think.

THE big news here about Britain lately has been the retirement of the traffic warden who inspired Paul McCartney's "Lovely Rita, meter maid." She got roughly ten times the amount of coverage Mrs Thatcher's Cabinet re-shuffle received. And quite right, too. She was a more interesting topic, and, I'll bet, the story has a greater long-term importance.

The most grotesque British image recently came in an advert for gin which appeared in the *New York Times*. Advertisers love symbols, and baseball here symbolises good times and a fine American tradition. Queen Victoria symbolises a stern regard for quality and a fine British tradition. Some clever clogs at the agency had the idea of combining the two, so that the ad shows Queen Victoria waving a baseball bat, ready to swat the ball. The witty caption reads: "Bombay Distilled London Dry Gin. A hit in any league." I'd like to see them try the opposite: dressing a baseball player in bombazine, and have him flog American drinks in England.

If you want to feel really warm and good about Britain while you're in America, you have to watch Public Broadcasting. These are the channels in most big cities which have no ads,

being run on private subscriptions and grants from big companies who wish to appear cultured. (The companies are allowed one short plug in each programme, e.g.: "This presentation of *The Jewel in the Crown* was made possible by The Napalm Corporation: defending our heritage without nuclear weapons.")

On a typical evening half the programming is British. Leafing through PBS's monthly mag, we find Diana Rigg in *Bleak House*, P.D. James and *Death of an Expert Witness*, Geraldine Chaplin, Laurence Olivier, Alan Bates in *Dr Fischer of Geneva* and Peter Bowles as the *Irish R.M.* One or two Americans sneak in there, but obviously to show willing, like the token blacks who crop up in TV commercials.

The reason for all this British material isn't that the rest of American TV stinks. It doesn't. Lots of it is made with a style and panache we rarely approach. But it is all what the writer William Goldman calls "comic-book" filming, in which the good guys always win, the bad guys always lose, and the comedies invariably finish with a heart-warming, twinkle-eyed chuckle which makes persons of sensibility wish to throw up.

The reason for this is advertising, a fact

which we may one day discover when it is too late. In the meantime the largely well-to-do and often influential people who watch Public Television think of British TV in the same way opera fans regard Italy and wine drinkers look upon France. No doubt Mrs Thatcher is working on a way to end this state of affairs.

Sometimes it can have faintly ludicrous results. The other night it was hideously hot and humid outside, so we closed the windows, drew the curtains, and curled up with the air conditioner to watch *Rumpole's Return*. The chaps at PBS were clearly scared that viewers wouldn't get it, so they called the series: *Mystery! Rumpole of the Bailey* and had Vincent Price introduce it in his usual role as a cross between the Abominable Doctor Phibes and the Duke of Devonshire.

Now, the pleasures of Rumpole are nothing to do with rattling skeletons or corpses in the library, but PBS was too nervous to dish out the truth. Who from a generation raised on *Perry Mason*, they must have thought, would watch a series about a fat old josser who loses half his cases? So they hired Vincent Price to do his guardian-of-the-crypt act and to make Hilda Rumpole sound like Dracula's au pair.

*"I don't pay you to think, Miss Bodwell."*

*"Is it any wonder we're endangered?"*

The faintly awed reverence for things British extends to the PBS news programme, the admirable *MacNeil/Lehrer News Hour* which treats news of our beleaguered island with a high seriousness not often found at home. Whereas *NBC News*, the nationally networked show, dismissed the Thatcher changes in six seconds and one sentence (roughly: "Worried by poor opinion poll results, British Premier Margaret Thatcher announced a string of Cabinet changes today."), *MacNeil/Lehrer News Hour* will on occasion devote long discussions to British affairs.

This can be oddly disconcerting for the expatriate hack. For example, these people take Vincent Hanna terribly seriously. There he was, on the day of the BBC strike, sounding off at sombre length, a symbol of the BBC's great mission, a herald of global truth. This is not quite the image most of us have of Vincent, chubby and delightful though he is in so many ways.

Things warmed up when they brought in Jimmy Breslin, a New York Irishman who is either drunk all the time or else a brilliant actor pretending to be. Breslin swung verbal broken bottles at Vincent, his chief complaint being that Hanna had married Gerry Fitt's daughter and was therefore the son-in-law of a traitor to Ireland. Since on an average day Gerry Fitt suffered more abuse and violence with more courage than Breslin has experienced in a lifetime, this had the curious effect of making Hanna look even more magisterial and statesmanlike. The son-in-law in this case refused to rise to the bait.

For a Brit, this sort of stuff is greatly preferable to the hackneyed images used by the networks. I remember a film report once about Barbara Woodhouse, a British TV dog trainer whom you might faintly remember from the distant past. "At four o'clock on a Sunday afternoon, everyone in Britain leaves the pub…" it began. The fact that everyone in Britain would have been lucky to linger in the pub beyond 2.15, and the fact that Barbara Woodhouse never got near the ratings, were ignored. British people spend all their spare time in pubs, except when Barbara Woodhouse is on, just as they frequently remark, "Gawd bless the Royal Family."

It's largely our own fault, same as it's theirs that many Europeans are convinced most Americans suffer from gunshot wounds the way we suffer from rain. People want bold, simple images of us, and we are happy to provide them. I wonder what America will make of *Mapp and Lucia* if they ever dare to show it.

Talking of images, I learned two interesting facts this week. The first was from a university teacher who has worked out that many of President Reagan's speech lines come from his films. The theory is that he sees his life in terms of the images created by movies, especially the ones he appeared in.

The best known example is the football coach, the Gipper, whom he played in *Knute Rockne, All-American*. The nickname "The Gipper" is Reagan's own creation, and is as artificial as "Ol' Blue Eyes" for Frank Sinatra. It is used by sycophantic members of his staff and by no one else, but it clearly means a lot to him. Another instance of the same thinking was his famous *Rambo* remark during the hostage crisis.

The second thing I learned was that he was approached for, and considered, the Humphrey Bogart role in *Casablanca*. "If she can stand it, I can. Play it…" as the military band starts *Hail to the Chief*. "Here's looking at you, America;" "Of all the legislatures in all the capitals in all the world, you had to walk into mine…"

It is, as Mr Reagan himself would remark, "unconscienceable". On the other hand, I think it might be nicer to be ruled by Rick than by Rambo. ✤

*"We'll both have the 'Idiot's Lunch' but without the boiled pebbles."*

# THEATRE

**WHEN WE ARE MARRIED**   TIMOTHY WEST *as Councillor Albert Parker*
JAMES GROUT *as Alderman Joseph Helliwell*   PATRICIA ROUTLEDGE *as Maria Helliwell*
SUE DEVANEY *as Ruby Birtle*   BILL FRASER *as Henry Ormonroyd*   PATRICIA HAYES *as Mrs Northrop*

**THE SEAGULL**   JONATHAN PRYCE *as Boris Trigorin*   VANESSA REDGRAVE *as Irina Arkadina*
JOHN LYNCH *as Konstantin*

# William Hewison

**MUTINY**    DAVID ESSEX *as Fletcher Christian*    FRANK FINLAY *as William Bligh*

**BOUNCERS**
CHRIS WALKER *as Judd*    PAUL RIDER *as Ralph*    STEVE WESTON *as Les*    RICHARD RIDINGS *as Lucky Eric*

N the days when I went to the pictures on every Saturday night, the film industry was still in its age of innocence. Perhaps the producers and directors, agents, writers and stars were dissolute and corrupt. But the fans were untouched by either their sins or their sophistication. We found *The Wicked Lady* shocking because she displayed a depth of cleavage which is regularly on view in central London on a summer's day.

There were two houses each evening in the provincial cinemas, the best seats cost one and ninepence and the usherettes sold fan magazines at the end of each performance. The magazines revealed nothing of the stars' private lives but concentrated on the most naïve of all human emotions, hero worship. The nearest that we came to admitting that Clark Gable and Lana Turner might be human were the affectionate cartoons in *Film Fun*. We would have found *Film Review* ("Britain's Best Selling Movie Monthly") profoundly offensive.

That is not because it attempts to diminish or belittle the stars. On the front and back cover of its February issue it has coloured photographs of Sylvester Stallone's bizarre torso in a way which I found reminiscent of publications produced by the Johnny Weismuller Fan Club. But inside it writes about him with an apparent frankness that we, Gary Cooper fans, would have found extremely shocking had anyone written such things about our hero. I say "apparent" because my innocence ended when the Hillsborough Park Cinema became a cash-and-carry. My suspicion is that the movie magazines still describe the stars in a way that pleases the fans. In the Fifties and Sixties we wanted knights in armour. Today, a different sort of hero is in vogue. "With stardom," the caption says, "came unwitting slips into self adulation." And the glossy picture shows sweat running down his neck.

The stills from pictures made in the more innocent age, which appear on pages 29 and 30 of the February *Film Review*, reveal how respectful the movies used to be. Ava Gardner survives an *Earthquake* without a hair out of place. James Stewart pumps a genteel trombone in *The Glenn Miller Story* and Rock Hudson and Doris Day pose like polystyrene sculptures depicting sanitised sex and dehydrated desire. The *Three Smart Girls* are excessively dowdy, but they look like palpable virgins. Even Lon Chaney and Boris Karloff seem more concerned with humour than with horror.

Deborah Kerr (as a nun in *Black Narcissus*, circa 1947) has not a single wrinkle under her wimple. She could easily be the prioress at the Convent of St Helena Rubinstein. Forty years on, Anne Bancroft as Mother Miriam Ruth in *Agnes of God* is all artificial crow's-feet and counterfeit wrinkles. Movie-goers expect more realism than they got out of the Hollywood dream factory in the years after the war. But the magazines write with a coy confidentiality that is ageless. The coded messages confirm that readers and writers share the comforting conspiracy of infatuation with the cinema. Outsiders might describe *Agnes of God* as being "beautifully filmed". Trainee enthusiasts would no doubt say "beautifully shot". The real buffs of *Film Review* think of it as "beautifully lensed". With his head stuffed full of such verbal vulgarities, it is not surprising that Peter Haigh, who reviews the recent releases, blithely observed that "A film centred on a convent doesn't sound to have mass appeal."

Robert Redford, of course, does. And *Film Review* tells us why. "He has the strong jaw, the youthful thatch of hair and the open smile that could sell us anything." That is the sort of hero worship that we of the Gary Cooper generation understand. With the magazine *Starlog* (subtitled "Science Fiction Universe"), we feel far less at home – even though the *War of the Worlds* was out of date before we were allowed to see "A" pictures. The January *Starlog* reveals that science fiction films have changed. In *Terrorvision*, for example:

> One day the father is fooling around with his Satellite TV dish and he actually attracts the garbage from a planet in another galaxy … This planet has a pet problem. Their pets are very sweet but they look hideous … This all becomes too much for the planet's inhabitants, so they throw the pets out with the garbage. One of these monster pets enters our house through the TV set.

The monster "slimes" anyone it fancies (as a verb, "to slime" makes "to lens" sound like a euphemism) and eventually "proceeds to eat everybody in the family and then reproduce them". At least we were told that the film was about garbage.

There is, of course, a lot of honest hokum in *Starlog* – *Dr Who*, *The Incredible Hulk* and *Star Trek: The Motion Picture*. There is even an account of the latest version of *Alice in Wonderland* with Karl Malden as the Walrus, Sammy Davis Jr as the Caterpillar and Telly Savalas as the Cheshire Cat. I had never thought of Alice as science fiction. But then I had never imagined that Sherlock Holmes evolved through childhood and adolescence, as distinct from leaping into the world fully grown and already armed with deer-stalker, meerschaum and magnifying glass. Yet Hollywood says that he was once a boy and has recorded his schooldays in a film now showing in London's West End. *Starlog* calls that science fiction too. It may be that there is not enough man-eating garbage to fill 75 pages.

The miracle is that it produces 75 pages at all. For it seems to exist – perhaps even prosper – without any conventional advertising. *Film Review* has a single page promotion for one of those brands of cigarettes which advertise without speaking their name, and relies for the rest of its supporting revenue on announcements of the latest films in town – usually called *Rocky*. As I read "*Teenwolf* Preview" (not in *Starlog* but in *Film Review*), I began to realise how such bizarre publications survive. They are subsidised by extraterrestrial forces determined to destroy the world. ❧

*"I'm sorry, but due to the recession, some of you will be issued with redundancy notices on the basis of first in first out."*

# CHRISTMAS WITH THE
# FAMILY
## Bill Tidy

"With or without, sir?"

"Yes, Poppa, we've got somebody on the inside at last!"

"You blew it, Rino...
He's still alive!"

"...Tonight Franco Polestra sleeps with the...what?"

"Don Pasquale says he'll see the D.A. now."

"Yeah, the Fusconi and Tattaglia families...looks like a Christmas truce."

"Where am I gonna get a stiff at this time of night?"

"C'mon, Toni – Clay-Liston had no battery but you fix them!"

"Giuseppina, how many times. .? Cards this side, contracts that side!"

"Gee, Ma, nobody else's mudder complains about the money coming from prostitution or…"

"Sanctuary…sanctuary!"

# DAVID TAYLOR TALKS TO:

OH Lordy. Don't ask. Spare him the inquisition. Golly, what a fuss and kerfuffle. It's been rather tiresome – one feels one's *dying* from exposure sometimes, and yet in a funny sort of way one's found it rather cheering, aged 50, still to be so much in the limelight. Rather curious. Heavens above and good gracious him. One might easily infer that never before in the history of museums had a director been so intemperate as to suggest – not to *require*, mind me – rather simply to *suggest* that visitors might make some modest contribution at the door. Goodness.

In point of fact, of course, the Maritime Museum and Imperial War have for ages done variants on what the V&A has lately begun, apparently without Colin Welland giving a hoot about that and no pickets and so forth. It's really rather extraordinary that as soon as it's our much beloved Victoria and Albert Museum, as soon as it is Director Sir Roy Strong, as soon as it is Lord Carrington, Chairman of the Board of Trustees, well then the whole thing goes up like a blessed firework. The telephones go quite mad. Pressmen are at every door. One begins to tire of the sound of one's own voice, almost. And yet one simply has to take it all in one's stride.

And to be grateful to an extent for all the publicity, which does the V&A no harm at all: coverage on a scale which one could not begin to buy. Inevitably there's been a degree of distortion and of ill-considered denunciation. Frankly one expected that. Yet, to be fair, the media on the whole did seem to appreciate that voluntary charges had properly to be seen as just a *part* of a much wider plan, a package of timely reforms which in effect *transmute* and re-state the ideological principles for the museum, for any museum, at a time of *irresistible* change.

What one has simply *got* to accept, willy-nilly, is that the nature of museums has quite fundamentally shifted since the post-war period – a fact which everyone at the V&A has now taken on board and which must in due course obtain more universal acknowledgement. Absolutely *must*. Ineluctably the fact is, or rather fact was, that museum visiting was sadly more often than not associated with some form of discomfort or deprivation. One connected with thoughts of dreadful dust and dirt, with indifference, irritation and closure. Those criteria which one would apply without hesitation to an evening at the theatre, or those thought usual for example in a good hotel, were imagined not to apply. A museum was a *frightfully* dreary place.

There is in fact no logic to this position. Even with such an illustrious museum as the V&A, one is obliged to take into account radical shifts in the *expectancy* of the public. One is obliged moreover to accept that we live in a society where what a museum has to offer will be lined up against what others have to offer. The old concept that a museum opened its doors and that was that has gone forever. One *has* to compete for attention. One *has* to be aware of one's presentation, one's *ambiance*. One's visitors are ever more discerning *consumers*. Like it or not, one's museum is in the marketplace. One's said it again and again.

Very well. How, then, is one to satisfy such demands, mmm? Is one simply going to mooch about, wringing one's hands, wretchedly hoping against hope that progress and change might suddenly pause or change direction? One means *crumbs*, what earthly *use* is it to pretend that we're still living in the 1950s, as part of that post-war period when museums were seen practically as a part of the ideology of the welfare state, of the sort of provision which created the Arts Council and so on? It just isn't like that today. One has got to get to grips with things as they *are*, not as one might wish them to be. The museum *must* change. The V&A *will* change: in its structure, in its management, in its methods of presentation, in its ways of financing its

> ## "Like it or not, one's museum is in the marketplace. One's said it again and again."

needs and in its entire *attitude* towards its obligations. In the next five years this place will change, mark one's words, out of *all* recognition, one is perfectly sure of that.

God. One does tend to get a bit *volatile*. Up, so to speak, and at 'em. Really one's here to care deeply and sound off, scream a bit, to love and chastise, cherish and chivvy, put it how one will. One accepts that one's style is either thought quite *wonderful* or else drives people into *paroxysms* of rage. One's used to that. Yet in a funny sort of way, one feels at the moment as if one is *directing* the museum for the first time, almost. Such has been the heady influence of one's Board of Trustees, a new set-up for the V&A, demanding reforms and quite rightly so, as the museum is freed at last from the deathly clutch of the Department of Education and Science. Great heavens above, if one is remembered for naught else, let one *please* be remembered for that.

It's absurd that when one came here from the National Portrait, quite a *decorative* era in one's career, one then imagined such freedoms – to be *roi de soleil* at the V&A. Imagine! Whereas what one in reality found was frustration, *constant* frustration, at the yawning *gulf* dividing one's

perception of what needed to be done from one's reluctant assessment of what the Department would allow. He *means*. A more consumer-orientated V&A was quite out of the question, then. Good grief, for years and *years* one has cherished the thought of floating off a company to produce a range of merchandise – to make the V&A the *Laura Ashley* of the 1990s and realise a quite *enormous* potential. That the Trustees will now allow and frankly one could not be more delighted. Not for one *second* could it have been done under the old system of Departmental governance.

Well. There are, of course, more immediately pressing concerns: the continuance at speed of the huge maintenance programme of repairs and restoration to the *ruinous* roofs, drains, electrical heating and security systems for which not less than £26 million is needed chop-chop. Then how in heaven's name to reduce a salaries and wages bill which eats up 82 per cent of one's vote from government, or at the very least to avert its continued rise in the face of reduced resources, pay settlements over which the trustees have no control and inflation in excess of what government sees fit to recognise?

Lord, lord, lord! One's *beset* from dawn to dusk by such perplexing problems. The challenge is to respond – through changes such as one has outlined, a programme of reforms *far* greater than any undertaken since the V&A was founded in the 1850s, through the encouragement of sponsorship, through realising the commercial potential of what one already has, through so much change in the fabric of the place – such as is presently to be undertaken by Michael Hopkins, who's an architect determined to have *fun*.

Now as Peter Carrington has forcibly said, *extra* help from the public is a necessary part of paying for it all. Whatever the colour of government in the next 25 years, one does not see pouring money into the national collections as one of its prime objectives. One is obliged to capitalise. One small part of that obligation is to seek *voluntary* payments from visitors. So there we are. Let some chastise, even vilify. One's skin must thicken accordingly, one fears.

Well of course it is, in sum, rather taxing: a strain. For the past fifteen years one has determined to spend four days a week in the office and the other three at home in the country. One's customary breakneck pace could not otherwise be supported, every blessed day from morning until late at night. One tried it once, five or six days a week, finished up on the carpet

# SIR ROY STRONG

*weeping*, demolished by fatigue. Typical is to be plunged straight from one's breakfast into meetings, snatching moments to do, or attempt to do, correspondence, to have formal lunches at which one's often called upon to speak, to be chasing about all afternoon, engagements almost every single evening until quite frankly one is *whacked*.

Work follows one home to the country – well it's between Hereford and Ross-on-Wye – but one has at least the solace of the garden, one runs for perhaps five or eight miles and finds that quite *marvellous*, rain or shine. Then one is usually attempting to write at least one serious book, or planning a lecture or a broadcast, snarled up with one's Arts Council work, whatever, whilst Julia (Trevelyan Oman, one's wife) will be hard at it on some theatrical design – and one simply *has* to put a foot down and say NO VISITORS!

A certain amount of time surely must be one's own. Whilst one *adores* the V&A and lives and breathes its welfare, wants to do great and wonderful things there and perhaps one day shall, yet one remains keenly aware of the need to maintain one's personal integrity, one's personal voyage of the night as it were. It may sound rather *pious* but really to make what one can of one's certain gifts and capacities, certain applications within one's chosen area, is all.

Life must remain vivid and full. A degree of, well, theatricality is a part of that. Perhaps one won't find too many museum directors prepared to dress up in 1820s costume for a Great Ball at Osterley where one dances the quadrille – to recall a recent to-do – but it's such *enormous* fun and, like it or not, one's *style*, just as is having Messrs Pirelli into the museum (another recent day) and drinking in their calendar of young ladies in gorgeous costume on the one side and not a stitch on the other!!! Or, crikey, that Saatchi evening which was – well! – an absolute *spectacle*!

One's not afraid of theatre and spectacle. One's never shied away from extrovert *verve*. One's a grammar school boy, don't forget, perhaps still a little bemused by one's own spectacular progress and – yes – *glittering* associations, for what is art, what is design, what is decorative skill, craftsmanship, if it does not include *vitality* and *fun*?

Up and down, as one says: mercurial, volatile. Lordy, one first said it all twenty years ago when one made one's first contribution to the museum debate: *Martini with the Bellinis*, the headline said. Rather amusing at that. ❧

# Aardvark's Fantasies

## ALAN PLATER

MICHAEL PARKINSON, momentarily forgetting it was sound radio, adjusted his forelock before asking the next question:

"Is there a simple explanation for the remarkable success you've enjoyed during the past year? A SWET Award, a BAFTA Award and an Oscar, all in the space of a few months, it's quite remarkable."

"Yes," said Aardvark, "there is a simple explanation. It's all down to changing my name from Albert Maltby. Now I'm number one in Writers' Guild of Great Britain lists, therefore I'm the one that gets the phone call. That was certainly the case when Steve called me from LA."

"Steve . . . Spielberg?"

"Yes."

"That's really remarkable," said Parkinson, "and talking of Steven Spielberg, what have you chosen for your next record?"

"I'd like the Glenn Miller orchestra playing 'String of Pearls' to remind me of Sid Norris, when I'm on the desert island."

"Sid Norris?"

"A drunken tenor saxophone player and man of letters who played a major part in my writing career."

"Ah yes. According to our researcher, he encouraged you in the difficult, early days."

"No. He told me to stop farting about and get a proper job."

"Remarkable."

Terry Wogan marginally adjusted his profile, without losing sight of the Autocue, then said:

"You really are quite a resourceful chappy, young Master Aardvark. And not without spunk, I might add."

"I wouldn't say that," replied Aardvark. "I haven't even hit you yet."

The audience laughed, then broke into spontaneous applause.

"But dash it all, man, look at the track record. Three Oscars, two BAFTA awards and the Booker prize, all in the same year. By the sacred drinks cabinet of the Director General, it isn't just your winsome smile and five o'clock shadow. Or is it?"

"It's mostly to do with being at home when the telephone rings. And don't forget, one of the Oscars was shared with Sid Norris. That was for Barbra's musical."

"Barbra, as in Streisand?"

"Yes. By the way, are you Terry, as in Wogan?"

The audience laughed, then broke into spontaneous applause.

"All that being said and very probably done, you have to be considered the greatest thing since William Shakespeare or sliced bread, whichever is the greater."

"We were talking about that in The Lower Case the other night. That's my local. Just chatting. The usual Tuesday night crowd. Steve and Barbra and Al . . ."

"Al, as in Pacino?"

"Yes. That one. And there was Sid, of course, and Pete Hall and Julie Walters and Dennis Taylor and Jorge Luis Borges. We played darts and pool and talked about genius and stuff like that. Why, for example, when Shakespeare decided to write a play about a King, did he end up with Lear instead of Kong?"

"And what conclusions did you reach, bearing in mind this is a family show?"

"As far as I recalled, we agreed it was Pacino's turn to get the beer in."

The audience laughed, then broke into spontaneous applause.

Melvyn Bragg waited for the camera crew to settle outside the window of Aardvark's basement study in Isling-

ton. There was space in the room for only the two men and Aardvark's desk and the director had decided to film the interview through the open window, hoping it would be considered a significant breakthrough in arts programmes.

On the call "Action", Bragg leaned forward with middle-range intensity.

"Mike Aardvark. A year after winning the Booker Prize, you have now been awarded the Nobel Prize for Literature. It seems to me something of a contradiction that you still work in this tiny basement room."

"I was discussing it with Sam the other day."

"Beckett?"

"Yes. I said all a writer needed was space for his body and a desk. Sam had serious doubts about the desk."

"Yet it seems to me astonishing that working in this monastic setting you produce such an intimidating range of work. In the last year alone, we've seen your Old Testament adaptation on Channel 4, your trilogy of plays at the National Theatre, the ten-volume cycle of novels that won the Nobel prize. I'm almost afraid to ask . . . what happens next?"

"The opera."

"You're writing an opera?"

"I had this phone call from Milan. At first I thought they were ordering a pizza. But it was an opera they wanted."

"It seems to me that's a very big leap, even by your standards. How exactly do you set about writing an opera?"

Aardvark picked up a sheet of paper. "It's like anything else, Mel. I take it a page at a time, a line at a time, a word at a time. Basically that's your only option. You can't plan too far ahead. Anything might happen. You might have a run of injuries or international calls. Or a bad referee. Basically, it's all part and parcel of the magic of the game. So we just push it around in midfield, close them down, use the whole width of the park, get round the back of the defence. Basically it's about sticking the ball in the back of the net."

Like most writers, Mike Aardvark basically wanted to be a professional footballer. ❧

*"Just hand over the skin, and there won't be any trouble."*

# CHARIVARI

## MONDAY

Never heard further from Sotheby's regarding what they were calling "The English Bed with Powerful American Connections". The sale was to have been held a week or two ago, "a magnificent state bed made in the reign of Queen Anne (circa 1710)". Who bought it? Is that how the rumours first started about Andrew and Fergie? To Sandhurst, to play war games with Brigadier Peter Young, the battle of Alesia, he to be Julius Caesar, me to be Vercingetorix, the Celts' last stand. Wargaming is an increasing sport, they tell me, over lunch in the officers' mess. Television shapes the trends. *By the Sword Divided* spawned a huge vogue for the Civil War. Next year will Romans v. Celts gain popularity? Vercingetorix, silly bugger, lost at Alesia despite his superior numbers. Caesar just dug in and laid long siege, with immense circumvallations, fourteen miles of watch-towers, ditches and rebarbative dykes (no, Colonel, we weren't talking about Greenham Common). Reading the rules proves fascinating. Among the Afterthoughts and Clarifications I find the following: "Interpenetration: subunits are normally permitted to interpenetrate with other subunits of the same body without penalty, but in most cases separate units may not interpenetrate without being disorganised." Tell that to the Page Three correspondents of *The Times* who follow Fergie.

## TUESDAY

Sophie, Susan's daughter, arrives for supper, bearing this advertisement for Blisteze: "For most girls a cold sore is one of the worst things that could happen to them." I riposte with the poster from Charing Cross Hospital, a perfectly ordinary photograph, showing two companionable women (fully dressed) and their young-ish children: "If you had a friend who was breastfeeding it would be easier." What would – legal studies, the theory of relativity, electrical engineering? I rush out into the street to find a breastfeeding friend. But no luck. Interesting conversation earlier with Malcolm Bradbury, he singing the praises of William Gaddis, the American novelist whose *Carpenter's Gothic*, his third novel in thirty years, has been receiving more attention than the previous two – but then *The Recollection* and *JR* were rather long, 926 pages, 756 pages. Over-smooth metaphor for this new one: *Carpenter's Gothic* is the style of architecture in which the house façade was first constructed, the rooms squeezed in afterwards, all very meaningful, very paradigmatic of American society, geddit? Prefer to read Malcolm Bradbury, actually: remember his Iris Murdoch parody? "Flavia says that Hugo tells her that Augustina is in love with Fred."

## WEDNESDAY

Dinner with Bob Gavron and Kate Gardner where, belatedly, I hear that Elizabeth Smart has died. Was ever a writer so well known merely for the title of a book? *By Grand Central Station I Sat Down and Wept*, described by Brigid Brophy as "a prose poem", splendidly dramatised on the wireless some years ago. Such a tale: how Elizabeth Smart and George Barker careered across America after she read his poems in a bookshop and sent for him. And how he arrived in America complete with unanticipated wife, and later, when he and Elizabeth were arrested on a morals charge, and the police questioned, "Did you have intercourse with this man?", she drew (hence the title) upon *The Song of Songs*: "My beloved is mine and I am his – he feedeth among the lilies." At the Edinburgh Festival Writers' Conference in 1980 I brought the lovers together: their appearance became a dejected occasion. His view of the affair was a book called *The Dead Seagull*. She read passionately for the sentimental matrons of Edinburgh, who wept. He pooh-poohed the whole thing and she said in her reedy, throaty voice, "O, George, how could you?"

## THURSDAY

A postcard from Scott Berg who, coincidence this, at the same Writers' Conference gave the best popular literary lecture I have ever heard: on "Maxwell Perkins: Editor of Genius", the Scribners editor in New York who promoted, edited, developed Scott Fitzgerald, and whose first-rate biography Scott Berg wrote. Now he is immersed in his biography of Sam Goldwyn, which promises to be superb too. Ironic that his editor on the Perkins book should have told him to write it as if he were writing a screenplay. Letter from John Ryan, author of *Remembering How We Stood*, my favourite book about Dublin, recapturing Behan, Donleavy et al. And Flann O'Brien – about whom there is to be a symposium, commencing on, O, yes, the first of April. What would Flann O'Brien – who developed Jamstutter's wonderful game – have made of wargaming? "Router rally, others fanatic attack" or "Charging enemy with longer weapon" or "Interpenetrate with routed friendly troops".

## FRIDAY

Question: if you have your car washed while it sits in the car-park, how many people must you tip? Robert Benchley, worn-out with tipping the elevator man, the telephonist, the desk clerk, is leaving a Chicago hotel. Says the hand-out stretched doorman, "You won't forget me, Mr Benchley?", who snarls, "Of course not. I'm gonna write to you every day." Andreas Whittam-Smith cancels lunch; he is still racing around the City raising money for his new newspaper. Robert Redford just happens to be free, but too late, I've let the table go. Nonie Niesewand to supper: we talk about people with bad teeth who refer to their clients as "Monsters". Again, I miss John Le Carré reading *A Perfect Spy* on *Book At Bedtime*, and I cannot join in now because I don't want the plot betrayed to me until I read the book. More notes from wargames: "Rear Facing: the direction perpendicular to the rear rank of a body towards its rear, i.e. the opposite direction to the body's direction of facing."

## SATURDAY

More coincidence, Peter Bologna's catalogue arrives from Kilbrittain, Bandon, West Cork. Can't afford the Joyce item, or Flann O'Brien items, but notice a book called *The Damnable Question, A Study in Anglo-Irish Politics* by – wait for it – George Dangerfield. You see, I am still exploring the life and times of Sebastian Dangerfield, whom John Ryan wrote about in *Remembering How We Stood*. Sebastian Dangerfield was the Ginger Man – in real life, Gainor Crist from Dayton, Ohio. And who turns up to see Susan but an American designer whose home town is Dayton, Ohio, and who as a little boy had as his next-door neighbours the Crist family? The post office in Galway added an "h" to the name when the Ginger Man landed in Ireland and wired to Dublin for money. Isn't it a small world, and speaking of which we take ourselves off to see *Ran*, the new Kurosawa film, his version of *King Lear*. All critical faculties have to be suspended, even the fashionably peevish ones which must descry everything. Is this the most encompassing film I have ever seen? The most overwhelming? All war games are redundant in face of the real thing.

**Frank Delaney**

37

# MELVYN BRAGG
# Art History Is Junk

YOU will no doubt remember the lavatory which failed to reach its reserve price of £18,000. Perhaps the extravagant figure was for the seat. Not a solid gold Brunei thunder-box encrusted with diamonds, presented, say, to Mark Thatcher. Nor a snake-skinned, ruby-embedded job struck as a tribute to Clive James Esq after his "I root for the real Dallas" television doc. Nor yet anything connected with the person of Princess Diana and up for an unexceptional charity.

No, this was a common or (more likely) garden bog-seat, but *fin de siècle* and likely – according to the Maigrets in these matters – to have been a little *14e arrondissement* item, manufactured most certainly by "*Les Toilettes Pères et Frères*", with the beeswax polish taken from that highly-bred swarm kept and refined through the centuries by the Little Sisters of Lax.

For you squire, £15.50? Wooden seats are very fashionable with Sloanies. What might seem a bum deal to most of us would, to a Sloanie, appear as the perfect finishing touch in that Victorian look-alike loo. Along with the olde brass-like taps (which don't quite work), the old SAS boots, the torn mags, the odd unread Penguin Classic and the serious range of "Foodie" books, ok, yah. We admire a good seat in the SW3 shires – £15.50 is a good buy, but £18,000? No way.

If you looked closely, you would have seen what many a neat and bad-tempered parent – whizzing about with a cloth and spray – might have wiped off as graffiti. Scribble lurks quite prominently. "Kilroy was here"? No. A ditty to the effect that "Once upon this seat I sat/And thought and thought but never completed the line"? (Bring out the Shakespeare scholars with the computers.) No. A signature. That of Marcel Duchamp.

Duchamp is a decisive figure in the history of twentieth-century art. His *Virgin Descending A Staircase* is a wonderfully complex work, drawing on Braque and Muybridge to create a very fine painting. Duchamp could do the business, which is why it is so provoking that he also played tricks. One of these was to pick out a manufactured artefact – perhaps a "john" – sign it and say, in effect, "With this signature I thee transform." It is the artist's recognition and conviction of what is a work of art which makes it so, and in our culture the authentication of a signature is all that is needed – isn't it?

This, of course, was a twister. Tongue-in-cheek, but by no means dismissible. And after all, there were deeper roots to it. How many of the monumental bronzes, how much of that marble statuary and how many of those great buildings which we speak of in the name of one man or woman, were in fact *made* by anonymous craftsmen, tradesmen, labourers? Was Duchamp drawing attention to this also? As well as to the increasing determination of many artists to seek their materials in what was "given". Usually rubbish, literally: rags, tatters, odds and ends, tat. And so, if anything went, why not a well-made lavatory pan which had the added merit of drawing dramatic attention to the state of the art?

The question then becomes "What price statements?" £18,000 it seems, and although the object was withdrawn because it did not reach its reserve price, someone had bid up to £15,000. Do we take it, then, that there is an ebb in the market for what led on to conceptual art? Not if we look at the pieces being thrown by the contemporary New York chic artists, self-publicists, agents' puppets, gallery marionettes, critics' creatures – whatever you want to call them. Any of those phrases would fit most of the fashionable, young millionaires snug in six-figure lofts in SoHo, Manhattan today.

L'Affaire Duchamp loped into mind when I took part in a recent charity sale, for which celebs had sent in bits and pieces. Some of them were very generous bits and pieces: gold and platinum discs from various pop stars, some fine classical music scores – and oddities, as I thought. It was the oddities which made the running.

Exhibit A: a wig worn by the Lord Chancellor, Baron Hailsham of St Marylebone, when he was a QC. I have to hold to accuracy here and describe it as a fusty, rather sweat-soaked, dull object – very like any wig in props in any amateur or professional theatre company the length and breadth of legal dramas. When examined closely, without the interference of a head, it looked as if it had been rough-hewn from a Herdwick Sheep. (Herdwick Sheep, peculiar to Cumbria, grow grey wool. Hence the line in "John Peel" so often misquoted – which should be "with his coat so *grey*", i.e. from the Herdwick. They're still there now, providers of very good-looking but very scratchy sweaters.) The ex-wig of this ex-QC went for a brisk £550.

You (or at least collectors) would expect a presentation Triple Platinum Disc, "Do They Know It's Christmas?", to bring £1,700. And perhaps those in the know were unsurprised that an acetate Beatles' "Do You Want to Know a Secret?/A Taste of Honey" went for £380. Or the Sex Pistols' "God Save The Queen", as a single, went for £250. But here were a couple of further exhibits. Exhibit B: What would you give for the indisputably limp, jiggered jacket – unwearable, I would guess – designed as a Union Jack and worn on stage by Pete Townshend (label inside pocket reads "Lew Rose, Savile Row, London W1"). Give up? £650.

Exhibit C: Here we have, from the same P. Townshend, what are accurately described as "Assorted Guitar Pieces". The description continues, "including two Fender bass guitar necks, one Saz neck, broken body of an SG Gibson guitar and miscellaneous parts". We are gravely informed, in the high-gloss catalogue, that these instruments were smashed during live performances in the 1960s, *and there is an accompanying colourplate*!

These splinters look like smashed bits of whatever Harry the cleaner swept up that night after the lads had left the stage and made for the party. Beside them, the lavatory was, well, a work of art. How much? £100? I shall keep you in suspense no longer. £1,100 for these genuinely shattered remnants. What price the Emperor's clothes?

Is that an opening bid from the back?

*"I'm sorry, my dears, but I'm afraid the Reformation won't go through without job losses."*

# MICHAEL BYWATER
# The Thing from Outer Spice

What first led Europeans to spread all over the globe? Was it religion and the rise of capitalism? Or was it more to do with pepper, which was essential to mask the flavour of salted meat, stinking fish and boring vegetables?

*The Times*

MILES off, of course. Absolutely out of order, as the chaps say around High Table at All Souls when the conversation turns to the influence of putrefaction and mildewed taste-buds on the course of European History.

Fascinating. One wouldn't, of course, expect you lot to know anything about it. Food? Oh yes, jolly good, push along to the *Manoir au Quat' Saisons,* shell out your £8 for a plate of soup, down the red lane, swill, munch, belch, upstairs to bed, *O God Susan we shouldn't we shouldn't but O God I've wanted to for so long you know you make me feel like a teenager all over again;* which is fair enough since the requisite mental age for that sort of nonsense is about 14, erring on the side of maturity.

Keep your pants on and your mouth shut and you won't go far wrong; won't in fact, go far at all, and nor will anyone else for that matter. As I myself said several hundred years ago, "The history of humanity is the history of war," but of course I was talking out of the front of my face: the *real* history of humanity is a confused, bub-bling, rasping cacophony of buttons bursting, zips unzipping and choppers gobbling, take it how you will.

Dredge around long enough and I would not actually bet three cabochons to a cake of Life-buoy that one or two of you don't come up with lampreys.

Lampreys! Surfeits of ruddy lampreys! Do not make me laugh. Lampreys are not the half of it. Have you any notion what they used to shovel in to stave off the pangs? Lampreys were definitely in the small time; come eleven o'clock, your average potentate would feel the pangs coming on and in would come the butler with a merry smile. "Your surfeit of lampreys, sir," he would wheedle, "slightly stinking, just like you like them."

"Whacko," the potentate would cry, "and how about a couple of rancid houris liberally smeared with boring vegetables to follow? Actually, make that four, will you? We feel a spot peaky this morning, and bung in a narcoleptic turnip while you're at it, and how about a couple of repetitive beetroot with a long story about their holiday in Corfu."

That is the way things were, with the spread of Western civilisation. Anything spotted scuttling across the rush matting would be seized, sniffed and either munched or mated, depending on whim. Admittedly the spice trade did have something to do with it, but backwards; far from wishing to (a) find spices or (b) spread Western civilisation, the early sailors were men of strong sensitivity. "Ye Godf," they would cry, "I cannot ftand the fmell any longer! Let'f bugger off and circumnavigate Ye Wurdle in my clipper, they have got places down fouth you wouldn't credit, aromatic trees, lovely fmell and women which wash every day in the fea!"

And off they'd go, and come back with something faintly ridiculous like a shrunken head for keeping cloves in, with Pago Pago tattooed across the lip. "It is a souvenir," they would say, proudly. "Oh," the King would reply. "Funny, that. It reminds me of something. And what are cloves?"

And the intrepid explorer would fiddle around a bit, sheepishly, and then say something like, "Ah. They are a rare, um, deodorant, due to where the natives stinketh in no small wise. You get a woman and make holes in her armpits and stud them with the cloves and there you are. Could I have lllxiv florinf, pleafe?"

And the King would say, "Lllxiv florinf? You musft take me for fome fort of fucker"! and the explorer would say, "Yef and no, but they have this remarkable fpice up Ceylon called Bick's Bar-B-Q-Style Hamburger Relish, you splat it on all over, guaranteed," and that would be that.

No mention, you note, about religion or the rise of capitalism. In those harsh and expan-

sionist days that was off the menu. You don't bull on about abstractions when you face problems of day-to-day survival, e.g., when you discover a nest of vipers lurking on the periphery of your feudal power-base, what do you douse them in to make them taste nice? There's not a lot can be added to that kind of consideration, not even if you were to lock up an entire roomful of merchant bankers and comparative theologians; as a matter of fact, look what's happening now that we have a hemispherical concensus up this end of the globe that government is best done by merchant bankers and half-baked dogmatists. Stuff them full of fresh-frozen cod pieces and terribly exciting vegetables and little slices of bloody kiwi fruit and what's the answer? Damn all. Admittedly we have actually lately sent quite a fistful of new tin stars unto the firmament but what have they brought back? When did you last hear of a satellite sending back a new kind of HP sauce or something to stop canteen fish sticking your fingers together? What is the point of it all?

The answer is, of course, none, and that's because of the food. Look at it this way: when Justinian sent missionaries to China and Ceylon to smuggle silkworms in 552, it was not silkworms he was after, but Baco Foil; the development of the Celtic crwth in 609 marked not a new era in music but was actually a form of *mandoline* designed specifically for slicing rotton hard-boiled eggs and throwing them away in one combined action. The Northmen's invasion of Ireland, long thought to have been an expansionist incursion, was nothing more sinister than an attempt to find out where they had left the mustard. The introduction of cotton into Arab countries in the seventh century was all jolly well but they thought they were growing Bovril. And so it goes on.

The entire history of humanity, that beastly prauncing pageant of lies and gore, turns out to be nothing more than an attempt to slake the appetites without poisoning the blood, and, discounting the Persians, who where wearing tightly-fitting leather clothes back in 600BC, as well as issuing the first known edict against sandwiches, the only honest man was Heraclius. Off went his armies, and back they came, round about 627, and what did they say? Did they say, "Hey, gosh, we have spread the influence of thingy all over the globe, or, at any rate, the flat bit?" No. They said, "We have discovered sugar," and the ruling class said, "What ho! Good show! Put the kettle on and we'll rub some in!"

Now we are grown dim, and if you ask me, it's because nothing stinks any more. If you don't believe me, pop down the passage and have a sniff at whoever is in the next-door office. If you can tell with the naked nose the difference between the occupant and your lunch, you are living in an effete society.

The lesson of history is therefore simple: the best thing to do to pull things together again is to lock the entire legislature in its room, turn the heating up to full, and chuck in a couple of goats, half a stone of limburger, two sacks of old cabbage, and Mr Bernie Grant, and if that doesn't reawaken the old pioneering spirit, don't come looking for me because you won't find me; I'll be hidden in the potting shed, boring the rhizomes. ❧

"They're auditioning at Notre Dame."

"No, I'm Alexandre de Toulouse-Lautrec. My brother couldn't come."

# ffolkes en ffrançais

"Poor devil. He was hopelessly outnumbered."

"It stood for Rest In Pernod."

"Well, Monsieur Robespierre, you've certainly given politics a shot in the arm."

# FRANK KEATING
# SUNSET STRIP

I NEVER went much on Wilson of *The Wizard*. He was the ageless chap who trained on exotic herbal tea, loped down from the Dales in a black leotard, would win Wimbledon, the Olympic 1,500 metres, or the Ashes at The Oval, mumblingly come out of his trance, refuse backslapping interviews, and lope back north at a rate of knots for a refreshing cup of tea. A bit of a G. Boycott, in fact.

I was much more of a Rockfist Rogan man: he was the dashing RAF prize-fighter who would get up early to rat-a-tat down a few Jerries over the Channel before the weigh-in of his services' title-fight that evening. I was rather partial, too, to the people's choice, Alf Tupper, the tough of the track, who worked such odd hours (as a lorry driver?) that he would have to sprint 20 miles or so, from breakdown or depot, to make it to the stadium just in time for the start of the AAA 10,000 metres or marathon. He'd win, of course, always chivalrously showing up the cheat or the snob – and then run 20 miles home to catch the fish-and-chip shop just before it closed.

Ah, chums, they don't write 'em like that anymore. Today's most widely read comic, *The Sun*, has just started a new children's sports strip. The operative word. The outline scenario is solidly traditional – Nick Jarvis, ace No.9 striker for amateur club, Oakvale (who just happen to have drawn Man U in the third round of the Cup thanks to Nick's last minute winner), is torn between studying for his engineering exams, his football, and his blonde, long-limbed girlfriend, Jennifer. At least, I think she's blonde – trouble is, just about every drawing of her in the first week, whether waiting for a bus, walking down the street, or sitting with Nick in the Red Lion, described only the contents below the hem of her skirt. The artist, Peter Nash, must be more of a midget than Lautrec. Jennifer also has nipples like sharply upcurving little Ottoman daggers. We know that because she is often naked in bed with Nick as they hammer out the merits of engineering or soccer – while back home, old Mr Jarvis is always in front of the telly, ruminating, "Playing Manchester United is biggest thing that has happened to Oakvale, and that randy idiot is going to throw away his chance to play."

I may be wrong, but by the time you read this I bet Nick has scored the winner against United, who will sign him up, but Jen won't go to the big city till he's passed his exams, so he'll love her and leave her, all the way to the World Cup with England next year, where he'll score the extra-time winner against Brazil in Mexico – where the girls will all have nipples like sharply upcurving little *Mexican* daggers.

Wilson of *The Wizard* was certainly celibate. Rockfist Rogan was never known even to wink at a barmaid. Alf Tupper lived alone in a railway shack. So I suppose Nick Jarvis is much more to do with real life. Perhaps the spur of Jennifer's nipples, knickers, and tousled sheets might at this minute be encouraging some spotty youth to train himself up to be a future England centre-forward. (To be sure, the need is pressing, after the twin spearhead of Dixon and Lineker missed so many open goals as to revitalise Irish football at Wembley last month.)

Come to think of it, I daresay I'm in this job after reading C.B. Fry's notes to young men each week in the *Boy's Own Paper*. He would ramble on about keeping the elbow up at the forward defensive, getting your left foot to the pitch of the ball, or how to float over inswerving corner kicks to the far post ... but just sometimes he would give glimpses of life as a sportswriter. And it very much seemed to be The Life. Digest the breakfast kidneys and kedgeree at Brown's Hotel, while seeing how *The Times* feller had commentated on yesterday's play by Middlesex, then a couple of champagne 'vivers before Brooks summoned you to the waiting Bentley in which you would process purringly to Lord's for the openin' overs. Those being bowled, you would dash off three paragraphs for the *Star*'s first edition, hand them to a breathless, guttersnipe messenger boy, hummingly twist the first hand-rolled, monogrammed Turkish of the day into your onyx holder, and call for your first chilled bottle of hock, and accompanying seltzer.

If luncheon was to be in the President's box that day, you could amble round slowly, afix the monocle and note the runners and riders on the Long Room teleprinter over a large whisky, place your bets with the ever-attendant Brooks – happy to miss the fish dish while waiting for the Côtes de Rhone to breathe a fraction longer. If Hendren got out early, you could summon the guttersnipe from the stairs and give him two pars insisting the wretched Hendren be left out of the next Test. If Patsy hit a couple of decent fours and carried his bat into lunch, you could demand his retention in the Test team. That could hold for the fourth edition – and, by Jove, Plum, this *is* a very decent brandy, ol'boy.

Alas for the day I read C.B. Fry. I have been pining to emulate such times at Lord's for years. The only remote resemblance to contemporary sportswriting, I'm afraid, might be the intake of alcohol – though the *carte du vin* these days is decidedly inferior. I would have been far better off relying on my spiritual inspiration from, say, upright, fresh-faced, short-back-and-sides

Nick Smith, captain of Redburn Rovers in *The Rover*'s "It's Goals That Count". Or was that *The Hotspur*? And in whose columns did the onliest Baldy Hogan do his stuff? He was pioneer of "total football", so loved now by the game's po-est of pundits. Baldy was an unpassable defender in shinpads of steel, a mesmerising midfield dynamo, and a snipe of a striker when there was a goal to get and a minute to go. His team, I remember, wore jerseys of multi-coloured concentric circles because they had a mysterious gypsy goalkeeper who was colour blind and could not otherwise distinguish his own colleagues.

Of the soccer men in those wholesome, sunny and uncomplicated pre-Nick Jarvis *Sun* days, I had a soft spot, too, for *The Wizard*'s "Limp Along Leslie". I suppose he was a bit of a wimp in a way, a self-taught teenage winger who could, as they say, "make the ball talk." Leslie – never Les – doubled in midweek as the British sheepdog-whistling champion. The secret of his success was that one leg was much shorter than the other. Thus, as he shuffled towards them, he completely unbalanced and bamboozled backs and goalies. Likewise, his starring role in the primitive, one-man-and-his-dog local events on Wednesdays was enhanced, for his unfortunate disability allowed him to scuttle up and down dales with goat-like abandon.

Talk about childhood being one's most impressionable time. It must have been 15 or 20 years after I first read of these schoolboy characters that England really won the World Cup on that golden Wembley afternoon in 1966. And there I was that day, thinking Geoff Hurst bore a literally striking and high-stepping resemblance to Nick Smith, of Redburn Rovers; right down to his haircut. Certainly Alf Ramsey was a dead ringer for Baldy Hogan. Likewise, in the previous World Cup four years earlier, hadn't Brazil's coruscating attack revolved round Pelé and the little bird-like figure on the wing called Garrincha (who baffled backs because he *had one leg shorter than the other*)?

Again at Wembley, on Derby Day evening in 1968, I was transported back a couple of decades, for when Man United became the first English club to win the European Cup, two of their four goals were scored by a tall, long-striding, tousle-haired kid called Brian Kidd. For a much earlier hero had, of course, been Cannonball Kidd, the slim, tousle-haired youngster who could shoot with deadly accuracy and power from any angle and who helped his team of middle-aged ex-Prisoners of War win the First Division the season after they were let out by the Jerries in 1945. I can rattle off

without a crib all of Cannonball Kidd's 1968 colleagues – as in Best, Charlton, Stepney, Stiles, Aston etcetera. Same with Kidd's 1945-46 squad – Danny the Diddler, Daddy Lucas, Old Man Dallas, Baldy Brown, Stiffy Miller, and not forgetting good ol' Wheezy Keys on the wing.

How would Wheezy, Baldy & Co have possibly coped in bed with Nick Jarvis's Jennifer? Women were simply never mentioned in this stuff I was weaned on (not even old C.B. Fry so much as gave a parenthesis for their presence on the planet). The sporting heroes of my literary youth had no wives, no sisters, and certainly no girl-friends. If ever a mother got even a mention, it was only to record her death in the opening *Story So Far* …

Had we had the slightest touch of healthy imagination, I suppose we would have taken it for granted that Alf Tupper was haring home of a Saturday night for his *extra* six-penn'orth from the woman who served him his staple diet of chips in the fish shop. If we had given it a thought, Rockfist Rogan was late for his title-fight weigh-ins only because he was bleary after a binge of bliss with a willowy WAAF – and it was nothing to do with dogfights at dawn over Dover or Dunstable.

One-and-a-half-legged Leslie, naturally, would sleep only with

his four-footed sheepdog friend. Wilson never slept with anyone. *The Wizard*'s wizard just has to remain a dedicated virgin. He did not even have a mother as far as I can recall – at the age of about 150 he "discovered" himself on a Yorkshire Moor after a fellow nut in a neighbouring hut brewed up for him his first herbal teabag containing "the elixir of life". Certainly, Wilson would never have won Wimbledon – nor climbed Everest without oxygen – if big-breasted Jennifer had been bringing in his morning tea.

Such a scenario might yet be something for *The Sun* to start working on. ⚽

43

# DICK VOSBURGH

# WRITERS' BLOCK

**"Hearing no sound
coming from the writers' building, Cohn yelled threats
and imprecations until a veritable fusillade of typing noises filled the air.
This infuriated Cohn even more and he bellowed: 'LIARS!'"**

*A writer does not own the chains
That bind him head and toe;
If, before he falls asleep,
He should count a lot of sheep,
They belong to the studio.*

SO WROTE George S. Kaufman in a 1945 Broadway adaptation of Gilbert and Sullivan called *Hollywood Pinafore*. In Kaufman's version, the common sailor Rackstraw became an even more common screenwriter, whose entrance was preceded by the studio doorman's contemptuous announcement, "Ralph Rackstraw! Writer! Seventy-five dollars a week!" At which point, poor shunned Ralph shambled in, wearing convict stripes.

No Warner Bros screenwriter of the Thirties or Forties would have found Rackstraw's costume incongruous; that studio made most of the prison films, and, as Barry Norman would say, why not indeed? Wasn't the atmosphere there ideal? Warners' writers were forbidden to park their cars on the lot, and had to work from nine to five in a forbidding building (all too appropriately called the Writers' Block), the walls of which bore such electricity-saving edicts as "When Not In Use, Turn Off The Juice". Rudy Behlmer's fascinating new book *Inside Warner Bros* offers a prime example of that film factory's passion for economy.

In 1942 Warners hired Clifford Odets to write *Rhapsody in Blue*, a script based on the life of George Gershwin. When the film eventually appeared – screenplay credited to Howard Koch and Elliot Paul – so little of Odets's material remained that the studio resolved to get its money's worth. Screenwriter Barney Glazer received a curious assignment: change the names of all the characters in the Odets script, and turn Gershwin into a violinist. The revamped film was given the title *Humoresque*, and John Garfield, Joan Crawford and Oscar Levant were cast in it. Shortly before shooting began, the film's producer sent an urgent memo to Jack L. Warner's associate production executive:

TO: Steve Trilling      DATE: December 1, 1945
FROM: Jerry Wald      SUBJECT: "Humoresque"

Dear Steve, If you wish to start *Humoresque* a week from Monday, I think you are making a mistake that is going to cost this company eventually an extra $100,000 on the picture. Let's face the facts for a moment: John Garfield arrived in the studio Tuesday. You expect him to know how to play the violin in two weeks – or even give the impression that he is able to play this instrument. For your information, nobody in the history of the music world or the picture business has been able to accomplish this feat, unless he has had some previous knowledge of the instrument. The studio is certainly placing a handicap on Mr Garfield's performance when they ask him to fake violin-playing in a picture which concerns itself primarily about a violinist, without giving him a reasonable amount of time to get up on it. After Mr Garfield learns how to handle the bow and the violin, he must next learn how to get the proper fingering for each number he is supposed to be doing in the picture.

Wald was worrying unduly. Soon somebody came up with a most surreal solution. Yes, this was the fabled movie in which Garfield, whenever he played a solo, went into a close shot and called for his Fiddlers Three. Fiddler One, crouching behind him, provided the arm that mimed the bow work. Fiddler Two, his hand sticking through a large hole in the elbow of Garfield's jacket, mimed the finger work. Fiddler Three was Isaac Stern, who did the actual playing. One day, while Garfield was conferring with his three violinists, Levant said to them, "I understand the Hollywood Bowl's free next week – why don't you four guys give a solo concert?"

But I digress; back to George S. Kaufman on the screenwriter:

*He should work ev'ry morning, ev'ry noon and night,
And all he should do is write and write
Till he falls right over and his eyes protrude,
And this should be his customary attitude.*

So thought Columbia's Grand Panjandrum Harry Cohn, the mogul Ben Hecht christened "White Fang". In his book *King Cohn*, Bob Thomas describes the day Cohn arrived at the studio and was enraged to hear no sound coming from the writers' building. He began yelling threats and imprecations until a veritable fusillade of typing noises filled the air. This infuriated Cohn even more and he bellowed: "LIARS!"

In the early 1950s, Edward Anhalt co-wrote an original screen story called *The Sniper*, which was sold to Columbia. He later received a characteristically frenzied telephone call from White Fang. "How the hell can we make a picture about somebody who gets his jollies by shooting dames?" shouted Cohn. "The guy's a God-damn pervert!" Thinking fast, Anhalt said, "Look Harry, if this guy achieved orgasm by shooting *men*, then he'd be a pervert. But he shoots *women*! He's just an ordinary heterosexual." Mysteriously, this satisfied Cohn, and Columbia made the film.

In the opinion of Samuel Hoffenstein (co-writer of the Frederic March *Dr Jekyll and Mr Hyde*), Bernie Hyman, MGM's nondescript production supervisor, was "like Jekyll in that uncapturable moment before he merged into Hyde". In 1938 Hyman was put in charge of *The Great Waltz*, which introduced Poland's nubile coloratura soprano, Miliza Korjus ("Rhymes With Gorgeous!"). When he first heard a recording of his new star's voice, Hyman was transported. "Perfect!" he shouted. "We'll have her sing that in our picture!" Gottfried Reinhardt, who'd written the original screen story, interjected, "But you can't, Mr Hyman. That's Mozart – our picture's about Strauss." Hyman pounded the desk. "And who the hell's gonna stop me!?"

In the late Thirties, Ben Hecht and Charles MacArthur came to Alexander Woollcott's island in Vermont to write their film adaptation of *Wuthering Heights*. The moment his guests arrived, Woollcott started telling them that no pair of Hollywood hacks could ever adapt Emily Brontë's masterpiece with anything even approaching sensitivity. Knowing what an inveterate snoop their host was, the hacks wrote ten pages of script just for him to find. As Hecht told it, "We dramatised a line in the book that said Heathcliff spent a year among the Indians of the New World. We wrote it in 'ugh, ugh, heap big pow-wow' dialogue between Heathcliff and Chief Crooked Head. Woollcott wouldn't speak to us for three days."

*His lips should tremble and his face should pale.
His steps should falter and his eyes should quail.
He should live somewhere in a 'dobe hut,
And he always should be ready for a sal'ry cut.*

Norman Zierold's book *The Moguls* tells of the day during the Depression when all of Hollywood's top brass got together at the Ambassador Hotel to agree on a fifty per cent salary cut for their contract writers and performers. The screenwriter Norman Krasna was fuming about the high-handedness of this when a massive earthquake shook the city.

Before the tremors had even subsided, Krasna was on the telephone to the Ambassador Hotel, asking to be put through to the meeting. Warner Bros studio manager, Bill Koenig, answered and asked who was calling. "This is God," said Krasna, "and that quake ought to give you some idea how I feel about your salary cut!"

In William Froug's *The Screenwriter Looks at the Screenwriter*, William Bowers, writer of such films as *The Gunfighter* and *Support Your Local Sheriff*, tells of one of his early assignments, the ghastly Cole Porter biography *Night and Day*. "They had two writers, Charlie Hoffman and Leo Townsend, working on *Night and Day*, and Cary Grant brought me on to the picture. That was one of those insane things when what I wrote in the morning, they shot in the afternoon. When we were halfway through, Charlie Hoffman called me up and said, 'Leo and I have decided that you have gotten all the dirty work

# BEAU JEST

𝖎𝖎𝖎𝖎𝖎𝖎𝖎𝖎𝖎𝖎𝖎𝖎𝖎𝖎𝖎𝖎𝖎𝖎𝖎𝖎𝖎𝖎𝖎𝖎𝖎𝖎

on this picture and you deserve a solo credit.' And I said, 'I've seen the rushes too, you sonofabitch, and you're going to take the rap right along with me!' "

In 1948, MGM released an all-star version of *The Three Musketeers* with a well written screenplay by the playwright Robert Ardrey. Imagine Ardrey's reaction when, to avoid seeming irreligiously pinko (the House un-American Activities Committee had its beady eye on every studio), Metro gave history a rewrite by robbing Cardinal Richelieu of his robes and turning him into Prime Minister Richelieu.

According to Max Wilk's *The Wit and Wisdom of Hollywood*, John Huston, director and co-writer of Warner Bros 1956 *Moby Dick*, received an urgent telephone call from Harry Warner. "John, I've just been reading the script. For Chrissake, there can't be a family in the country that hasn't had somebody wounded in the last three wars! So how come you got Greg Peck with one leg?"

> *A writer fills the lowest niche*
> *Of the entire human span;*
> *He is just above the rat,*
> *And should always tip his hat*
> *When he meets the garbage man.*

Twentieth Century-Fox was hardly a screenwriter's haven. Sol Wurtzel, its "B" movie supervisor, kept ordering the Broadway playwright George Middleton to rewrite a screenplay with the words "Where's the menace?" After the fourth rewrite and the fourth "Where's the menace?", Middleton looked his tormentor straight in the face and said, "Mr Wurtzel, *you* are the menace!"

George Oppenheimer bit the hand of *his* employer in a most unusual way. While under contract to the anti-semantic Samuel Goldwyn, Oppenheimer suggested to a handful of fellow writers that each should throw ten dollars into the kitty and coin a Goldwynism, all the money going to he whose line first reached print. Oppenheimer won with "It rolls off my back like a duck."

Born in 1900, ("At 7.35 p.m. in time for dinner and the theatre") the witty Oppenheimer first came to Hollywood at 33 to work on *Roman Scandals*, and stayed on for such assignments as *A Day at the Races*, *A Yank at Oxford*, *A Yank at Eton*, and *Born to be Bad*, a Joan Fontaine stinker that Oppenheimer renamed *Too Bad to be Borne*. Many of these represented "patch-up jobs" on other men's scripts, on which he was billed last. The film composer Bronislau Kaper, on being introduced to him, said, "I always thought your name was 'and George Oppenheimer'." Eventually tiring of screen rewriting, Oppenheimer returned to New York, where he applied himself to drama criticism and, in 1966, his memoirs. In the delightful *The View from the Sixties*, he looked back on Tinseltown so greatly changed from the place where he'd begun his screen career 33 years earlier.

"Graustark is no more, its towers razed by reality. Yet, despite its fears and follies, I shall always be grateful to Hollywood. It gave me enough money to escape from it." 🌝

"WHEN I was young," Oscar Wilde is quoted to have said (so my morning paper affirms), "I thought the only thing that mattered was money. Now that I am older, I know it is."

Just the sort of line which could have been inserted into the text when I was pretending to be him all those years ago at the Gate Theatre. In those days, many of his contemporaries survived; they were often in my dressing-room after my performance, examining my make-up in the mirror and opining that Oscar was altogether more rubicund and, because of poor teeth, invariably crooked his forefinger over his mouth when he saw fit to open it. Later on, when I came to make the film, they were all dead or had stopped going to the pictures.

It is safer when the illustrious dead whom one is struggling to recreate have been dead a good while. Even then, one is never entirely safe. Who would have suspected that my performance as George III – or was it George IV? – in *Beau Brummell* could have been the subject of classified criticism thirty years ago? Or that Her Majesty would disapprove of it so strongly that she declined to appear at subsequent Royal Film Shows? The trouble with Bader and Gandhi is that survivors who once shook their hands like to recall such occasions: "Hardly my recollection of Lady Mountbatten," or "Thomas Beecham, you know, had very bony knees." There follows a long anecdote of the amateur critic perching briefly as a child on the great man's knee.

Not, of course, that anyone ever sat on her Ladyship's knee, at least not in my presence, but I do remember Edwina (here I go) taking the chair at committee meetings and invariably courteously remarking that, "For Mr Morley's benefit, I will try and simplify this paragraph." When I caught a brief glimpse of the actress portraying her on screen recently, she hardly stirred my recollection of that beautiful firework that used to light up my sky.

Since Rod Steiger played Al Capone and lived to tell the tale on chat shows, the threat of being placed in personal danger of assassination (except by critics) has been lifted, although I suspect there is little desire in the profession to be currently cast as Yasser Arafat or even General Gaddafi. On the whole it is safer and professionally more rewarding to stay on the sunny side of the street.

But to return to *Beau Brummell*, nobody told me that they planned to show it to the Monarch, or I might have toned down my performance of one of her royal ancestors strumming on the organ and trying to strangle Peter Ustinov. "You are not going to enjoy this one," Stewart Granger assured me as we assembled in the throneroom of Windsor Castle. "The director is a Nazi." At that moment the Reich Marshall demanded of no one in particular if he might be brought a cup of tea. Mr Granger pinched my arm. "Sarcastic into the bargain," he affirmed, "and the script is unactable."

So it was to prove. Later in the morning he enquired of the good director how often he proposed to shoot the scene. "Until you get it

right," the director assured him patiently. Things had not got off to a good start. Besides the script, I was worried about the casting. The role of the Prince Regent had been awarded to Peter, despite the fact that I had played it for two years at the Savoy. I had, as it were, been kicked upstairs in a nightdress hunting for the lost chord. I did rather enjoy the strangling scene, though Mr Ustinov thought I had been a shade heavy-handed. "In a scene like this you have to go all out," I told him. "But you could have got the same effect without breaking my toe, which wasn't even in camera," was his limping reply.

There was a picture of him in *The Times* only this morning, looking like the elder statesman he has become. No one steps on his toes these days, but in those days it was different. Leafing through an old press-cuttings book, I see that the critics apportioned the blame fairly evenly. Most agreed that it had not been the sort of dish to set before a Queen. But the great thing about filming is that you are not the one expected to pick up the pieces from the cutting-room floor.

Opinions divide as to the correct way for mummers to depict the famous. As far as I was concerned, the question was answered by the late George Arliss: "Play them in costume, taking care they all look alike." Such has been my policy. Oscar, Dumas, Fox, a succession of French monarchs, Nehru and members of the British Royal Family, Father Christmas and even old Father Time himself all looked and spoke, not entirely to my surprise, uncommonly like myself.

I recall, as very few others may, the extraordinary resemblance between the Duke of Manchester and myself in a film about Oliver Cromwell. I had arrived late on the casting scene and only acquired the role by personally ▶

# LET'S PARLER FRANGLAIS!

## Dans le Knob et Knocker Shop

**Salesman:** Oui, monsieur?

**Client:** Je cherche un door-knob.

**Salesman:** Et vous êtes dans le right place! Ici nous avons 9,000 pairs de door-knobs, tous différents. Simples, compliqués, nouveau riches, néo-brutaliste, Thatcheriste...

**Client:** Thatcheriste?

**Salesman:** Oui. C'est un door-knob avec une effigie de Michel Heseltine. Vous prenez M. Heseltine dans la main – et squeeze!

**Client:** Hmm. Très satirical.

**Salesman:** Aussi un door-knob pour les millionaires.

**Client:** Solide gold, peut-être?

**Salesman:** Non. Il est hollow, pour stocker le heroin et cocaine. Nous avons aussi un door-handle végétarien, qui est fait en burnished broccoli stalk...

**Client:** Non, non. Je cherche seulement un knob comme *this*.

**Salesman:** Hmm. Un straightforward job, ordinaire. Dead boring.

**Client:** Oui.

**Salesman:** C'est difficile. Nous avons beaucoup de fancy knobs, mais les no-frill knobs sont un peu tricky. Look, donnez-nous 2 ou 3 jours pour trouver un counterpart pour votre knob ici, et donnez-nous un bell, Friday.

**Client:** Friday? Mais ma wife sera une dead woman par Friday!

**Salesman:** Votre wife? Dead? Friday? Je ne comprends pas.

**Client:** Ma wife est dans son bedroom. Ce knob est le knob du bedroom door. Ce matin, le knob est détaché du door. Ma wife est stuck dans le bedroom! On ne peut pas ouvrir la porte! Si j'attends Friday, vous aurez une histoire de "Wife Starved in Bedroom Shock Horror Story. Knob Salesman Held".

**Salesman:** Ah, je ne crois pas. Ce n'est pas un cas pour moi, mate, c'est pour la police.

**Client:** J'ai déjà téléphoné à la police. Ils étaient out. Pas available.

**Salesman:** La police était *out*?

**Client:** Oui. Il y avait un recorded message. "La police sont à Hendon pour riot control practice. Si vous avez un message, parlez après le beep. Mais si c'est un complaint contre la police, forget it."

**Salesman:** Blimey. Il est worse que je ne pensais ... J'ai une idée! Insérez une tube par le key-hole et nourrissez votre wife avec chicken noodle soup!

**Client:** C'est une très short-term solution.

**Salesman:** Hmm. Ah! J'ai la very thing. Un door-knob de Libya! Vous attachez le door-knob. Après 20 secondes, il explode! Le door collapse, et voilà votre wife, shaken mais free!

**Client:** Excellent. Je le prends.

**Salesman:** Et vous avez complimentary life insurance, aussi. Bonne chance.

**Client:** Merci.

---

presenting myself in the producer's office, taking my seat on the casting couch just before the cameras were set to roll. "Fully cast," he informed me. "Nonsense, let me look." I detached the schedule from his cigar-laden hand. "There is no one down here for the Duke of Manchester," I chided. "Thank goodness I am here to fill the gap."

Not that in the early shooting this was exactly the case. Eager young horsemen thirsting for fame and battle were constantly cantering forward towards the camera while I proceeded at a cautious trot, arriving too late to complete the set-up envisaged by the director. This was made more noticeable, alas, by the script, which called for me to enquire as to the location of the proposed confrontation, thus allowing the audience to catch up with the plot, supposing the unlikely circumstance that they had heard of Edgehill or Marston Moor.

Once having arrived, and been obliged to wait for the customary tea-break which rightly signalled the printing of the fifteenth take, the rude mechanics returned to find cameras hopelessly out of alignment. They puzzled for several minutes before discovering that my horse, unaccustomed to the weight allotted to him while others munched sausage-rolls, had sunk up to his fetlocks, or whatever it is a horse sinks up to. There was ribald laughter and the eventual procurement of a coach in which I subsequently attended the proceedings, tardily alighting from the vehicle to demand, "And where are we now, my Lord Grantham?"

Long before Richard Attenborough was raised to the nobility, I too made a film about Gandhi. The proceedings necessitated a visit to India and a ride seated on the Mahatma's coffin along the funeral route. Ducking the marigolds thrown by over-enthusiastic extras, we reached Lutyen's folly only to be informed of the director's dissatisfaction, and his demand that the whole proceedings should be repeated.

He was thwarted by his principal Indian assistant: "A lot of these good people believe this is really the funeral of Gandhi, and would not allow the event to be restaged." In any case we had lost the sun. The latter argument finally clinched it, and I was off to the races. It's wonderful how often the sun comes to one's aid on location and prolongs employment. Unless a cloud chooses to pass across the heavens in view of the camera, no self-respecting lighting expert allows the proceedings to be recorded lest he be blamed for the sudden change of shadow.

But to return to the film, or rather the London studio where shooting was completed. Everyone had been telling the gentleman who played Gandhi how impressive was his resemblance to the original, and – unversed in the market conditions prevailing – he volunteered to play the part for practically nothing. It would be honour enough, he unwisely remarked. He was not a popular figure among his fellow countrymen, some of whom he had previously employed in a managerial capacity, and they took the opportunity, whenever it arose, to remind him of the fortunes they themselves were accumulating. "Mr Morley, I have bought a large house in Notting Hill which I am shortly opening as a hotel. I am advised to furnish at Heal's, would you agree?" "Undoubtedly," I would assure the conspirators, whereupon

Gandhi would hurry to the men's room. He had the weakest of professional bladders, or possibly he didn't care to weep in public.

Another who has gone about her business in the manner of Arliss is, of course, Dame Anna, a magnificent survivor of Nurse Cavell, Queen Victoria, Nell Gwyn and a prominent French Resistance leader, Odette. She may have made us share her belief that she was temporarily *The Lady With The Lamp*, but she never let us forget for a moment that she was also Anna Neagle.

My distinguished brother-in-law Robert Hardy, who also specialises in representation, would not agree with any compromise. Whether playing motor-boat enthusiasts, hotel-keepers or Winston Churchill, he goes all out, as it were. Even to the extent of half-swallowing a device which might have originated, but didn't, in a Christmas cracker, to give the effect of over-abundance of saliva and bring an uncanny resemblance to the late Prime Minister's delivery. One day he'll swallow it, I told myself, and was equally convinced that his hair would never grow back when he had it specifically thinned and shaved for the role. I was wrong, of course, on both counts; all he got, and I trust still does so, are almost incessant residuals, whereas I can truthfully say that no one has ever paid me twice for any of my performances as one of the illustrious dead.

There is a world of difference in the approach of, for instance, Paul Scofield and the late Charles Laughton: the former played Thomas More to the manner born, while the latter approached similar conflicts as if exploring how Rembrandt or Henry the Eighth would have behaved when asked to depict the actor himself. There are more ways than one of winning an Oscar – or, as Peter Finch, Michael MacLiammoir, Laird Cregar, Vincent Price, and countless others including myself discovered – of playing Mr Wilde. Let his aphorisms never be ignored. ❧

---

## ROGER WODDIS

### Reds in the Bed

"History is made in the class struggle and not in bed" – Alex Mitchell, leading member of the Workers' Revolutionary Party.

The Trotskyist who fills his role
By pressing on towards his goal
Is not to be confused with one
Who thinks the struggle should be fun
And takes time out, when waging war,
To maximise his chance to score.

Whether by rumour or design,
The news has travelled down the line:
The function of the working class
Is making history, not a pass.
To get the masses roused does not
Mean thirty women on the Trot.

Those who have cuddled 'em and kissed 'em
Do less to overthrow the system
Than comrades who are more inclined
To raise the flag and hope to find,
Before their youthful ardour fades,
The strength to mount the barricades.

# BANX

# FREE!
## BUT EXTREMELY SMALL
# PUNCH BOOK OF THE ROAD

A section of ROAD, viewed in plan (NOT TO SCALE)

## Contents

## IT PAYS TO KNOW YOUR VEHICLE

When your vehicle hisses, makes metallic "grinding" noises or goes **chuff-chuff-chuff** and then stops, perhaps bursting into flames, there could be a riot about or perhaps a fault in THE ENGINE.

In the case of rhythmical thumps or "shrieking" sounds, it pays to ensure there is no one inside the boot, or sundry items stuck to one or more WHEELS. Use the **Handy Symptom Sorter** to help you find where these sorts of things are located.

NEVER get out to investigate a noise whilst the vehicle is moving at speed. It pays to wait until the vehicle can be brought to a place of safety beside a warning triangle, uniformed police officer, or community liaison spokesperson. Most breakdowns occur because something or other has GONE WRONG. Often there are TELL-TALE SIGNS of neglect, such as NO PETROL or NO OIL or a BROKEN PART. Sometimes INSTRUMENTS can help you to identify the trouble (**see chart**).

It pays to keep babies or small children well away from hot or moving PARTS and to keep them illuminated at night, when it can be dark.

If trouble persists, it pays to ensure you know how to MEND various things around the vehicle, perhaps using a few easy TOOLS. A handy tip is to carry a SPANNER, wrapped securely in a lint-free oil-rag. It pays to carry a SCREWDRIVER too. Be sure to mark or embroider **both** lint-free oily rags with the words SPANNER or SCREWDRIVER, as the case may be.

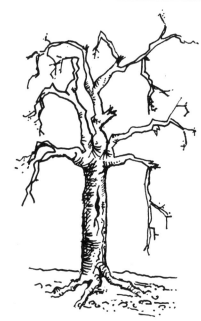

### The Up-to-The-minute Wonders of Acid Rain

The Once-Verdant Roadside Tree
© READER'S INDIGESTION 1985

## WHAT TO DO WHEN SOMEONE HAS AN
# INCIDENT

A prudent motorist knows that his or her vehicle, as the case may be, might one day suffer, or become involved in, a vehicular INCIDENT.

It pays to be prepared. The following items should be stored in a cool, dry location in the car for use at an incident:-

**1.** Notebook and pen or pencil, or fibre-tip, rolling ball biro, proprietary propelling pencil, or box of watercolours.

**2.** A length of string, knotted at 2in (5cm) intervals.

**3.** A piece, or length, of chalk (colour white).

**4.** A torch complete with bulb and fully-charged batteries.

**5.** A loaded ciné camera or portable VTR unit.

**6.** A night stick, aerosol pepper gun and/or alarm klaxon.

The following information should be noted at the scene:-

**1.** The make, model, year, registration and chassis numbers of any vehicles within $100m^2$ of the alleged incident.

**2.** The names, addresses, postcodes, blood groups and NI insurance numbers of no fewer than one dozen independent witnesses or their immediate next of kin.

**3.** The precise nature and extent of any damage to persons, vehicles, property, horses, cattle, asses, mules, sheep, pigs or dogs under the meaning of the Immunisation Act.

**4.** The type and condition of the road surface to a depth of 2in (5cm) and sketch-map of prevailing winds, barometric isobars and any other pertinent information, e.g. hurricane.

## EMERGENCY FAULT-FINDER

| SYMPTOM | CAUSE | SYMPTOM | CAUSE |
|---|---|---|---|
| ENGINE WILL NOT START | Engine faulty<br>Starter faulty<br>Car gone wrong<br>Not your car | LIGHTS DO NOT WORK | Switch set to "Off"<br>Switch set to "On", but faulty<br>Light unit or "bulb" broken<br>Other fault |
| ENGINE SPLUTTERS AND DIES | Spluttery or dead engine<br>Fault in vehicle systems<br>Worn or damaged components<br>Parts need changing | VEHICLE GETS HOT | Engine overheating<br>Brakes "on"<br>Windows set to "shut"<br>Vehicle on fire |

# THE WONDERS OF ROADSIDE LIFE

'Twixt kerbstone and hedge, beside rolling hard shoulder or under cracks in the concrete criss-crossing the length and breadth of Britain (see **Gazetteer of Concrete Cracks The Length and Breadth of Britain**) lies nature's half-hidden refuge for a myriad of miraculous living things in bold profusion, from the noblest big tree (see **The Book of Big Bold Roadside Trees**) to the delicate little Devil's Boletus or Edible Dormouse (see **The Big Digest of Little Roadside Wonders**).

Once forests covered these isles, sanctuary for all manner of species great and small. Ice Ages, wet summers and wars ensued, then later came road-widening schemes to exact a heavy toll upon the erstwhile teeming habitat of Buxbaum's Speedwell, Mouse-Eared Hawkweed, Ivy-Leaved Toadflax and Brimstone Fritillary.

In days of yore, Old Albion's yeomanry explored this pageant of untamed grandeur (see **Old Albion's Pop-Up Pageant Book of Untamed Grandeur**) but in today's modern times the motorist can re-discover the joys of roadside life **and** win a FREE set of reversible, wipe-clean, toughened Jolium™ ring spanners with every FIVE volumes ordered, yours to treasure and to peruse without obligation in the comfort of your own vehicle (see **Our Nation's Proud Heritage of Boring Roadside Books, Vols I to CLXVIII**).

## IDENTIFYING ROADSIDE MOTHS

(Condensed from **The Roadside Treasury of Nature's Wonders In The Moth World And Complimentary All-Weather Wingspan Gauge**)

One of the proudest, most timeless pleasures of motoring along today's busily congested roads, midst all the "hustle and bustle" and "hurly-burly" of life as we know it, lies in the fascination of spotting our native roadside moth life and the richly absorbing panoply of lepidopterous visitors to these historic shores.

Perhaps the most spectacular of all is the night-flying, mottled umber **Bombyx Woddisii**, or **Devil's Pollinater** with its thread-like cousin, the ocean-going **Crepuscular Boatman**. Both can be found basking on warm, south-facing bollards or, in season, skittering gaily between the proud cohorts of fluorescent cones which are such a colourful feature of our network of "highways and by-ways".

To observe and correctly identify the **Ermine-Bellied Nettle Moth** (poisonous if eaten with fish) is by no means an easy task in swiftly-moving traffic when it is easily mistaken for a piece, or length, of broken twig. Tell-tale knobbed antennae on its comb-like offside rump are the key, but it pays to keep a watchful eye for predators like the Common Moth-Eating Ringed Whimbrel or "Saint Agnes's Swatter" (**Eradicus Buzzboxii**) and for heavy vehicles in the inside lane which may run out of control, especially in fog (see special section: **So You Think It Might Be Foggy**).

# You and Your GUDGEON PINS

It pays to maintain your gudgeon pins in tip-top condition, for otherwise your gudgeons may fail to operate smoothly or could become "un-pinned". This can lead to "flasking".

The pins are easily located beside the wet-pinioned flange's journal-piece and should be inspected at regular intervals. Apply a few droplets of proprietary lustralising agent or anticoagulant flux, ensuring it is well bedded in between the splines. Do NOT over-tighten the crux bolt.

Check periodically for signs of seepage where the gaiters rub against the main rostrum on the "up" stroke. Wipe BOTH ends with a swatch of lint-free scrim, then use a strobe and calipered (or nib-ended) pargeting tool to check the inner tension. If EITHER the bezel OR variable arm is thwarted or "tram-lining", switch OFF and replace the grommets without delay.

# RESTORING OLD TREASURES OF THE ROAD

**BEFORE**

**AFTER**

Unless a motor vehicle is thoroughly rinsed, soaped, rinsed again, leathered off, waxed and "buffed up" at least once or twice a day, "corrosion" can quickly take hold and may mar the "showroom" finish or **lustre**. Where "rust" or extensive "rot" is present, remedial action may be time-consuming but is full of interest and excitement for the d-i-y automotive enthusiast or "crushing bore".

With patience and a little "elbow-grease" there are hours of fun to be had for

**(continued pages 2-599)**.

# QUICK ROUTE-FINDER

(arrows indicate direction of travel)

M25 · B303 · ARMSTRONG · KERBSTONE · Wadham Stringer · Stirling Moss · Damper · A246 · GIRLING · M25 · Grommet · SIDDELEY · JUDD

# HRH THE PRINCESS ANNE
# One's Travels

THE camel next door to me let off a series of the most revolting, flatulently bilious noises I have ever heard when asked to rise to its feet. He, she, or it was apparently not pleased about the position of its passenger, somewhere behind its second or stern hump. The noise only stopped after it was made to kneel down and the passenger moved to behind the forward hump. My camel was much more amenable and ambled off down the road on its well-worn path through the old town of Jaisalmer in Rajasthan. Just a little taste of the local form of transport on my way to visit a Save the Children Fund project in India. Next time I want to try a proper thoroughbred riding camel and not the equivalent to a tourist bus, but the beast is the only way to travel long distances in this part of the world.

Before I became President of the Save the Children Fund, I had done a little travelling of a fairly conventional kind – although with not very happy memories of my early experiences in the air or at sea – with my extraordinarily bad sea keeping capabilities, it's a wonder I ever got further than the overnight train to Aberdeen! I do recall that when I was small the train was an adventure, and in those days you got an excellent breakfast as well.

However, a whole new dimension of my experience of travel really began the first time I went overseas to visit a Save the Children Fund project in Ethiopia, back in February 1973. As a result of a previous drought, the Fund had been asked to help in relief work and in setting up long-term mother and child health care projects. Ethiopia is a large country with very poor roads and a few fairly basic airfields, and flying anywhere in Africa is uncomfortable if you cannot fly at dawn or dusk. The heat during the day causes tremendous thermals and one of my worst memories of any flight or landing was getting into an airstrip 8,000 feet up in the mountains but with much higher mountains rising all round so that the aircraft had to be flown in ever decreasing circles before it could land. If that was not bad enough, I then had to climb into a Land Rover (looking like a green being of average size from outer space and feeling worse) and drive 2,000 feet back up the mountain. But the trip was well worth it just to see the Coptic churches at Lalibala, carved down into solid rock. They are surely one of the less well known wonders of the world.

After an inspection of a Save the Children Fund clinic, I was allowed the luxury of three days in the Simien Mountains – the huge central plateau of Ethiopia, rising to some 14,000 feet in places. Fortunately, we started climbing from about 8,000 feet and had help from some local mules. They were nothing like the mules normally illustrated in the children's books of my youth or as used by the British Army or Gold Rush prospectors. They were barely the size of an English donkey and decidedly thinner, but their lungs were infinitely more efficient at that altitude than the lungs of those of us more accustomed to sea breezes. We spent two nights under canvas at about 12,000 feet and we walked to the edge of the plateau to look for *moufflons* which graze on what can only be described as precipices. I say "walked" but wheezed and tottered would be a better description of our movements at that altitude. Also on that trip we passed several nomad settlements and it was already apparent that the demands being made on the limited resources of trees and soil were creating trouble for the future. However, a centuries-old way of life is not easily changed by outside interference, especially when there is no real alternative to the traditional form of agriculture. This situation is found in many places and similar problems must be appreciated by those who wish to make a genuine contribution to developing countries.

It was a memorable trip for me in so many ways, not least because of all the little "friends"

> ## "Looking like a green being of average size from outer space, and feeling worse, I had to drive 2000 feet back up the mountain."

who shared my sleeping bag, and the amount of weight I lost. So far, I have (regrettably) not managed to achieve a similar reduction again!

Since then my travels have taken me to many other parts of Africa, Asia, and briefly to the Middle East. The greatest distances were covered in Andovers of The Queen's Flight, not fast, but very practical, especially for some of the very rural areas that I need to visit to catch up with our Save the Children Fund teams. In Africa the most basic air-strip I have experienced was Goram Goram on the edge of the Sahara in Burkino Fasso (or Upper Volta as it was when I visited it). The strip was barely distinguishable from the desert around it and certainly had no control tower, landing aids or services such as fire extinguishers. However, a fire engine was found and persuaded to drive all the way up there and fortunately was not required.

In India I made the mistake of accepting the invitation of the Captain to view the hills from the cockpit, but by the time I could see the airstrip we were really quite close and it did *not* look long enough. I reminded myself – not for the first time – that ignorance is bliss and I would have been better off in the rear where you cannot see what is about to happen to you and therefore don't worry about it. Watching air shows, where they demonstrate how quickly a particular aeroplane can stop, I have often wondered what it must be like for the passengers within the aircraft. Now I know. As my trainer used to say, "Put it down to experience and don't do it again!" The whole exercise was, of course, perfectly safe – or at any rate as safe as, or safer than, taking to the roads. The roads themselves vary considerably from the recognisably tarmac variety to those indistinguish-

*"I'm going to call it football!"*

able from the surrounding countryside. Again Burkino Fasso comes to mind – this time for the slowest of road journeys thanks to the ruts and bumps. In fact I abandoned the estate car provided for me because of the rotten ride, and took to the Save the Children's brand new Land Rover County, kindly donated by the Worshipful Company of Carmen, since its rather more basic suspension ignored most of the bumps. But driving through the countryside really brought home the problems of these Sahel areas. Camels, sheep, goats, donkeys and even horses are all competing for much the same limited grazing. The acacia trees are few and far between, where once, I was told, there used to be an almost impenetrable forest. There were one or two small areas that had been fenced off where the vegetation, while not exactly lush, was considerably better than outside the fence, which just showed what could be done to improve the viability of the land. It was also on that drive that I came across a piece of international "aid". It was a bright, shiny and very large set of disc harrows that many farmers in the affluent West would have thought twice before buying – partly because of the size of the tractor required to pull it, never mind the cost. The harrows had been in the same place for six years, there being no tractors for hundreds of miles and certainly no diesel.

Running a car is difficult enough, but essential for the Save the Children Fund if its field workers are to reach the three clinics they run, each a minimum of 60 miles from the next. It was dry when I was there and the travelling was slow but possible. When it rains – if it rains – the roads simply disappear and, short of a hovercraft, no transport moves. In those conditions, the ubiquitous Land Rover is still the best bet (and I'm not even sponsored by them!).

In Bangladesh we had to abandon planes and cars and went by train, by boat and Shanks's pony. It is a very flat country: good news if you are walking, but bad news when the water level rises, as it does every year. Whether or not you get flooded is "Inshallah" – "The will of Allah". That day we walked through three villages, visiting the locally trained Village Health Workers and Traditional Birth Attendants, who looked after the villagers' minor health problems and the vaccination programme. On foot you have time to see how well kept the houses are on the inside and the efforts the people have made to follow the example of their Health Visitor. The boats, some powered by outboard motor and some by manpower, are essential in a country which is basically a river delta. The river, and the sea into which it flows, control life completely and often very harshly.

Finally, I think I must mention one other form of "transport" – although I did not use it on Save the Children business. It was as a result of a visit to Nepal in order to see the Fund's projects. I was allowed a couple of days in the Royal Chitawan National Park down on the Indian plain. We flew in to a grass strip and were met by our transport for the journey to the lodge, some way away into the jungle. We went down one set of aircraft steps and up another set, rather older and a bit wobbly, but really the only practical way to get a lot of tourists on to their first elephant! We climbed on to a reasonably well covered platform with a wooden running rail and four little uprights at the corners. The passengers sit at the corners with a leg each side of the upright and under the rail. At this point the elephant, which had been kneeling down, rose to its feet, a sensation that feels like I imagine a small earthquake would. Uplifting? It then marched majestically off towards the river. I will not describe any more because it would turn into a story of its own. Suffice to say that a young lady asked me the other day if I would rather drive a tank or ride a horse. The answer was a horse, but if she had asked me to choose between an elephant or a horse – well...!

*"Don't move an inch, Findlay, I think he's trying to sell us something."*

51

"Frankly, I'm at my best in character parts. Remember Champion the Wonder Horse, Elsa in 'Born Free', the shark in 'Jaws'? All me."

# THE WILD BUNCH

"Keep it under your hat, but she does Streisand's singing voice."

"…And your great grandfather's great-great grandmother starred with Errol Flynn in 'Robin Hood'. He pulled her leg off and threw it at Friar Tuck."

"He was a child star in the early 'Tarzan's, but then the talkies came along."

# DONEGAN

"I wouldn't mind him doing his own stunts if he was paying for his own insurance!"

"I don't care what the union says! Mooching about or stampeding, the money's the same."

**BBC TO SUSTAIN VIEWERS' VIEW**

**By Our TV and Radio Correspondent**

BBC Television's "Points of View", to which viewers contribute their opinions about BBC programmes in hundreds of letters a day, is to be kept on the air without a break.

When Barry Took, the regular presenter takes his summer break, in August, he will be replaced first by Nanette Newman, the actress, for four weeks, and then by Andrew Sachs, the actor, for a further three weeks.

*Daily Telegraph*

Why oh why must all your letters start with

must this behaviour permeate even "Postman Pat?"

ineffable

OUT-BLOODY-RAGEOUS: I HAD HOPED THAT SEX WAS A THING OF THE PAST...

I bet you don't dare read this out

WE say "NO, NO, NO:" yrs, *[signature]* (DR.)

Whenever Richard Bak comes on, my dog Baggin (a loveable mongrel with 6 paddy-paws and a roguish glint in his good eye) see

# Points of View

**GUSHING FEMALE VOICE:** "Thank you thank you thank you Auntie Beeb!"

**BARRY TOOK** (*deadpan feline grin*): Writes "Gushing" of Baldock.

**GUSHING FEMALE VOICE:** "When I heard that Barry Took was going to take a break from the wonderful programme he presents so well –"

**BARRY TOOK** (*writhing modestly and giving mock-saucy glances at camera*): Well, normally we don't give your comments on this programme, but can we really afford not to on this occasion?

**GUSHING FEMALE VOICE:** "My pet Siamese loves him and miaows along with his impromptu jokes…"

**BARRY TOOK:** And many more of you wrote in to say the same.

**GUSHING FEMALE VOICE:** "So it was something of a relief to discover that instead of some long-haired trendy intellectual person from the BBC taking over we have purring, tabby Nanette Newman and butch tom-cat Andrew Sachs who I know my pussy will love."

**BARRY TOOK:** Not such a dumb dumb friend. But yes it's true, with me in the studio are gorgeous, purring Nanette, hot from her latest film, *Restless Natives*, and hectic, Torquay-based waiter, Manuel, or Andrew Sachs to his friends both dumb and human, if he has any.

**ANGRY FEMALE VOICE:** "No, no, no, no, no, no, a thousand times no!"

**BARRY TOOK:** Writes "Narcolept" of Flint, but what can she be saying "no" to? Surely not Nanette and Andrew? (*Grins slyly and sticks tongue in cheek.*) Surely not?

**ANGRY FEMALE VOICE:** "I sat through *Raging Moon* from beginning to end and I was sickened by the smutty behaviour of everyone concerned with this tastelessly orchestrated farrago of lewdity amongst disadvantaged persons, or spastics as some tasteless people call them. I have suffered from narcolepsy for some time now and I can assure you it is no joke, so I was heartily sickened by Ms Forbes's or whatever her name is portrayal of the so-called 'attractive polio victim' who shamelessly makes up to Malcolm McDowell in the film – at least, when I was awake to see it. Am I a rare specimen or do many people feel the same way as me? Can someone explain to me why we are forced to sit in front of our screens and watch such a crippled and warped view of life being perpetarted (there is no other word for it)?"

**BARRY TOOK:** It's our old friend, "Disabled Lib", again. But never let it be said that I don't give both sides of the question.

**MORONIC MALE VOICE:** "If only if only if only!"

**BARRY TOOK:** Writes "Concupiscent" of Cirencester in wistful vein.

**MORONIC MALE VOICE:** "If dear old Auntie Beeb as I believe we have to call it now would only pull her finger out –"

**BARRY TOOK** (*Kenneth Williams impersonation*): Ooh!

**MORONIC MALE VOICE:** "And take the advice of our superb Prime Minister and show advertisements, then we could see more of gorgeous, purring Nanette Newman or whatever her name is in her excellent series of advertisements shown recently to a grateful public on the other channel as I believe we must call it. We have seen her shapely undesiccated hands. Can we perhaps also be vouchsafed a sighting of her legs also?"

**NANETTE NEWMAN:** We move on now to our next letter. And it has an Irish flavour to it.

**BARRY TOOK:** A drisheen-flavoured epistle forsooth.

**ANDREW SACHS:** It's from "Buggered" of Bognor.

**BAD-TEMPERED MAN'S VOICE:** "I watched *A Better Class of Person* for the full two and a half hours and I have never been so nauseated in my entire life!"

**BARRY TOOK:** There's no point to this interruption. I just like to show my face as often as I can. I know you like me to do that because I get a hundred letters a week telling me that you do. The fact that only madmen write to programmes like this does not seem to deter me or discourage me in any way. But back to "Buggered", Bognor.

**BAD-TEMPERED MAN'S VOICE:** "The good old BBC is to be congratulated on failing to show such filth. The scene in which tight-lipped Eileen Atkins is blown off the lavvy by a German bomb, her knickers round her ankles, and the full frontal of the great Shakespearean actor Alan Howard falling down the stairs in his birthday suit (I suppose we have to put up with this kind of thing since we joined the EEC) are a gross slur on the reputation of the people of Bognor where these scenes are alleged to have taken place. Do the trendy intellectuals, so-called, at the BBC who make such programmes ever stop for so much as one single second to consider the difficulties involved in running Select Holiday Homes With Telly In All Beds, H&C laid on?"

**BARRY TOOK:** He's got a watertight point there, you have to admit. (*Looks very serious and stern.*)

**BAD-TEMPERED MAN'S VOICE:** "Besides which, it is common knowledge that the Urban District Council as we must call it now, the Germans and the Developers have all competed to show their loyalty to King George III's command with regard to this town without upstarts such as John Osborne, whoever he may be, muscling in on the act. Besides, it was not King George III at all who mentioned the unnatural act concerned but King William of Orange who, when told that Littlehampton was smaller than Bognor, said, 'It's bigger begorrah.' Being Irish, that was the way he spoke, of course. 'Buggered', Bognor."

**BARRY TOOK:** Or Bognor can't be a chooser to adapt dear old Maurice Bowra and go upmarket all in one fell swoop, something which this programme normally does not try to do.

**NANETTE NEWMAN:** Anyway, I quite agree with the viewer that the good old Auntie Beeb is to be congratulated on failing to show such a programme. I do not think that that kind of drama is quite nice and I am sure such things do not take place in Torquay?

**ANDREW SACHS:** Don't you believe it, I remember –

**NANETTE NEWMAN:** As an actress I often have to do quite a lot of ad-libbing but I always try to keep my act clean, which is why, after a lot of thought, I decided to take part in an advertisement for washing-up liquid.

**BARRY TOOK:** Did you know when you promised to love, honour and *obey* it would involve appearances in such films as *Restless Natives*, which has been universally vilified to coin a phrase? But now we turn our attention to cakes.

**TETCHY WOMAN'S VOICE:** "When oh when oh when oh when?"

**BARRY TOOK:** It's our old friend "Egregious" of Egham again, I fear.

**TETCHY WOMAN'S VOICE:** "I suppose the clever, fashionable people at the BBC who make children's programmes such as *Tales From Fat Tulip's Garden*, so called, do not stop for a moment to consider what the effect on children may be when they see Fat Tulip (whose very name is an incitement to abnormal obesity levels in infants) trapped in his bedroom by a giant cake. That would be too much to ask, I suppose. When oh when oh when oh when will these long-haired *graduates* from some of our best universities ever learn that this kind of programme blatantly encourages pre-school infant-level children in their low-nutrition oriented eating habits, which as many experts now agree are the cause of many of the social evils in our society today as we know it?"

**NANETTE NEWMAN:** As a children's writer I agree with the viewer and though the programme involved did not go out on the dear old etc, nevertheless we are sending a written apology *from* the producer who now realises that it was a wrong emphasis to place and a negative set of signals may have been going out to children there and indeed adults. So it's a big "sorry" to "Egregious", Egham there.

**BARRY TOOK:** Thank you, "Sorry" of Surrey.

**ANDREW SACHS:** I say I say I say: what did Barry Take?

**NANETTE NEWMAN:** I'm afraid I don't understand what you're talking about.

**ANDREW SACHS:** All the fun out of fronting this, well, programme, so called.

**BARRY TOOK:** And there we must leave you with some irrelevant news pictures which show disabled kittens having a boxing match and dressed as waiters in Torquay. Goodnight.

*"Tell me, Smithers, if all the world's a stage, how come all the clowns are employed in this office?"*

# LET'S PARLER FRANÇLAIS!

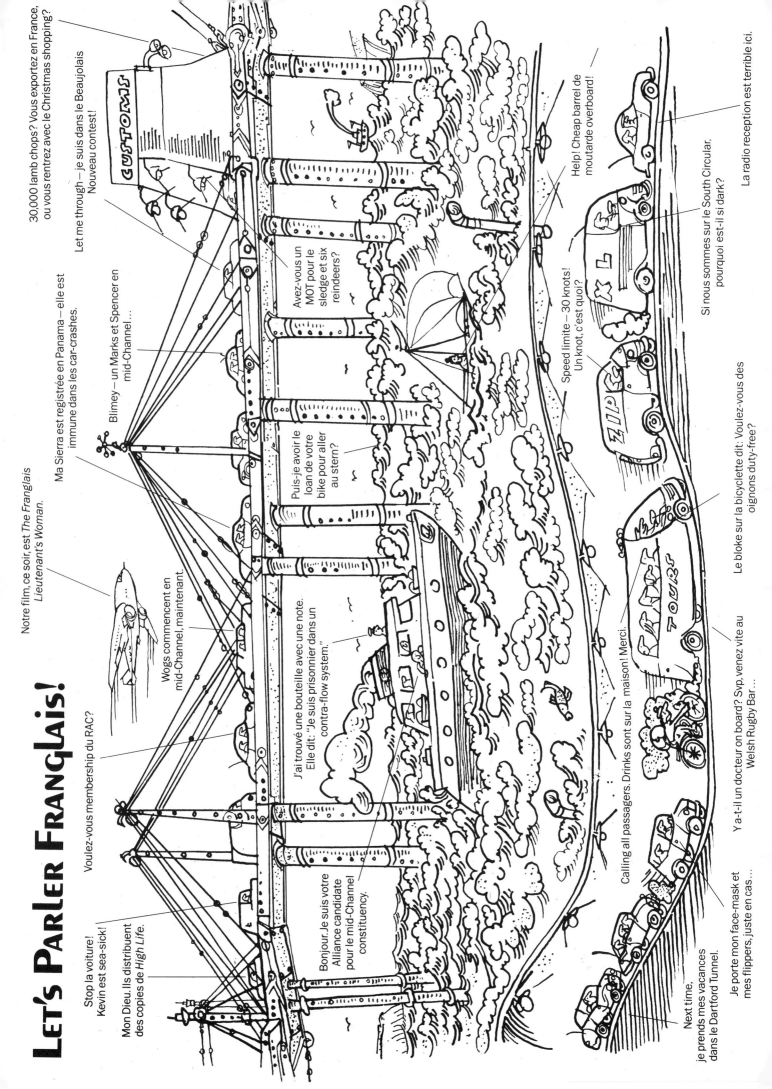

MALE and female prisoners should be imprisoned together with shared facilities and supervised by staff of both sexes, according to an independent inquiry into women prisoners to be published this week.

*The Observer*

Dear Claire Rayner,

Oh dear me, I am in a pickle! Since 1981, I have been walking out, not literally, ha-ha, with a wonderful guy from wing, he is strong but never smelly, and very considerate, for example he has promised that as soon as he gets out he will have *Terence* tattooed on his left bicep with a little ring of teeth round it in memory of our first date.

But suddenly, horrors, this has all changed! Last week, they introduced women into our nick, since when he has been all over a fat redheaded bitch doing three for dishonest handling, and seeing her standing next to him in the slops queue this morning, I am here to tell you the jury were not wrong!

I am at my wits' end to know what to do. He seems to have lost all interest in me. Worse, my attempts to win back his undying affection seem doomed. Last night, I stuffed a couple of oranges up my singlet in the hope of beating her at her own game, but he just pulled them out, gave one to her, and they ate them in front of me.

I don't mind humiliation, as a matter of fact I have made bob or two out of it in my time, but what I can't bear is not understanding. Up until last week, he was a normal, healthy prisoner. What has made him go peculiar, all of a sudden?

*Weepy, Strangeways*

---

Dear Claire Rayner,

I am at my wits' end. I was recently moved here to Broadmoor from Holloway because I kept shaving my hair off, and they put me in with a very attractive arsonist, slim, little moustache, nice personality, likes Chinese restaurants – apparently they're very slack on fire regulations, you learn something every day, don't you? – and we have been getting on like a house, anyway, to cut a long story short, he wanted to know why I had no hair, and I didn't like to tell him it was only because I had nits and didn't want to let on at Holloway because they make you wash in Lysol etc, so I told him it was because I was Joan of Arc, she is always bald in pictures e.g. Ingrid Bergman, Jean Seberg, I thought that might impress him, due to where most of the women in here are Florence Nightingale and Queen Victoria and Edwina Currie and boring old rubbish like that.

I think it was a mistake. It has made him fall in love with me. Every time we are alone, he starts breaking up the chairs and putting them into a pile and throwing me on top. It is not really risky, because they do not allow him matches, so he has to get down and start rubbing two chairlegs together, which gives me plenty of time to run, but that is not my problem.

My problem is: if I tell him I am not Joan of Arc, will he stop respecting me? I suppose I could tell him my voices had suddenly come to me and informed me that I was non-inflammable, but would he believe me? Worse, if he did believe me, would he stop loving someone he could not get to light?

Desperate,
Broadmoor

---

Dear Claire Rayner,

Please use your enormous influence to help me!

On our top corridor, the authorities are shoving four women in with every four men. Do people outside have any idea what conditions can be like with eight prisoners crammed into a titchy cell originally intended for four, all pressed up against one another?

Well, down here they have given us sod-all! We are four blokes rattling around like wossnames in a bloody pod.

The undercrowding is a scandal.

*Disgusted,*
*Durham*

---

Dear Claire Rayner,

I am doing a ten stretch for using a hammer on my wife without due care and attention, i.e. failure to throw same off bridge, and I have recently took a fancy to a nice big woman who is in for running a disorderly launderette.

Recently, she took 2oz best snout off of me, so I know I am in there with a chance, there is a romantic language of snout, and I have asked her to come away for the weekend to a nice little place I know behind the boilers. But I have been in here since 1981, and fashions change, and I do not wish to look a prat, so can you tell me whether I should knock her about on our first date, or would it be more sensible to wait until we know one another better?

Confused,

Brixton

PS I mean failure to throw the hammer off a bridge, not failure to throw the wife off.

PPS Oh, I don't know, though.

57

# YOU AND WHOSE ARMY PENKNIFE?

**TONY HALL**

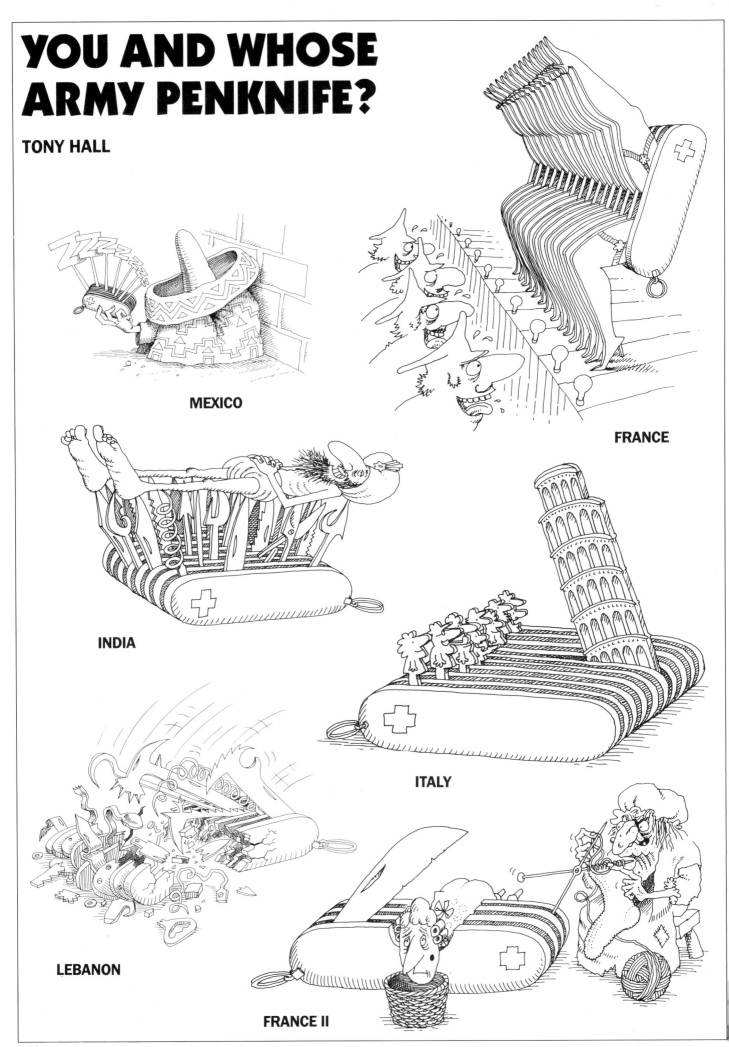

MEXICO

FRANCE

INDIA

ITALY

LEBANON

FRANCE II

# Screen Play

COUPLE of years past, when the NY and LA arbiters of "in" began popping up on their respective *Times* fashion spreads sporting flat-tops and pleated pants, I was among the first of the rural nerds correctly to identify this phenomenon as the Fifties Fad. My principal seat of dismay at that juncture lay in having so rashly abandoned my poodle skirt, crinolines, Capri slacks and ratting brushes to the Salvation Army only slightly prior to retooling my radically straightened wardrobe in basic black turtlenecks and wire-rimmed spectacles. Latter-day dismay, however – perma-fitted, as I am, with your standard Sixties-style expanded consciousness – springs chiefly from the observation that all of America has since fled, en skittish masse, back to the snug haven of the Fifties fantasy for indefinite asylum from contemporary Reality.

I know, for I have been watching TV. And television, mirror of the mind of middle America, has little to offer of late beyond recycled or reconstructed reflections of that simpler day, when bad guys wore black, father knew best, and Ronald Reagan's Death Valley Days were but ephemeral flickers of black and white fancy.

Scores of second-hand family situation comedies, spanning the spectrum of cable and network frequencies, daily enchant '85's recidivistic masses. *I Love Lucy*, though, earner of over $3 million in re-runs since going off the air in 1959, seems to be suffering a certain displacement lately as burgeoning legions of *Leave It To Beaver* fans, splicing three generations, sigh with wistful nostalgia at family life *à la* fabulous Fifties. Therein, Mr Cleaver arrives home from work, looking the very picture of respectable provider, and accords a chaste kiss to the cheek of impeccably groomed, mild-mannered wife, June. Mrs Cleaver, ever frosting a cake (baking a pie, drying a dish, tossing a salad) then declares anxiously, "Oh, Ward, I think you'd better have a talk with the boys." (Or else He says, "June, I think I'd better have a talk with the boys," upon which She wails, "Oh Ward! But they're just BA-bies!") After that, Ward either does or does not have a talk with Wally and/or Beaver, the adorable, affectionate kids who always get into mischief but only through innocent thoughtlessness or bad companions. In any case, father never loses his temper, and always arrives at a firm decision that illustrates yet again to June the vast superiority of her husband's Solomonesque judgment, and inspires the boys to sit up in the bedroom they share without ever quarrelling (Mr and Mrs Cleaver, parenthetically, do not have a bedroom), and discuss their parents' infinite goodness and wisdom.

The Cleavers do not use cocaine or rubber underwear.

Westerns, for decades the grit of America's film mill, seem to have disappeared into the celluloid sunset in recent years. "Why then," one might logically cogitate, "are re-run TV westerns thicker 'n wild injuns? Especially such venerables as *Lone Ranger* and *Cisco Kid*?" To this I should reply, because Hollywood fiddled with its formula. When outlaws like Butch Cassidy and the Sundance Kid mutated into Byronic heroes, inaugurating a whole new anti-Establishment cinematic trend, ambiguous distinctions between good and bad guys got the ingenuous American Everyman all mixed up. Traditional western heroes and villains have been refitted in foil jumpsuits, certainly, but some of the dear old formulaic elements have sadly slid to the cutting-room floor.

Like sexism and ethnic prejudices. In the westerns of the good ol' days, ladies were dim and defenceless victims of ruthless men or critical circumstances, urgently requiring the swift assistance of ethically immaculate champions. Unmarried women requiring less were not Ladies. Married women were presumably all June Cleavers in longer skirts. Fifties' comfy convictions of national and racial superiority were validated by stereotypical villains, dark-skinned and primitive. Indians and Mexicans, whether singly or in legions, were unscrupulous, greedy, violent, and in direst need of a hot shower and shave. They kicked their horses, double-crossed their pard'ners, and usually lived in rocks. Semi-enlightened exceptions, like the Lone Ranger's Tonto and Cisco Kid's Pancho, knew their places and left decisions to their Betters, yet could never quite grasp the civilised intricacies of English pronunciation and syntax.

New programming, picking up where re-runs leave off, preserves not only those fanciful facsimiles of intact institutions and simple solutions of decades past, but generally attempts to do so with the same old faces and places as well. *Leave It To Beaver*'s recent television movie, wherein all the old characters are reunited after 20 years, was so successful, it promptly evolved into a new weekly series, *Still The Beaver*. Ageing stars of other old series are riding the same wave: Sally Field and Barbary Eden, of, respectively, *Gidget* and *I Dream of Jeannie* ▶

*"No, I don't think you're extravagant, Mr Mellors. We've got to overdo it a little. It keeps the economy strong."*

*"He'd been looking depressed for some time."*

the Fifties, are again growing enormously popular, both in re-runs and replicas. *Wheel of Fortune*, once an enervated old veteran, has suddenly surged to the most successful show on TV, with millions more viewers per week than *Dynasty*, *The Cosby Show* and *Dallas* combined. (*The Cosby Show*, incidentally, in its second season, is a wildly popular little Fifties sit-com set in the present, featuring your standard solid family unit with affectionate, intelligent children responding sensibly to the guidance of wise and loving parents. Mother, though, is a lawyer; so father, a doctor, helps her cook dinner.)

Even TV commercials are geared to the Good Old Days, featuring '57 Chevies, hula-hoops, and Ed Sullivan impersonators. Magazines have "All-Time Favourite" re-run polls, urging readers to send in votes for such categories as "Best Horse" and "Best Neighbour"; while newspaper features bring us serial updates of whatever became of so-and-so.

It's not just the Fifties on TV, either. Old clothes, old records, and even old slang are brand new. And the Fifties, so far, show no sign of progressing toward the Sixties – which suits, of course, the Administration of the Eighties just dandy. Star of Death Valley Days would no doubt find managing his transcontinental spread a good bit trickier if constituents started scratching their heads and checking their calendars. Pray God we'll nonetheless survive the slide into the Nineties.

► fame, are cases in point. *Twilight Zone*, the late Rod Serling's late TV series, became a popular movie, and several old black and white *Alfred Hitchcock Presents* shows were recently touched up and coloured in for a widely-bruited network special.

All America went hysterically happy a couple of months back, when sufficient unused old film was unearthed to create 75 new *Honeymooner* episodes. Jackie Gleason, looking much

the same, suddenly appeared on every imaginable televised chat show to tell us all about it one more time. His appearances, however, were hardly conspicuous; TV interviewers for cable, breakfast TV, magazine and talk programmes had long before that discovered media diamonds by digging up dusty not-quite-gone-nor-forgotten series stars for vacuously redundant personal reappearances.

Game shows, another old television staple of

*"I think we're all agreed then – Blend 79 just about has it all."*

# OH MY GOD, IT'S A PAGE ABOUT
# *STRESS*

## *FEARS RISE AS MILLIONS CAN'T PULL THEMSELVES TOGETHER*

In tests, many people shook like leaves or felt all sick and peculiar. One in quite a few got hot and/or bothered. Some were a bit blotchy, too. Especially at certain times. Lots of us, experts believe, can't cope with everything. Millions more sometimes "go all of a doo-dah".
Now doctors are concerned.
Whether or not you are up to it, rushed off your feet, going up the wall etc, it is IMPORTANT that you find time to relax and do this simple test. If you DO NOT, you might well go down with something AWFUL.

### *NOW WASH YOUR HANDS*

## CHECK YOUR STRESS RATING
### CAN *YOU* COPE IN TODAY'S BUSY AND EXCITING WORLD?

**1** Do you feel "on edge" when:
  **(a)** Plotting to strangle smokers or South Africans?
  **(b)** Parts of you rasp a bit, more like pins and needles really, or knocking, worse at night?
  **(c)** People make fun of your interest in model railways and Satanism?

**2** Are you the sort to "make a fuss" when:
  **(a)** Coshed in error by hard-pressed police officers?
  **(b)** Suffering "upset tummy" from poisoned confectionery?
  **(c)** Beaten senseless by bored teenagers?

**3** What with one thing and another, are you "fed up" with:
  **(a)** Acid rain, rape, AIDS, fats, fouled pavements, etc?
  **(b)** Shortness of breath, accompanied by "clonking" in the lower abdomen and being covered by an all-over rash which flashes in the dark or "squeaks" when you walk?
  **(c)** Surly chimney-sweeps OR the shape of your neck?

**4** Do you have "nightmares" about:
  **(a)** Hairline cracks?
  **(b)** Indigestion caused by radiation sickness?
  **(c)** Blurred vision, like people who have got something rare or have fallen into a Moulinex?

**5** Are you easily "irritated" by:
  **(a)** People who mix Molotov Cocktails in a no-smoking compartment *without asking for your permission*?
  **(b)** People who sniff or use catapults or waste water?
  **(c)** Happy-chappy television weathermen?

**6** Do you ever get "impatient" when:
  **(a)** You are held to ransom by Middle Eastern fanatics?
  **(b)** Staff take time off with Legionnaire's Disease?
  **(c)** You overtake some drunken half-wit of a glue-sniffing slowcoach on the inside who then decides to turn left without bothering to signal, thus forcing you to mow down a bus queue and demolish an old people's home, losing your No Claims Discount?

**7** Do you find yourself "biting your lip" when:
  **(a)** Drug-abusing toddlers try to cut your head off?
  **(b)** A Channel tunnel ventilator shaft is driven through your sitting-room on the night you generally watch *One Man and His Dog*?
  **(c)** Beings from space have stolen your tranquillisers?

**8** Do you tend to feel "jumpy" when:
  **(a)** You are mugged at knife-point?
  **(b)** You are caught shop-lifting?
  **(c)** People stare at your uncontrollable facial tic?

**9** Do you sometimes "worry" that you might:
  **(a)** Be telephoned in error by The Pope OR Melvyn Bragg?
  **(b)** Get lumps EITHER on a gland OR in gravy?
  **(c)** Find it hard to stay calm if you were drowning?

**10** Have you ever felt "hot under the collar" when:
  **(a)** Bound and gagged by burglars?
  **(b)** Teaching infants not to talk to strange in-laws?
  **(c)** Told to suit yourself by shop assistants?

**11** Does your heart "thrum" or "murmurate" when:
  **(a)** You are upset by disadvantaged kids hitting animals or parked vehicles with a crowbar?
  **(b)** You are startled by a bomb or exploding gas main?
  **(c)** A close relative or friend defects to Libya?

**12** Are you "sick to death" of:
  **(a)** Being made to feel insecure by pundits?
  **(b)** Most things, these days?
  **(c)** Multiple-choice questionnaires that go on and on?

### CHECK YOUR SCORE

**If you scored whilst reading this you should seek immediate medical advice or a good agent.**
**If you answered YES or NO to any of the questions, YOU MAY BE AT RISK from not having enough things to do.**

# ANTHONY BURGESS

# On Having a Book Written About One

I UNDERSTAND that a book is being written about me and that my response ought to be one of excited anticipation, not to say gratitude. After all, books are usually written about people only when they are dead – Dr Johnson, for instance – and to be written off at length when alive is to be granted a parcel of that immortality that should only come when one has proved one's mortality. I wish I could feel excited about the prospect of seeing a book with my name on the cover as title, or part-title, and not, as has already happened nearly fifty times, in the merely authorial slot. The excitement should properly derive from the knowledge that this book is to be a British book, since the British are not good at paying attention to their men of letters until they are safely dead. To be noticed by one of my own people between hard covers is, true, something I never expected to see. If I am less than excited it is because books have already been written about me in other countries.

Chiefly, inevitably, in the United States, where, to quote Alroy Kear in Somerset Maugham's *Cakes and Ale,* they prefer a living dog to a dead lion. There are at least three books published in the United States about yours truly, to say nothing of vast volumes of exhaustive bibliography. This is the sort of thing that American professors of English do: it is something they have to do to obtain what is called tenure. It is easy to write a book on a living author, since you can send him a long questionnaire and use his answers, something difficult to do if you are writing about Mark Twain (though there are helpful spiritualistic mediums who will tune in for you at a price

and dredge great Emersonian truisms from the afterworld). Evelyn Waugh's Mr Pinfold is disdainful of those authors who reply to academic aspirants at such length that they find their theses virtually written for them. I am disdainful too, chiefly because I find writing a wearisome business if there is no money in it, but, especially when drunk, I have failed to notice cassette recorders in surplus US Army rucksacks. I fear, like most authors, that there are a lot of my less discreet obiter dicta lying around.

But what precisely would a book about yours truly be about? Not the life, since no writer really has a life unless, in the American manner, he succumbs to block and becomes a dipsomaniac. Most of the literary biographies

that I have recently read have been about American novelists who took seriously to the sauce – Scott Fitzgerald, John O'Hara, Raymond Chandler, Dashiel Hammett, Hemingway of course, most recently John Cheever. They make good reading, what with their outbursts at parties, their ramming cars into New England snowdrifts, their serial polygamies which are called divorces. Hemingway did more than drink: he went on safari and to bullfights and liberated Paris, as well as having four wives. My life, in comparison, looks pretty thin, has kept out of the newspapers, and has not been talked about much by me. Much of it has been taken up with what I am doing now – hammering an Olivetti for gain.

So if the life can't be written about, except in a preliminary chapter with apologies for its dull exiguity, it has to be the work. The writing about the work which appears in a book usually gets serially into print long before, usually in literary periodicals which are tolerant of length and positively welcome footnotes. Such writing could be termed reviewing, but it is reviewing on a scale not known in Great Britain: it should really be called criticism. If the reviewer has a book in prospect he cannot review as we do here – taking the work under consideration as an isolated construct to be treated on its own merits or demerits, without reference to other works of the author (which we probably haven't read anyway). No, the American reviewer with a book in mind has to find a pattern, and each new work of the author dealt with has to exhibit some new aspect of the pattern. The pattern, presumably, was there before the author in question even began to write: he has to write, and to go on writing, in order to let the pattern unfold. And God help him if he breaks away from the pattern and tries something new. That is not playing the game.

The patterns in my own work vary, natural-

*"A host? You call that a host! Why, back in the States. . ."*

ly, from author to author about it: after all, it's his book and my books are only the raw material. Some years ago, in North Carolina, a young professor formed a very interesting pattern based on his discovery that the name of my first fictional hero was R. Ennis. This, he declared, spelt SINNER backwards. Undeniably true, and I wish I'd discovered that before he did so that I could change the name. I'd chosen Ennis as a name because it means island and the character so named was pretty much on his own. Now he, and I too of course, was concerned with trying to hide sin or else commit it backwards. Of course, the young professor was doing what critics are supposed to do – dig into the writer's unconscious and show what was going on there. But it's an eerie business, having one's unconscious laid bare on the butcher's slab. And the nature of my unconscious seems to differ from analyst to analyst.

According to one book about me I've been retailing homosexual propaganda in disguise as something quite different. I'm pretty sure that this isn't so. I've always been a straight man, interested in wholesome heterosex with a few fetichistic appendages but rather shy of laying it on the literary line. The best writing about sex is in Book IV of the *Æneid*, where Virgil describes the orgasm, and everything leading up to it, as either *nota flamma* or *flamma nota* – the conflagration you all know about. I've tried to follow Virgil; in doing so I've achieved a diffidence open to bizarre interpretations, of which necrophily or bestiality may be one. I think I would prefer this to the morbid approach of another writer on this writer who finds in every book I produce an allegory of dyspepsia, though that writer may well be right. *Wind of Release: Borborygmic Symbolism in Anthony Burgess.* No, no, please no.

Let the homegrown book on this homegrown author be written by all means, if it helps its author. It may be enlightening to the only person who really counts in its connection – namely, the subject. And there's one thing I know, since the book will be British: it will not be French and it will not be Russian. The Sorbonne produced an astonishing book about yours truly, full of deconstructionism and post-Derridaism. The French are usually right about intellectual and aesthetic matters, so I must be what they say I am: thin, subtle, corrugated and very Gallic.

The Russians, on the other hand, have to be wrong. I am not the dying voice of a dying system, with clockwork in my orange head. Russian littérateurs are permitted to say such things about me, but the Russian public is not allowed to read my texts. But what does the public matter anywhere anyway? Once there is a book written about you, your own books may as well be ignored. Increasingly people don't want to know, they want to *know about*. I don't blame them. I look forward with mild interest to knowing something about me. Perhaps the revelation will induce the ultimate block and then, like Scott Fitzgerald and the other sauce merchants, I'll be a fit subject for a biography. 🙃

"Were there any messages while I was gone?"

"Cheer up, fellers – the pale-face just came back to sell us black coffee."

# Hacks to the Wall

WHAT with the forthcoming Daily This, the planned London Evening That, the promised Sunday Other and the projected Saturday Something Else, the big question, or possibly the small question, on the nation's lips is: where are the people who are supposed to *write* the things? Where will the proprietors of the future find the men and women able-bodied enough to tap out front-page leads like "Fergie – It's A Boy" or "Fergie – It's Another Boy"?

As a service to any of you who may be toying with the idea of starting up a newspaper in the near future, I can pass on the names of a few likely lads and lasses who are currently available for work, names gleaned from two directories which are by way of being the Yellow Pages of journalism, emanating from the two rival organisations (to use that word loosely).

There are some, alas, who had better be told that they are never going to make it in the cut-throat hell-holes that men call Fleet Street, Wapping, Vauxhall Bridge Road or wherever it is that word-processors are in overdrive. For a start, the NUJ's *Who's Who in Freelance Journalism* lists a couple of souls who claim the ability to turn in pieces couched in the Latin language. What is the Latin for "Palace in Aids Shock"? Or "Botham in Terrorist Alert"? As a hardened news editor might put it, they must think he is absolutely and completely *non compos mentis*.

One Alan Bold is quoted as being "able to supply high quality cultural features and in-depth literary articles about any part of Scotland". Sorry, sir, not much call for that, although there *is* a demand for cultural features on nude Satanism and in-depth articles on any part of Samantha Fox. Danah Zohar of London NW6 is unlikely to find much work at any futuristic cut-price tabloid, not if she can offer nothing but "feature articles on intellectual and academic subjects".

And if Nick Barrett claims only "Ecolo-journalist! socio-economic trends and pluralistic broadcasting" as his qualifications, he isn't going to get very far with the pornographer hoping for a knighthood who is making up the Identikit picture of the new press barons.

No, the best way for a thrusting freelance to put himself on the map is to put himself on the map. Like John Charity of Wester Ross, Scotland, who declares himself to be located at a point that is "Ullapool 8 miles, Inverness 55 miles, Kyle 80 miles, Thurso 125 miles". The only map reference missing is Fleet Street 500 miles, and that can't be for long, given a little faith and hope.

There is no need to check the Wester Ross-Ullapool mileage, of course. We can take the word of Patrick Roach of Netley Abbey, Hampshire, that he has an answering machine and "own photographic boat", whatever that is. But watch out for Len Richmond, NUJ member living in Hollywood, who declares "I am a feature writer for *Cosmopolitan*, *Penthouse*, *Punch* and *Forum* magazines." No you're not, Mr Richmond. I can't speak for *Cosmo* and co, and I haven't blown the dust off enough back-numbers to state that we have never used your Californian outpourings, but *Punch* feature writer is not something to put on your CV. And if you can't trust his CV, how can you believe the rest of his work?

The Institute of Journalists' scribes featured in *Freelances* are fewer in number but make up for it by having more names; noms de plume abound. Percy Barsby, whose qualifications include the fact that he has "visited Indian reservations" and produces "readers' letters" (what's the point of writing readers' letters? I thought readers did that) goes by the name of "Joe Bee". Michael Arton, "former county swimmer", writes fiction under the pseudonym of "Michael Fonda", for all the world as if he were Jane and Peter's long-lost brother.

For reasons best known to himself, Mr Donal K. O'Boyle chose the alias of Ciaran O'Ferry. And for reasons even better known to himself, he decided to use another alias, this one being Mary Mooney. "Vera-Brigitte" conceals the identity of Brigitte Von Sternberg, who produces scripts and puzzles, writes about fortune-telling and the occult, and has a photo library of cats. Look in the crystal ball for her rates.

John Harcup's photo library provides extensive coverage of everything from the Malvern Hills to acne. What does that leave? It leaves room for John Watney to corner the market in, among other things, "gardening, life, love", in all of which he claims personal experience.

That's nothing. Alec Beilby of Farnham has "visited Magnetic North Pole". Mr Denys Branch, aka "Jay", has pix of anything that moves in "South Essex, especially Canvey Island". Assuming, that is, that anything does move in Canvey Island. While some members of the Institute claim to have "ten years experience of East Midlands" (whether boasting or complaining, is not clear), a Mr Ernie Husson covers anywhere "within a 40-mile radius" but then there probably isn't much going on within 40 miles of Llandrindod Wells anyway. Gillian Riley, alias Gill Sharp of Sharp Enterprises, Putney, and with "School Cert 10 distinctions" under her belt (highly qualified, these IoJ members) will go anywhere so long as it's in "Putney area".

It's the scope of these writers which should have the new generation of proprietors banging on their 24-hour answering machines. Mrs Margaret Briggs of Runcorn specialises in "soccer results, modern ballroom dancing". Reg Batchelor of Weybridge ("own darkroom") can turn his hand to dental science *and* caravanning and not just caravanning but "caravanning (all aspects)".

Mr William Crossan can file a crisp item on art restoration (please state if "ceramics, enamels or pictures" required) and also "boxing"; it is not true, as he would doubtless explain, that ceramic restoration damages the brain. John Ebbs has a flow of words that covers "winemaking, windmills". Maybe he only does "W", leaving other letters of the alphabet to journalistic all-rounders. Don't sniff; there are men on Wapping tabloids besides whom Mr Ebbs is a *Mastermind* winner.

If Magnus Magnusson ever has Lance Fisher-Skinner in the chair, he could ask him probing questions about "the politics of war and peace". Or he could throw him a few trick questions about "motoring"; either way, Mr Fisher-Skinner will forge through to the next round. Bill Eykyn copes with "bathrooms and other related subjects including finance and law". There's a new magazine on the way entitled *Bathrooms*, so he should be good for a series on "The Hot Tap – A Lawyer Writes".

So there we are. A potential staff of thousands of all-round Renaissance hacks, rarin' to bring cats, Canvey Island and caravanning to a wider public. But how wide is wider? It may well be that the fledgling newspapers can survive only if everyone who is halfway literate (and *Sun* readers) buys at least three different nationals every morning.

The proprietors' only hope is for kind souls to club together to form a National Union of Readers and a rival Institute of Subscribers, people who live in Thurso and specialise in scanning articles on bathrooms, or are prepared to travel all over Putney for a piece on windmills in Latin, or love looking at pictures of skin diseases. It is unlikely that they would have to hire the Albert Hall for their AGMs. 🌿

*"For heaven's sake cheer up, Lascoux. This is champagne country."*

### The Italian Girl, Sorry, Woman, in Algiers

MUSTAFA, THE MIGHTY BEY OR DEY OF ALGIERS, HAD GROWN TIRED OF HIS CHIEF WIFE.

You never ask me to come with you to the Casbah any more.

It's bizarre.

Worse, it's a flipping flea market.

HE OFFERED HER TO HIS ITALIAN SLAVE, LINDORO.

She is very nice, Bey or Dey, but I love another! However, I'll think it over.

That's what I like — a slave who thinks things over.

You will be proud to learn that I have ordered my corsairs to abduct another Italian. A female one — I like the way they wiggle.

COINCIDENTALLY, THE ABDUCTEE WAS NONE OTHER THAN ISABELLA, LINDORO'S FIANCÉE.

A Moslem pirate? Didn't know they had them! Brute, does your religion countenance the capture of innocent people?

It requires it — otherwise no paradise! A whole new section of the Koran deals with that.

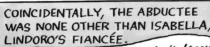

Here is your eye-tie, a trifle overweight but fetching withal.

Have I stumbled into a hotbed of chauvinistic sexism?

Well — we try to keep it fairly thermal.

Come, snuggle up to your little Musty.

Good God, it's my fiancé! Pretend you don't know me, Lindoro.

OK, but we are in trouble, Isabella. His Bey- or Deyship is making me a present of his wife.

So, Italian, I am to be supplanted by you?

And I by you! Laughable, no?

No.

Allow me to raise your consciousness...

HOURS LATER

...There! All raised?

So that is feminism! I am terribly interested! Tell me, how does one become one of these "sex objects"?

MUSTAFA WAS SO TAKEN WITH ITALIANS THAT HE HAD TAKEN HUNDREDS OF THEM.

It makes me feel more European, less of a savage — yet something is missing...

Mascalzone! Cornuto!

Prosciutto! Fegato macinato!

THIS PROVIDED ISABELLA WITH A PLAN.

Musty, dear, if you wish to be with-it and First World, you must join the Order of the Colpevole.

Count me in! What are the duties?

Feeling guilty! You must practise every day.

MUSTAFA PROVED SO APT A PUPIL THAT ALL THE ITALIANS WERE SOON ABLE TO LEAVE.

Come back here, scum! I'm sorry, I shouldn't have said that...

The truth, Lindoro! You were fond of the chief wife?

Addio, peste di pesto!

Oh, I suppose if you like arabic numbers...

The truth, chief wife! You were fond of the slave? Sorry...

Oh, I suppose if you like the italic type...

MORAL: Bet your money on the bobtail nag; nobody bets on the Bey or Dey.

# ALICE IN PROBLEMLAND

Alice heard the Rabbit say to itself, "Oh dear! Oh dear! I shall be too late!" She very slowly took a sniff from the tin he had handed to her.

"Curiouser and curiouser," cried Alice as she opened out like the largest telescope that ever was. "That's the last time I'll ever sniff glue!"

"Pervert!" screamed Alice. "My Mummy said I must *never* accept elegant thimbles from strange men!"

As Alice wandered in the wood, she came across an enormous rabid puppy. "I knew this would happen as soon as they opened the Chunnel!" she muttered.

The Caterpillar and Alice looked at each other for some time in silence. At last Alice said, "What were you before smoking pot turned you into a caterpillar?"

"You are old, Father William," Alice said, "and your hair has become very white. And yet they incessantly put you on the dole. Do you think that at your age it is right?"

"Please would you tell me," said Alice to the Duchess, "did your baby look like that *before* you visited Sellafield?"

Uncle Arthur turned crimson with fury and began screaming, "Off with her head!" "Nonsense!" said Alice, "I only asked was it *easy* to become a transvestite?"

Alice didn't know what to make of the Jabberwock. "It *seems* very nice," she said, "but it's *rather* hard to understand."

"I know what you're thinking," said Tweedledum. "Being very good friends can be great fun," agreed Alice. "But contrariwise, having AIDS can be no fun at all!"

"Oh, do stop complaining!" said Alice irritably. "It's a new EEC regulation that all mutton should be dressed as lamb!"

"What's this?" said the OAP, looking cold and hungry. "Government orders," replied Alice. "The PM said, 'Let them eat cake!'"

67

*"It's an acceptance slip! I'm rich, Friday! I'm rich!"*

# A LIFE IN THE DAY OF

## SPRING

IF I have had a good Winter's kip I am usually awake by mid-March – could be later, could be April. There is a cuckoo that gets me up, it is very reliable, too reliable in fact, it has been known to give me a bell as early as February. I would not mind but it gets you into the papers. I like to keep a low profile. In like a lamb, that is my motto, though not one I have always lived by, I am sorry to say. Sometimes I go out like a lion – I am like a season possessed, I just cannot help myself. But that is not the real me. I always reproach myself afterwards, and promise that next year I will be a better Spring. But you get no credit for it. "Worst Winter This Century", yes; "Hottest Summer Since 1947", certainly; but when did you last read the headline "Mildest Spring Since Nineteen Nought Ten"? It just does not get reported.

After a quick cuppa I have a wash, in cold dew if there is any, then, first thing, go out and look at the sheep. Sometimes they may have to be dug out of the snow before they can get on with their lambing, so I might fix them up with a bit of a thaw to help them on their way, if this is within my power which is not always the case. You have got to balance sheep with snowdrops when it comes to pushing up through the snow. There is the publicity angle to be considered. I do not go in for gimmicks but you are expected to present a good image.

If the lambs are already gambolling I just leave them to get on with it, but you have to keep an eye on the press photographers who are inclined to throw them up in the air to get a good picture.

I try to get in a bit of gardening before breakfast. I grow tulips and daffodils mainly, as well as quite a lot of grass. I see that everything is budding nicely, then have a big fry-up and glance at the paper. There is often some snide item about myself in it, especially if the weather has been at all dodgy – there may even be a joky little leader, "Woe! To be in England, now that April's here" style of thing. You get used to it. You do not let it affect your work.

After breakfast I do a few rustling exercises then deal with my mail, fan letters mainly. Many of them are in verse – it is amazing the number of odes I have had addressed to me. There is a kind of Spring groupie called Words-worth who must have written me hundreds over the years. I send out a standard acknowledgement card, also in rhyme, it says "Thank you for your Ode to Spring/Much happiness to me it did bring." It tickles them pink when you take the trouble to reply in verse, the same as they have written to you. I got the idea when I heard on *That's Life* about an income tax inspector who did the self-same thing, they read it out. But beyond that I do not like to get involved with the punters, otherwise you start getting a lot of hassle. They want you to breathe on them and stuff like that. Some of them can be really weird.

I like my job, though. I definitely would not change it for any other, not even Summer's. Summer may look glamorous on the face of it with everyone going on holiday and fruit ripening et cetera, but in reality it is dead boring, it is just the same old thing day after day. So is being Winter – you never hear of anyone writing odes to Winter, although admittedly you do get some nice carols. No, the only job I wouldn't mind having a crack at, if I ever had to jack in what I'm doing now, is Autumn's, the reason being that it is very similar to mine – you get a lot of variety, there is something different every day, even if it is only the leaves turning brown.

I have no set routine. I am supposed to work to a rough timetable, but really just so long as I get everything sprouting up it does not matter too much what order I do it in, in fact for a laugh I sometimes like to bring the daffs out before the crocuses. It gives the punters something to talk about and at the end of the day who cares? The main thing is to have all the flowers and fruit and that ready for Summer, which of course then takes all the credit, even though having done none of the donkey-work. Still, it does not bother me. When the critics can write "When birds do sing, hey ding a ding ding, Sweet lovers love the Summer," that will be the time to start worrying.

I have got to admit, though, that what we used to call the hey-nonny-nonny side of the business has taken a bit of a knock in recent years. It is the times we live in: sweet lovers and their lasses just do not want to wait for the corn-fields to turn green in this day and age, they are at it like knives all year round. I blame it on double-glazing, myself. But it is still part of the job to provide a minimum service for lovers – full moons, soft breezes, May blossom et cetera, I have never tried to change the formula, though I must say it is a bit discouraging when you have laid on a rainbow across about ten hectares of expensive soft grass and the little sods are stuck indoors watching soft porn videos. That is when it gets you down.

I always try to leave the blossoming till last. It is a messy business with a lot of spillage and you always end up with purple blossom in your hair and up your nostrils, it is amazing how it clings to you. But the job has to be done otherwise you have totally knackered yourself in your working relationship with bees.

Once I have got the blossom going I like to get back for a good swill-down and call it a day. Like everyone else I relax in front of the telly. The weather forecast is a good programme, I really like that Michael Fish, I tape it if I am going out which is rare, as I have to be up early. I do not read a lot. Because of my way of life I like romances, James Herriot books, and anything I can get my hands on about early cabbage, but otherwise it is just a quick flip through the gardening mags.

I think a lot about the future. I feel really, really sorry for the young. There are just four jobs for us seasons and we have them for life. It is security for us but nobody else gets a look in, we are like the dockers of old. What is wrong with a youth opportunity scheme whereby there are apprentice seasons, with youngsters being entrusted (under supervision of course) to look after a short period between Spring and Summer which could be called Sprummer or Sumpring, I care not which? It is just an idea. I have put it up, but nothing has ever come of it, they do not want to know.

*Keith Waterhouse*

## E. S. TURNER

# FIFTY THINGS YOU NEED TO KNOW ABOUT THE MEDITERRANEAN

**1.** "The grand object of travelling is to see the shores of the Mediterranean," wrote Dr Johnson, who unaccountably went to the Scots isles instead.

**2.** The record for the most indulgent short-haul journey along the French Riviera is held by "Bendor", Duke of Westminster, who ordered his steam yacht *Cutty Sark* down from Scandinavian waters to carry a party of guests from Cannes to Monte Carlo, 30 miles away, for a tennis match. He then sent the yacht, with its crew of 40, back to base in Scotland.

**3.** From the Amalfi corniche one may descend into an Emerald Grotto with an underwater Bethlehem crib, possibly the best underwater Bethlehem crib anywhere.

**4.** On the same corniche the opulent villa of Carlo Ponti is succeeded by the opulent villa of Sophia Loren.

**5.** Although some Mediterranean resorts are American in aspect, the coast is refreshingly free of natatoriums, sealariums, spongearamas, Santa's caverns, bear creeks and painted canyons.

**6.** The best people do not build homes on horizontal surfaces but on vertical cliff-faces. They hang swimming-pools on cliff-faces too and reach them by limousine.

**7.** Seafarers are often startled to see lustrous grubs emerging from holes in cliffs, wriggling along shelves above the sea, and vanishing again, with strange noises, into netted precipices. These are called coaches.

**8.** Edward Lear was so carried away by the Gozo landscape that he called it "pomskizillious" and "gromphiberous".

**9.** The ugliest Mediterranean city is Tel-Aviv.

**10.** The most glorious port of call is Grand Harbour, Malta.

**11.** There are no good winds in the Mediterranean. The bad ones include the bora, the mistral, the sirocco and the levanter. From the sirocco one may contract *le cafard*, the desert madness.

**12.** Spain has her own Gibraltar-style possessions in Morocco, like Ceuta and Melilla, but nobody is supposed to mention them.

**13.** From the cable car ascending the Rock of Gibraltar one may hear, booming down from the summit, the BBC's *World at One* grinding on about South Africa.

**14.** The oldest ruling family in Europe is found in a pink palace in Monaco and on the front page of every tabloid.

**15.** *Pin fan Pin* is a Monegasque proverb. It means "Pine trees can only produce pine trees." Which means "Like master, like man." On second thoughts, forget it.

**16.** In Monte Carlo an "unknown Italian industrialist" incurred the "world's biggest loss" in one session at roulette: £800,000. (*Guinness.*)

**17.** A guide to Monaco lists Accountants under "Liberal Professions".

**18.** There used to be two Sicilies, but one was wound up.

**19.** Permanent British residents on the Costa del Sol include a luckless garrison which, drawn up defiantly on parade, was engulfed in a great fissure of the rock of Alicante when the French exploded a gigantic charge underneath.

**20.** The slopes of Etna are perilous, not from lava but from *macho* motorists.

**21.** The Barbary Pirates used to put Britons in the galleys. Now they just lock them up in Tripoli.

**22.** Alexandria invites you to forget Lawrence Durrell with local wines called Omar Khayyam and Grand Cru des Ptolomées.

**23.** The most exciting poem about a Mediterranean sea battle is Chesterton's "Lepanto". Drop everything and read it.

**24.** The boy who stood on the burning deck whence all but he had fled was a young Corsican, Casabianca, blown up aboard *L'Orient* in the Battle of the Nile.

**25.** If Suetonius is right, the Emperor Nero, on approaching Baiae in the Bay of Naples, insisted on being greeted by a row of temporary brothels, each with a noblewoman acting as madam to solicit his custom.

**26.** Somerset Maugham lived in the Villa Mauresque at Cap Ferrat. According to Robin Maugham, he once told a young guest not to eat his zabaglione as if it were gruel, because the stuff was expensive to prepare.

**27.** In the Aeolian Isles one may occasionally find groups of exiled *mafiosi*. They are not particularly dangerous.

**28.** To the south, the former military adventure playground of Libya is now a Socialist Peoples Jamahiriya. It is very dangerous.

**29.** It was thought at one time that cutting the Suez Canal might send the Indian Ocean rushing into the Mediterranean, or vice versa, but suitable precautions appear to have been taken.

**30.** The eastern Mediterranean once exported large numbers of rich and oily Levantines, who are now called something else.

**31.** Both Lenin and Stalin attended Gorky's school for revolutionaries on Capri, a paradisal spot from which to subvert the world.

**32.** While on Capri, Lenin lost at chess and did a McEnroe. He then nipped over to see the grand job Vesuvius had done on the bourgeoisie of Pompeii.

**33.** Venus rose naked from the sea near Paphos. As Shakespeare testifies, she did not spare herself in seducing the young Adonis ("Her face doth reek and smoke, her blood doth boil...").

**34.** Venus was not suffering from Mediterranean Fever. That is brucellosis.

**35.** Tobias Smollett, the novelist, found the air of Nice to be dry and elastic, good for weak nerves, blocked perspiration, relaxed fibres, viscidity of lymph and languid circulation.

**36.** The same bracing air has stimulated Graham Greene to accuse leading citizens of Nice of nefarious practices.

**37.** More than 1,000 feet below the level of the Mediterranean lies Sodom, the best place for it.

**38.** Along the Mediterranean there is now a grave shortage of convents, monasteries and bishops' palaces for conversion into luxury hotels.

**39.** Aristotle Onassis's home on the rock of Skorpios required three boat-loads of water a day.

**40.** The Mediterranean *maquis*, or scrub, shelters songbirds, lovers, bandits, kidnappers, maniacs and Resistance fighters.

**41.** Trieste is where James Joyce, a Berlitz teacher, was arrested in a scuffle with drunken sailors on what he was pleased to call his honeymoon.

**42.** On the Yugoslav coast men climb up towers to look for fish.

**43.** A shocked Gladstone abruptly left a ballet performance in the San Carlo theatre, Naples, saying that if that was ballet he hoped never to see any more of it.

**44.** In Italy it is considered unlucky to have a cheque refused by the Bank of the Holy Spirit.

**45.** The Riviera's answer to Radio Tirana (Albania) will shortly come from SuperRadio 101, organised by William Davis, former editor of *Punch*.

**46.** The Mediterranean littoral exercises an irresistible fascination for "misfits", beach boys, gigolos, cat burglars, smugglers, topless starlets, estate agents, press barons, PLO saboteurs, ex-editors of *Punch* and the sailors of the American Sixth Fleet.

**47.** Wise travellers flee the northern Mediterranean on those periodical Heroes' Days when every living thing and every road sign is shot.

**48.** Heterosexuals should exercise special care in any Italian resort ending in the letter "o" and on any Greek island ending in "os".

**49.** The beach at Tangier resembles every other beach in the world: it is unsafe after dark.

**50.** The Mediterranean temperament is volatile, noise-loving, lascivious and un-English, ill-suited to a region purporting to be "the cradle of civilisation".

*"Woke up this morning, couldn't even afford a guitar…"*

*"Holy mackerel! You can't leave anything for five minutes!"*

# 30 YEARS OF

# ITV

"YES, I CAN REMEMBER WHERE WE WERE THIRTY YEARS AGO TODAY! WE WERE SITTING HERE."

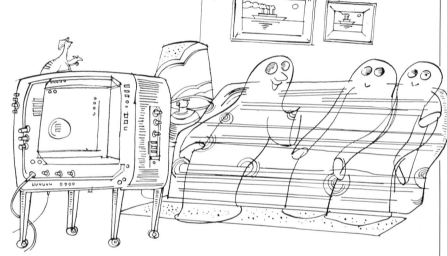

"I'VE NEVER MISSED AN EPISODE OF *CROSSROADS*."

"IT'S AMAZING – ALL THESE YEARS OF *THIS IS YOUR LIFE* AND NO TRANSPLANT."

"MY OLD MAN'S REALLY OLD – HE KEEPS GOING ON ABOUT SOMEONE CALLED HUGHIE GREEN."

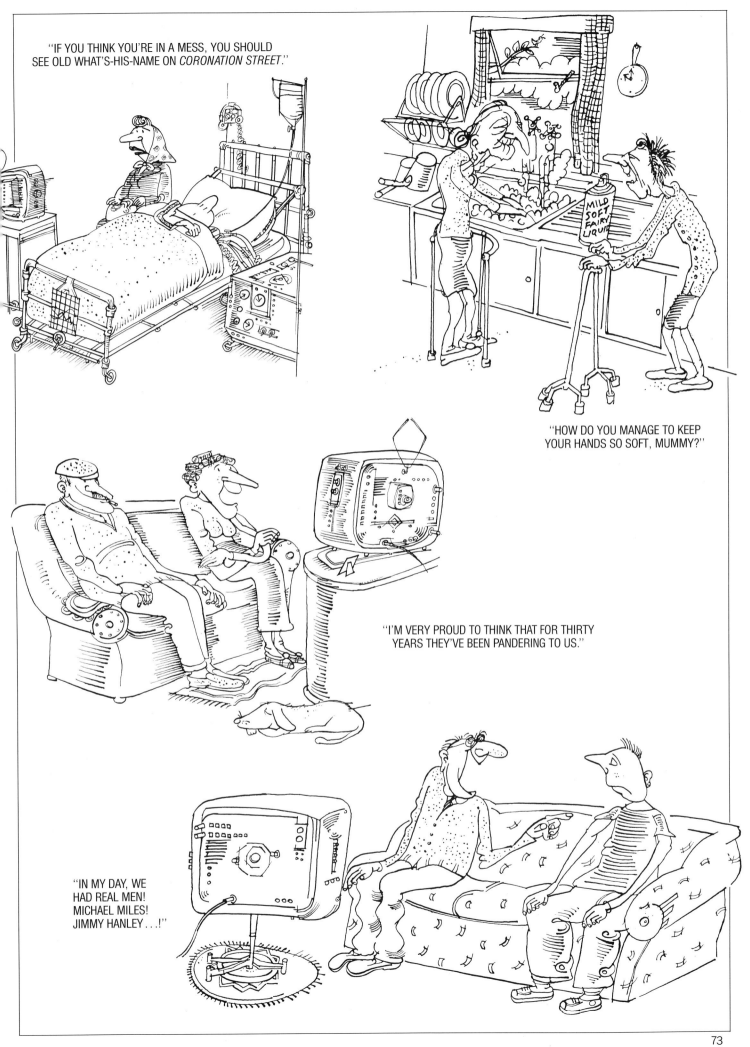

# The Big Boys' Wonder Book of All-Time Classic Motor-Cars

## 1952 CAMPARI VONGOLE BERLINA QUATTROVALVOLE

Ettore Campari's magnificent Turin-built Mk IX V-8 "Tipo KK" Vongole Berlina Quattrovalvole, nicknamed *"Ecco La Bella Macchina Meravigliosa dello Principe del Fabbrice Anonime Automobili Piedmontese"* was perhaps the most handsome of all the 1950s "Mamma Mille" fast tourers.

With its "superleggera" bodywork designed by Umberto Frascati, its characteristic Giovanni Bucci bonnet straps, and its flamboyant "flying chrysanthemum" motif (from an original commissioned by King Carol of Rumania for the 1928 Sofia Motor Fair) the big Campari had the looks to match its performance figures of 0-62kph in 7.1 seconds, or Turin to Reggio Calabria in a morning, not using the Padua by-pass!

Works-entered Vongole speedsters were driven to seven successive victories in the "Mamma Mille" by Austria's ace Count Otto Seikel and were placed no fewer than 44 times at Le Mans during the 1950s when all of Europe flocked to watch the swashbuckling Bonaventura Bangio using every ounce of the Vongole's remarkable torque to execute breathtaking handbrake turns with half-tucked somersault and pike.

Sadly Campari never mastered undersealing and none of his magnificent cars survived the harsh winter of 1963.

## 1933 BATTENBURG TWENTY-FIVE GRAND OTTOMAN SJ

Walt and Tyrone Battenburg's 25-tonner supercharged limos of the 1930s were easily mistaken for ocean-going liners. Their legendary "Ottoman" landaulette featured coachwork modelled on the Sultan of Baghdad's richly fortified slipper baths and was reputedly the most lavishly chromium-plated "car for the stars" ever made in Beverly Hills, or anywhere. Ottomans sat 22 at a pinch, plus the chauffeur and a bell-hop.

All Battenburgs, more luxurious even than Detroit's famous Spondulic limousines, had such fabled glamour, elegance and crankshaft-bending performance that they soon became favourite flashy transport for such style-conscious Hollywood immortals as Ronnie Reagan, Rin Tin Tin and Gladys Cooper. The Maharajah of Opdaipur ordered a bottom-of-the-range pick-up in 1935, but defaulted on the hp.

With a 24-cylinder Lycoming bomber engine capable of turning out a lazy 600bhp on tick-over, a zebra-wood inlay to the back fender, fur-lined trunk, retractable flagpole and twin running-boards which could stand up to 56 chorus-girls in comfort, the 130-mph Twenty-Five Grand SJs had what it took to cut a dash on the turnpikes, but proved martyrs to rust and woodworm. Nice examples can still fetch between 2 and 3 million dollars, more if autographed.

## 1946 CROSSBEAM TURBOT

First, and many believe the sturdiest of the 10hp side-valve "vets' workhorses" which were mass-produced post-war in the old "Jubilee" ball-bearing works at Manifold, just outside West Bromwich.

Back in civilian production after over six years of manufacturing helmets, snoek and munitions, Crossbeam Bros. abandoned their old supercharged four-litre in favour of the more austere 10hp they had used to such good effect in military sluice pumps.

The chassis, sketched on the back of a ration card by world-famous Alec "Tubby" Issibonnis, was a typically inspired variation on the famous triangulated box-frame he used for his 1927 Basil Rathbone tourer – incidentally the first British car to feature streamlined vacuum wipers and 18-inch hickory-spoked wheels as standard.

Two years later a Crossbeam Turbot tourer, driven by Nellie Van Der Vat, was placed 119th in the trans-Belgian Antirrhinum Rally. The saloon was a classic of the popular "sit-up-and-beg" designs which characterised West Bromwich cars in the late 1940s, yet curiously the convertible never really caught on and production ceased in 1952. A superb example is still in everyday use near Staines.

## 1938 IRENE ADLER TWO-STROKE

Few outside Dresden's Reichsmotorenwerken imagined in 1938 that the diminutive, "corrugated henbox" 663cc two-stroke people-carriers designed by Dr Irene Adler from an idea by Ferdinand Goering would one day become the first air-cooled three-wheelers to be made by the million in Brazil.

Yet such was the "Sehenswürdigkeit" of the tortoise-shaped bodywork and "Unburstigheit" of the wet-lined iron "boxer" twin that Adlers quickly took on "cult car" status all over South America and parts of Turkey besides (where they were used as minicabs).

Though they lacked the overall sophistication of their great French rival, the 664cc Citoyen "Marche Avant" ragtop utility with such refinements as a syncromesh gearbox, four wheels (five, counting the spare) and a back window, Adlers were nevertheless versatile, economical machines which could chug along all day on a litre of 1-star adulterated benzine or even a bucket of poultry droppings.

During hostilities, they served as nippy two-man troop carriers, mobile cultivators, amphibious mine-sweepers and regular transport for millions of 24-hour military plumbers. In later years, Adlers were destined to achieve a similar "street-smart" popularity as part of South America's wild "Swinging Sixties".

Though today superseded by the best-selling fwd Wolf, a great many Adlers are still in running order and continue to attract derision from passers-by when pluckily taking part in *concours d'élégance* or racing against such famous trains as The Orient Express or Blue Train. 🐾

# Canned Heat

## RUSSELL DAVIES

Tired of Sardinia? Surely not!

With its sun-dappled shingle and shin-stippling sea-foam, this apple-fresh fun-spangled Shangri-La will always call Come Ye Back. But — let's face it — it's getting hard, especially in the skin-grilling supersun season, to find those slumbering, breeze-bereft glades where you can read your flyaway tissue-paper *Guardian* in pluperfect peace. So this year, why not give lovely Sardinia the Elba and go for her beautiful sister island?

Yes, Pilchardia! Be fickle — she'll thank you for it!

**LOCATION AND HISTORY:** Pilchardia, sometimes called the Isle of Teeth, is a fabulous rocky outcrop – the seventeenth largest island in the western Mediterranean measured by surface area, though no less than fifth largest by volume. Pilchardia enjoys a year-round climate and is immersed in water throughout the full twelve months, though very little seems to soak in underneath. The Romans, no doubt attracted by the watertightness of the land-mass, chose to make Pilchardia the site of some of their vastest tin, lead and manganese mines.

In 423 AD approx, Pilchardia was briefly invaded by the Etruscans, who left upon the island their characteristic pot thing. In 1801, Nelson sailed past the southern tip of the island, his ship running so close to the cliff now known as Precipizio Nelson that the great hero bet the Officer of the Watch that he could hit the sheer rock-face with a tea-cup. Each man threw a cup from the Admiral's personal service – Nelson using his existing arm – but neither missile attained its mark. The British fleet always avoided the island thereafter.

In 1962, Pilchardia was the setting for Umberto Adiposo's film *Paparazzo Mon Amour*.

**RESORTS:** Porto Schifo, the island capital, has been a haven for storm-tossed voyagers since the dawn of pre-history. With its natural rocky harbour and firm, golden inhabitants, it offers something to suit all tastes, and more besides. The town centre, spectacularly obliterated by the 1979 earthquake, has youth on its side.

**EATING OUT:** Pilchardian cuisine is justly famous. Spicy, peppery, and violent in its juxtaposition of tastes, it carries us directly back to the Dark Ages of the Mediterranean, when Etruscan *plonki* (delicatessen ships) were regularly wrecked on the island's reefs and nobody quite knew what had spilled out of where. Great pride is taken in serving all foods piping hot, even at the height of summer, and it is a matter of politeness for the visitor, on his inaugural visit to any eating place, to burn his mouth loudly on his first spoonful of *stufalù* (charcoal soup) – a gesture that will be greeted with unfailing applause.

The most famous restaurant on the island is the difficult-of-access **Ernesto's** at Alto Schifetto, but it is worth the mule-ride across the precarious rope-bridge, even if the mule is hard to convince. Ernesto's *neraccio* (burnt barracuda) and *zuppa di nastolo* (horned viper soup) are unsurpassed anywhere, and every customer is served on a bed of fluffy rice.

**SHOPPING & SOUVENIRS:** Being the beneficiaries of thousands of shipwrecks down the centuries, the Pilchardians are experts in the field of luggage. There is no form of case, trunk, bag or crate that they have not seen and adapted to their own traditional woodcraft stylings. Nothing delights a Pilchardian more than to take your luggage, and turn it, by dint of marvellously skilful joinery and appliqué work, into something resembling a cross between an ornate sea-chest and a giant picnic basket. Sometimes you will scarcely believe that your own little valise is really still in there! Two words of warning: do make sure you have contracted legally for the work (official rates are posted outside the Communist Party offices in Via Nelson); and do remember that the material used is chiefly *lumbone*, a local form of hornbeam that is exceedingly heavy. It is therefore advisable, lest excess baggage charges be incurred, to submit only one item per family to the skills of your friendly chiseller.

## SIGHTSEEING:

Unmissable highlight of any Pilchardian holiday is a visit to the amazing drowned church of **Santo Stufo Sotto l'Acqua**. No one knows how this remarkable Romanesque basilica came to be sited some fourteen feet underwater off the extreme eastern point of Pilchardia. Local legend has it that the whole island dipped in that direction, as a form of salute, the day Christ was welcomed into Jerusalem; but this theory is discounted by geologists.

**How to get there:** hire a *sinca*, the local coracle (do not be put off by the name – they are lively, but seaworthy) and row vigorously south from Porto Schifo harbour. After three nautical miles, pull into the well signposted Bay of Sunk Kirch (*sic*) and pass through the turnstile (entrance fee varies according to saints' days, etc). **NB** Admission is by sanctified snorkel only, licensed by the Vatican and available from Fr Ginocchio, the official custodian and parish priest. Ladies must wear hats and long-legged bathing drawers.

## FESTIVAL:

Also unique to Pilchardia is the White Cliffs Cinema Season. During the Twenties and Thirties, feature films were the subject of a harsh local ban by the Bishop of Pilchardia, who was instrumental in forcing the closure of the island's only cinema. However, an enterprising fisherman smuggled in a projector under his nets. Having no screen of sufficient size, nor any chance of erecting one without attracting the attentions of the church authorities, this bold experimenter, on a calm night, rowed the apparatus out to sea and projected the film on to the white marble cliffs, attracting a large and enthusiastic crowd of fellow fisherfolk. Every August the success of that pioneering season is commemorated with a sea-borne Film Festival, using the same "screen". It is always hugely enjoyed by the native populace, if a trifle queasily by visitors.

(There is still no conventional cinema on the island, for it has been found that Pilchardians do not believe in cinematic action unless the entire image is sliding up and down.)

## ACCOMMODATION:

Porto Schifo abounds with lively hotels and cafés, each one striving to serve you more quickly than the last. Longest-established of the inns is the **Hotel Nelson** which, thanks to an enlightened government scheme, commemorates the English sea-dog by employing only one-armed and one-eyed staff. The waiters work in matched pairs, thus bringing a left arm and a right arm to bear on the problems of table service. To watch them tackle a typical Pilchardian *flambé* is to savour the joys of Nero!

Family-owned since 1974, the **Hotel Corleone** offers a pleasantly shady outlook. Legends cluster about the venerable owner, who does not deny that he was once a knife-thrower in an American circus! The most strik-

ing feature of the hotel's decor is Sig Corleone's collection of hats – dozens, possibly hundreds of mysterious trilbies, each allotted its own peg on the enormous lobby wall. No wonder the *Corleone* has become the meeting-place of the local Surrealist group.

**Howard Johnson's Motor Hotel** is not, strictly speaking, part of the American chain but aspires to similar standards. There are no motor cars on Pilchardia, but the charm of the establishment is that Mr Johnson (one of the Corleone family who changed his name while working as a stonemason in America) carries on exactly as though there were. Fuel pumps, inspection pit and workshop are maintained in perfect working order, glasses are given away with every order of petrol (there are two lawnmowers on the island, both available for hire by visitors), and Mr Johnson pays a cousin of his, a local character, to be stationed permanently by the bar should you wish to discuss the best route you might have taken across the island, had you had the opportunity.

It all adds up to a sun-steeped, sand-smudged sojourn in unforgettable Pilchardia, saucy old queen of the Western Med. You'll be glad you came across!

*"Never mind the wheels – what happened to the car?"*

## ANNA RAEBURN on men

# "You can have a big nose like Philippe Noiret or your ears can stick out like Clark Gable's. Women, like the film-making process, will adapt to everything."

THE best you can say about men in the movies is that there's more chance of seeing a man who looks like a human male in the movies – I mean, the ordinarily flawed variety – than of seeing a woman ditto. A less than perfect woman of one type or another may get work, usually in the form of featured roles, but a less than perfect man is more likely to be elevated to a new kind of stardom and stay up there twinkling in the firmament for much longer.

One of the great illusions about the movies is that the camera doesn't lie, as if we could blame it all on the machine that men do so much better for so much longer in this medium than women. But in fact the camera, far from being impersonal, has its own eye. It perceives, distorts and enhances in the most bewildering way. Yet, as the industry increasingly slots performers into screen personae they must inhabit in the modern edition of the old studio star system, we sometimes catch a glimpse of the real face, rather than the one the camera – and all the publicity and marketing machinery – have decided we should see.

Celluloid heroes, past and present, are often required to have a regularity of feature which in real life makes them look curiously flat, albeit pretty. If that soft-edged amiability is absent, you are left with a face of such symmetry that it gets in the way of anything else. It must be just as trying to be a conventionally good-looking man as it is to be a pretty girl with brains. Nobody wants either of them to think. They should just *be* – and preferably agreeable and acquiescent.

But the sterner types are just as back-to-front. A face which on the screen has always seemed menacing is seen to be chubby, even benign. The denizen of semi-psychopaths, Oliver Reed, was once brought to a television studio as an example of gung-ho male chauvinism, a role immediately undermined by his squeaky petulance and a resemblance to nothing so much as a slightly overstuffed, worn, pink plush teddy bear. Outside their movie incarnations, heavies like Vincent Price and Brian Dennehey turn out to be the possessors of rare charm and wit, antique collectors or scholars of oriental art. What, after all, constituted the menace but the lines and the lighting?

Once upon a time, the actors on the silver screen were offered to us to be what they seemed to be. Now, after sixty years of stories about lead dildoes and mother fixation, about meanness, violence and alcoholism, we know that, be they ever so gilded, most actors are still performers first and people second, with a few remarkable exceptions in which the people are as interesting and in some cases as blameless as

the characters they inhabit to entertain us. Why should it follow that because a man has a lovely voice, he must be a lovely person? A large proportion of the American public currently venerates John Rambo, in the second instalment of whose story the last chapters of the American War in Vietnam are rewritten. But do they therefore by extension also worship Sylvester Stallone, a man with overdeveloped muscles and of severely average height, who has difficulty in facing the reality of his irreparably handicapped child – a son at that?

The fascination about meeting the men in the movies, hearing stories about them, being witness to them off-screen, is that acting is always a peculiar business and even stranger when it becomes part of the extremely expensive, volatile, illusory world of film. The first shock is that they are not flat. They take up space and they almost always inhabit it differently from the way you had imagined. Then there's the conflict of how the camera made you see them and how you see them now. Some are taller – both Michael Douglas and Richard Gere look smaller on film than they are in life. Many more are smaller. Their personalities fill the screen but their inches do not dent the bar.

Remember, too, that the publicity is to a very large extent built around the image and how people would like to see them. Reality takes a back seat. The big men are less remarkable for their statuesque proportions and more appealing for some other part of their personality which is unexplored in the success of their films. In many ways Sean Connery *is* James Bond but he is also a brave actor, a tough Scot a long way from his beginnings and, incidentally, he looks better bald, brown and heavily lined than he did years ago as Ian Fleming's Mr Fixit.

And who cares about John Hurt's height, weight, girth or pallor? What counts is the voice.

To be in the movies is to feel that you would be (if you were the lead or even second lead) the focus of everyone's best efforts to make you look great. Leaving aside the miracles which can be wrought by the lighting cameraman, you'd have the tailoring, the helpful makeup man, the barber – and Clint Eastwood alone proves what a good haircut can do for a man. Look at him before he had it. Or maybe I should say look for him before he had it. He just doesn't happen on the screen in the same way.

But the fact is that the movies will work with less in terms of men than they will with women. The movies take a man and enhance everything he's got, as long as he's got something somebody wants to start with. It may be his size, his movement, his voice, his eyes, his smile, his dancing, his acting, his camera quality (what the director Billy Wilder called "flesh impact"), his charm – they'll build on it. Unless you have a certain degree of physical good looks as a woman, you won't get as much of a shot at success in the absolute terms of playing leads. This is true in life.

In life, a woman looks at a man to see what she can like. Too many men look at a woman to see if she's physically attractive first. Yet men can learn from the movies how better to present themselves because of this initial acceptance. You don't have to be tall. Neither Paul Newman nor Robert Redford is as tall as they're supposed to be; Al Pacino and Dustin Hoffman are frankly short. You don't have to have all your hair. William Hurt has a high forehead in advance or a hairline in retreat, depending on your point of view, but either way, it hasn't done him any harm. You can have a big nose like Philippe Noiret or your ears can stick out like Clark Gable's. You can walk as if you've wet your pants like Warren Beatty, or knock-kneed like Richard Dreyfuss. You can balloon with weight like Marlon Brando. You can be as cadaverous as John Carradine. Women, like the film-making process, will adapt to all of these.

What so many men could learn from the movies and do not is meticulous grooming, scrubbed and creamed hands, close shaves, clean teeth and no fluff in the navel. What movie-men offer is a representation of the best and worst that men can be and, too often, the elements of appeal are disregarded while a new set of attitudes is noted to be struck. Of course, it takes a very particular type of woman to be interested in an actor because they are, for the most part, in love already; inextricably with themselves and disappointingly all too often with each other.

# LARRY'S

## AMBULANCE MEN

# ALAN COREN

# THE REVISED VERSION

### *Appointed to be read in Supermarkets*

## from GENESIS

…beast of the earth, and to every fowl of the air, and to everything that creepeth upon the earth, wherein *there is* life, I *have given* every green herb for meat: and it was so.

31 And God saw every thing that he had made, and, behold, *it was* very good. And the evening and the morning were the sixth day.

**2** THUS the heavens and earth were finished, and all the host of them.

2 And on the seventh day God ended his work which he had made; and he was about to rest on the seventh day from all his labours, when he looked again at every thing that he had made, and, behold, *it was* not quite as good as he had thought. For some of the coving *that there* was in that place had come away, nor was there a host of shelving; also there were bubbles in the wallpaper, and a drip from somewhere.

3 And God said, I was about to bless the seventh day and sanctify it, because I had planned to have *a bit of* a lie in and rest from the work which I had created and made, but plastering will not do itself, there is no peace for, there is no peace for, it will come to me in a minute.

4 And the LORD God said, I wonder if there is anywhere open?

5 But there was not anywhere open.

6 Therefore the LORD God formed man *of the* dust of the ground, and breathed into his nostrils the breath of life; and man became a living soul.

7 And the LORD God planted a garden centre eastward in Eden, and adjacent *to it* in that place set he a homecare mart; and there he put the man that he had formed.

8 And the LORD God went back to make a list.

9 And behold, in the fullness of time, God went again to that place and called unto Adam and said unto him, Where art thou?

10 And Adam cried unto the LORD God, saying, I am out back stacking PVC guttering, I cannot be everywhere at once unlike some people I could mention, I have only got one pair of hands.

11 Whereat the LORD Customer waxed exceeding wroth, saying: if thou art not satisfied with the hands that I

have made thee, that can be fixed; and while I am at it, perhaps I will throw in a trunk and a couple of antlers.

12 And Adam came out quickly from that place where he was.

13 And he spake unto the LORD God, saying, Can I be of any assistance?

14 And God said, here is my list.

15 But when the man looked at the list, he straightway *smote* himself upon the brow, crying, I can do the half-inch Yorkshire joints, the eau-de-nil undercoat is always *in* stock, the Polyfilla is no problem, we are up to here with ready-pasted Vymura, but I can not do the two-inch pre-cast coving. There is no call *for* two-inch pre-cast coving.

16 And God spake in a voice like thunder, crying, I am the LORD thy God and I have set thee above all the beasts of the field, never mind all the builders requisites; if I call for two-inch pre-cast coving, is there not a call for it?

17 And Adam thought apart awhile, and replied in this wise, saying: it is possible that it is out back somewhere, we only opened this morning, I have not yet taken stock; if the LORD my God would care to hang on a minute, I shall see what I can do.

18 But God spoke unto him again, saying: The LORD thy God is not in the habit of hanging on, I shall find thee a help meet for thee.

19 And the LORD God caused a great sleep to fall upon Adam, and he slept: and he took *one of* his ribs, and closed up the flesh instead thereof.

20 And the rib, which the LORD God had taken *from* the man, made he a woman, and brought her unto the man.

21 And Adam cried aloud, saying: where did he come from?

22 And God replied, I have fashioned a rib *to be* thy assistant, and make the tea.

23 And Adam said, truly thou art a fantastic handygod, O LORD, thou hast done a remarkable job in the time, despite the odd structural flaw.

24 And God said, it is a woman.

25 Whereat Adam marvelled, crying: If I could get a couple of gross of ribs *from* somewhere, they could be a very big seller.

26 But to the woman, he spake in this wise, saying: nip out back, Sid, and see if we have got any lengths *of* two-inch pre-cast coving.

27 And they were both naked, the man

and the woman, and they were not ashamed.

**3** AND God took from the man all that had been *on his* list, and went away from that place and set to work speedily, for it was almost noon on the seventh day and there were many cracks to be made good due to settlement, and much paper to hang, and a great *deal* of shelving to be put up; and many sashcords had already perished, and subsidence had caused many doors to stick so hard *that* the LORD God had to remove the hinges.

2 And some of the screws rolled under cupboards where even the LORD God could not reach them.

3 And much of the glass that he had brought with him to that place was one millimetre larger than he had measured and shattered *when* he tried to force it in.

4 And however much paper of whichever pattern he had brought back from Eden, and no matter which room he was papering, he found that he was always one roll short.

5 And no matter which shade of emulsion the LORD God put on, it was invariably just a tiny bit darker than it had looked on the colour chart.

6 Or a tiny bit lighter.

7 And God grew great in his anger, crying: I have made the giraffe and the orchid; lo! I have fashioned the spider and the snowflake and the jellyfish after their wondrous fashion, I even did that duck-billed thing with the flat feet for a laugh, and all was as a piece of cake, compared with this. Yea, though I go back a bit, mind, was the Milky Way not knocked up in the twinkling of an eye, and everything fitted? How, then, shall it be that with this that I do now *there is* never enough of anything even though there was more than enough at the beginning, or, if there is, it is always a bit different from anything else?

8 But there was no answer to that.

9 And God said, I wonder if they are still open?

10 And he took *his* new list, and he returned eastward to Eden, and behold, they were still open.

11 And the LORD God went in unto them; and a bell had been put above the door, and it jangled.

12 And God made a murmuring in the wind, saying: what is it, that they have

need of a bell? And he called unto Adam, and said unto him, Where art thou this time?

13 And lo! a voice came *from* afar, crying: Be with you in a minute, due to where we are up to our eyes stocktaking.

14 Yet the LORD God did not wax wroth upon this occasion, for he believed truly that the man was going about his business; and he saw that it was good to do so, for it was the seventh day, and it was *as* it should be.

15 But after much time passed, the LORD God began to wax ever so slightly irritable, for there was a host of plumbing still to be plumbed, and rodding-out to do in great measure; and he had still not even so much as touched the garden.

16 Yet the irritation was as nothing to his wroth when Adam and his assistant came at last to that place *where he* was; for they were both clad in long brown warehouse coats.

17 And the LORD God spake unto them through his teeth, saying: well?

18 And the man said, I heard thy voice in the garden centre, and I was afraid, because I *was* naked; and I hid myself.

19 And God said: I?

20 And Adam said, all right, we.

21 And God said, Who told thee that thou *wast* naked? Hast thou eaten of the tree, whereof I commanded thee that thou shouldest not eat?

22 And Adam replied, saying: Sid said we should, she said we ought to taste the stock, they could be a duff consignment of apple trees, we might be taking money under false pretences; am I right, Sid?

23 But the woman answered him not; and looked at her nails.

24 And the LORD God cried unto Adam, saying: I gave thee the seventh day to run a nice little business, that it would keep thee out of mischief, but thou hast heeded me not; the moment the LORD thy God's back is turned, the pair of you are at it, yea, even like knives.

25 And Adam spake unto God, saying: all work and no play, et cetera et cetera, I trust I do not have to draw pictures, you are a God of the world.

26 And the LORD God said, Behold, the man thinks he is become yet mightier than one of us, to have a lie in *on the* seventh day and not do a hand's turn, and let the business that I have given unto him go unto pot; it will be golf next.

27 Therefore the LORD God sent him forth from the garden centre and home-mart of Eden, and caused a notice *to be* put in the window, saying: closed for alterations.

28 So he drove out the man; and he placed at the east of Eden Cherubims, *and a* flaming sword which turned every way; and he caused to be brought in the six-day week for a punishment and a sign, until such time as the earth was ready to receive his saints.

"I'm wanted in every state in the country. Why don't *you* want me?"

# BASIL BOOTHROYD
# Something to Play with

Dear Design Marketing Ltd,

My answer is 31. I have treated the numbers as sheep, or bicycles. It's just that I can't hold anything in my mind too abstract.

So multiply 9 by 5, add 12 and take away 6, and it gives me 31 eggs or whatever they are. I expect this is wrong. Still, I have had a go, and hope to qualify as a player of your "latest chic parlour game" as described in the paper.

In case this letter gets into the wrong hands and is puzzling, I should mention that your game has so far only been played by consenting Mensa members in the privacy of their chic parlours, but caught on so well it is now being thrown open at £22.95 per kit to the wider public, viz, ordinary muttonheads who have to think twice before making an anagram of honorificabilitudinitatibus, or spotting the link between John o' Groats, VAT and a week-old turbot.

Talking of VAT, your Mensa players probably don't have it. You can't be using your mind for fun all the time and have any left over for the higher income bracket. But here is a tip when they get a bill for £22.95 including VAT but not showing how much. Divide by 115, multiply by 15 and you get £73. Or I do. And I have not added my IQ in by mistake, as it has never been taken. I don't think about it much. I would guess it at about sixteen. And if that's centigrade another tip is to make it Fahrenheit by doubling

it, taking away the left-hand figure and adding thirty-two.

This could, of course, be kilometres if I have made a slip somewhere, as I used to when friends asked me the one about if a herring and a half cost three-halfpence, what was the engine-driver's name; or, if they were Mensa material, how many bones in Cleopatra's corsets, based on the trigonometry of the pyramids. Used to be called brain-teasers in those days, and were sometimes in statement form, e.g., that man's father was that father's son. When I took their word for it they were furious. What else did they want, for heaven's sake?

I am writing pre-Budget, by the way, in case by now they have changed the VAT from 15%, or put an import tax on corset bones used other than for medical research or foodstuffs. Please allow off for any error on that score which could damage my chance of winning a chrome statue, though I do not know who this is of, as the paper does not say.

Perhaps Clive Sinclair's brother, as he invented the game. It does say this, but not whether only the founding group of Mensa menschen got one, or it is being thrown to the wider public now in the market to answer questions about who invented cheese or the date of Cromwell's first wart.

What a game, eh?

But I think it's good for ordinary brain cells to have their potential stirred up, and not only mine. Not mine at all, quite honestly. I am no games player. My view is that rather than know my phone number is Disraeli's inside leg measurement multiplied by 188, I would use the cells to work out postages to America, such as 29p for ten grammes+11p each extra ten or part thereof, when your letter-scales are in ounces and you can only play safe with what

you've got handy in order to make 52p-worth of five old second-class 13p's still kicking around. Which actually I see come to 65p, what the hell.

For games of that kind I envy Mensa people. They look at a 2½ kilogram parcel packed up for Papua New Guinea and just get licking in their heads, 49 at 17p=£8.33, just right. Any lip from the sub-postmistress and they stop her off with the addressee's latitude of 11°S, longitude 160°E, and rainfall figures in 1886. They are by no means limited to arithmetic. Their geography is also OK. Also all you need to know about why the cubic capacity of a bull's stomach is $E=mc^2$ on the Beaufort scale. This isn't a lot of good in the post office, and holds up the man behind wanting a dog licence, but, brother, it puts them right up there for a shot at the chrome statue of that man's brother inscribed with the engine-driver's name.

And though none of this is for me, unless I have now qualified to send you my £22.95, it doesn't mean that lots of people don't feel differently. After a day's work and a guards' walk-out at Clapham they come home with more brain cells than they know what to do with. They want to be stretched. Coat off, straight to the games cupboard for the latest chic dice, board, counters and questions on the density of zinc and who designed Mungo Park.

Incidentally, I am making up these problems, so if you need help at your end with material do not hesitate to contact me. We are moving more and more into the age of leisure, and the demand for something useless to occupy it will increase by a factor of something chronic, say the square root of its quotient, long before I personally, not to talk about myself all the time, keep asking who's got Mr Sole the fishmonger at Happy Families, when junior Mensa members scream that he's actually the shoemaker and pelt me with Play-Doh.

Though in a way I am lucky in having a large and happy family who are always dropping in with their problems, such as a Sheik leaves 11 camels to his 19 sons and how do they end up with six each. Never mind Why does a chicken cross the road, grandpa, and tell me the answer while I'm still thinking.

Please let me know how I have done. To show I am worth encouraging there are some hidden problems in this letter, with solutions below, as I would not want to leave you dangling. It will mean you or Clive's brother finding where they are hidden, but if you are in the popular growth industry of games people play, it can't be a bad thing to see how the other half lives.

Yours playfully —
Design Marketing Ltd,
Andover,
S+P÷10+2×Q−X

*"It's a compulsory purchase order – to make way for the Okehampton by-pass."*

# GREAT WINE NATIONS OF THE WORLD

## No. 3 – USSR

Currently the world's third largest producer, the Soviet wine industry has remained a shrouded mystery to all but a few devoted sommeliers and bio-chemists. Its recent emergence as a major export force is partly due to the extensive introduction of new technology to replace traditional methods (tractor-driven rémoullade turning racks etc) and a reluctant change to fungus-free American vines after many unsuccessful years experimenting with Pinaud Noir, before realising that it was a hair tonic.

All wine production is State controlled. As is all distribution, bottling, marketing and drinking.

## HISTORY

Quite how the grape vine (*Vitis Vinifera*) arrived in Russia from the Roman Empire has never been proved. Apocryphal tales abound claiming it to have been a talisman brought by the Firebird, or a fertility symbol conjured by the witch Baba Yar and even a household pot plant surrendered to the Court by marauding Tartars. The most likely explanation, however, is that they stole it.

The history of Russian wine is dogged with misfortune. After its first documentation in an eleventh-century seed catalogue until well into the 1600s, nobody had chanced upon the idea of using it for drinking. Throughout these gastrically unabused years, Russian wine was variously bottled as a horse linament, a dye for staining the inside of lacquered Palekh boxes and an organic fertiliser and compost accelerator; while at Court the grape found much favour as disposable costume jewellery by the vegetarian Tsar, Count Nicolai the Bland.
Catherine the Great, popularly known by her voracious appetite for pleasures of the flesh, was particularly fond of what she used to call "*drinski-poos*" – a sweetish Kazbek sherry that she reportedly poured down herself in bed (q.v. Hitting the sack). The Tsarina used to say that she would drink one bottle for every lover she took. She died of alcoholic poisoning on her wedding night.

## TOURISM

The hills are alive with the sound of mujhiks, treading barefoot their relentless path through hectares of semi-crushed grape, often humming to themselves a peasant chastushka as they follow the age-old search for some dacha or wayside collective selling decent vodka.
Tourists are welcomed in **Georgia** and **Soviet Armenia** to any of the State Grape Collectives, especially around the time of the State Grape Collection. **Moscow**; guided tours are offered daily in the magnificent Caves under Lyubianka and Djerjhinsky Square, currently sublet to the State Security Bureaux for laying down dissidents.
**Wine Lovers' Tours** (c/o The Lenin Institute for the Rehabilitation of Perrier Drinkers) take parties of visitors through the national production centres around the Black Sea, the Caucasian Mountains and on self-paddling ferry trips across the great Euro-Baikal Wine Lake. Latest bargains include fourteen days sightseeing the 1800 miles of barbed wire along the lush Chinese/Soviet border, under test as a self-contained, combination vine support and anti-tanker trap; threatening to crush the Chinese pea-stick farmers and Mowtoy-smugglers in one fell swoop.

## Export Labels to look out for (Les grands Marx)

**Mukuzani (RED):** Produce of Georgia. Imagine the subtlety of ikon-printed wallpaper, the body of a netball team prop-forward, the bouquet of dew-gathered beetroot . . . in fact, anything you can to take your mind off trying to drink it. Suitable only for de-icing your troika (and then only an old one).

**Tsinandali (GREY):** The "Gold Medal" boasted of in point-of-sale advertising material in State pharmacies refers to the 1952 Concours des Vins de Pays Etrangers (Havana) when it scraped home a close second to a mislabelled bottle of Alaskan battery acid. Favoured years 1917, 1945, 1987.

**Champanskoye (BRUT):** If you're offered the choice, plump for the aftershave (recognisable as the slightly fizzier one). Ungoverned by French chauvinism for its nomenclature nor the Shops, Factory and Railway Premises Act as a gastronomic hard hat zone.

**Crimean Cognac:** A description that particularly infuriates the European wine trade as this eau-de-vie style spirit does not actually come from the Crimea. Often drunk as an after-dinner accompaniment to coffee in order to speed home recalcitrant guests.

**Grain Wine:** Often distilled and exported as unlabelled *white box* vodka; whence it is reimported (attracting considerable import tax), rebottled/labelled as Moskovskaya (generating year-round employment) and sold at inflated prices in Airport Berioska shops to unsuspecting Libyan tourists – a practice known in vintners' circles as *The Soviet Economy*.

**Bluecol Nun:** A Rhine-style, big-end of the market, schlossleader. Pick up an expansion bottle or two, cheap, in end-of-sump sales at Mosplonk.

**Graves:** Brand leader is *Karl Marx* from the sunblessed slopes of Highgate Hill. (See also *Kremlin Wallbanger*).

**Vino Ordinarski:** A last-ditch attempt to popularise cheap wine drinking in a manner more suited to western marketing values. Non-vintage, biologically engineered grape ferment, produce of more than one regime; usually supplied in Chianski style, raffia-wrapped trendy bottles, complete with ready-to-wire table lamp fittings. Marketed under pop brand names like *Peter the Grape* and *Communist Party Seven* and *Little Cyrillic Ray of Sunshine*.

## What to look for in a Soviet Wine label

WHERE THE KHOLXOZ LEADER WENT FOR
HOLIDAYS AND DRANK A LOT_____

IN CASE OF COMPLAINT, BLAME_____

BRAND NAME_____

VINEYARD PATRON_____

FRENCH HONESTY THAT RUSSIANS
WON'T UNDERSTAND_____

*Mosel*

Apparatchik Contrôlée

762534/BP/A4

*The Novolush Shipyard, Winery & Model Laundry im. Lenin*

**VINOGRAD**

*Mis en bouteille dans nos laboratoires*
*(Best before uncorking)*

# PARTING SHOTS

"OK, men, I'm just a burden – go on without me!"

"Goodbye, Shane! . . . . Goodbye, Mom!"

"Spiffer didn't make it. We thought you might like his breakfast."

"Cochise has given up smoking. I hope you like hazelnut whirls."

"Geoffrey, you won't ever leave me, will you?"

"George, this is Harry, my brief encounter on the 4.30 to Watford. Harry, this is George, my brief encounter on the 5.30 to Liverpool Street."

"You're giving little Sparky the best gift you can, son. His freedom."

"It's gonna be OK, Dad. Lassie's brought us the phone!"

"Here's lookin' at you, kid."

# Rough Drafts

## A Christmas Carol by Charles Dickens

Marley was ill: to begin with. There is no doubt whatever about that. Old Marley was as sick as a parrot.

Mind! I don't mean to say that I know, of my own knowledge, what there is particularly sick about a parrot. I might have been inclined, myself, to regard a dodo as the sickest creature in the avian kingdom. But the wisdom of our ancestors is in the simile; and my unhallowed hands shall not disturb it, or the country's done for. You will therefore permit me to repeat, emphatically, that Marley was as sick as a parrot.

Scrooge knew he was sick? Of course he

Marley was off-colour: to begin with. There is no doubt whatever about that. Old Marley was as off-colour as

Marley was out of sorts: to begi

Marley was not in the best of health: t

Marley was poorly
Marley was was was . . .

## Three Men In A Boat by Jerome K. Jerome

There were four of us – George, and William Samuel Harris, and myself, and Fido. We were sitting in my room, smoking, and talking about

There were four of us – George, and William Samuel Harris, and myself, and Rover. We were

George, William Samuel Harris, myself, and Spot.
And Rex/King/Bonzo/Butch/Killer/Spike . . .
. . . Champion Yellow Fang of Henley . . ?

## Gimlet, Prince of Norway by William Shakespeare

ACT ONE: Scene I. The guard-platform of the Castle. FRANCISCO at his post. Enter to him BERNARDO.
*Ber.* Who's there?
*Fran.* Nay, answer me. Stand and unfold yoursel

## Humbert, Prince of Sweden by Willia

## Goblet, Prince of Schleswig-Holstein by

Hambone, Prince of Latvia
Hogrot, of Estonia      Two Gentlemen of Lithuania
The Merry Wives Of Finland . . .

## The Cask of Amontillado by Edgar Allan Poe

The thousand injuries of Blenkinsop I had borne as I best could, but when he ventured upon insult I vowed revenge. You, who so well know the nature of my soul, will not suppose

The thousand injuries of Snodgrass I had borne as I best cou

The thousand injuries of Wilkinson
of Bloggs
of Bollweevil-Smith
of, of . . .

## Tarzan of the Monkeys by Edgar Rice Burroughs

I had this story from one who had no business to tell it to me, or to any other. I may

## Tarzan of the Gibbons by Edg

Tarzan of the of the the
Chimpanzees/Gorillas/Orang-Utans
Tarzan of the Lemurs
Tarzan of the Marmosets
Tarzan of the Tarsiers . . .
. . . Tarzan of the *Ants* . . . ?

## The Gremlin by J. R. R. Tolkien

In a hole in the ground there lived a gremlin. Not a nasty, dirty, wet hole, filled with the ends of worms and an oozy smell, nor yet a dry, bare, sandy hole with nothing in it to sit down on or eat: it was a gremlin-hole, and that means

## The Gargoyle by J. R. R. Tolkien

In a hole in the ground there lived a

The Goggit – ?
The Gadjit – ?
The Hoggit – ?
The Hogrot – ?

## The Final Problem by A. Conan Doyle

"You have probably never heard of Professor Montmorency?" said Holmes.

"Never."

"Aye, there's the genius and the wonder of the thing!" he cried. "The man pervades London, and no one has heard of him. He is the Genghis Khan of crime, Watson

"You have probably never heard of Professor Montressor? He is the Attila the Hun of crime, Watso

"You have probably never heard of Professor Marley/ Marlborough/Montezuma/Muggins . . .

"He is the Palmerston/Gladstone/Disraeli/William Pitt the Younger of crime, Wats

# ROGER WODDIS

# The Green Eye of the Little Orange God

"Let us not ask for whom the bell tolls, it tolls for her" —
Enoch Powell, Official Unionist MP for South Down,
on the Anglo-Irish agreement.

There's a one-eyed orange idol to the north of No-Kan-Du,
There's a little-noticed seat in County Down;
There's a stony-hearted woman shakes her fist at You-know-who,
And the Orange God still claims to serve the Crown.

He was known as You-know-who by the bluest of the blue,
He was harder than they felt inclined to say;
But for all his classic pose, there were rumbles when he rose,
And the grocer's daughter wished he'd go away.

He had served her long ago, till the blood began to flow,
And the fury of his fire was plain to all.
Now agreement with the South tasted poison in his mouth,
And he warned her she was riding for a fall.

He was moved to pitch it strong, saying what she did was wrong
And would set the Papist high above the Prod;
But she said in tones of ice nothing else would now suffice
But the green eye shining in the Orange God.

She upbraided You-know-who in the way that women do,
Although her eyes were strangely hot and wet;
But what occupied her mind on the day that he resigned
Was the pact that she had done her nut to get.

There's a one-eyed orange idol to the north of No-Kan-Du,
There's a little-noticed seat in County Down;
There's a stony-hearted woman shakes her fist at You-know-who,
And the Orange God still claims to serve the Crown.

# OLIVER PRITCHETT
# Cutting Remarks

I HAVEN'T got the items, you see. That is the trouble. That is why I cannot write for *Punch*. You need the cuttings. So many of the articles are headed by a photograph of a tear-out of a four-line news item (usually from the *Daily Telegraph*) which then inspires a magnificent flight of fancy. Given an offhand reference to a report saying there are more cage birds per head of population in Wales than in any other part of Britain, your average *Punch* writer is away. Before elevenses he has keyed in an immaculate Dylan Thomas parody called "Under Millet Wood" and featuring Polly Garter and Who's a Pretty Boyo.

Where do they find these items? When I go down-page in the papers for an hour or two looking for something offbeat I come up with "Three Die in Gales", or "Date Set for Bolivian Elections" or "Rise in Interest Rates Expected". These do not trigger off mirth. Yet I know that somewhere on the inside pages there is a little gem and if I could find it the pastiche would be unleashed. I try the In Memoriam column one more time; I go through the names and addresses of the winners in the Prize Crossword.

Sometimes I lurk in Tudor Street at six o'clock in the morning watching the humorists arrive at the *Punch* office in their armoured buses with heavy grilles over the windows. They clamber off the buses with their metal lunch-boxes, laughing and joking and wondering what the day holds in store for them. Occasionally I make an effort to infiltrate the group and learn their secret. I crack my double-glazing joke or allude to my skiing accident, but they shun me. The great wrought-iron gates of the *Punch* building slam shut before I can arrange to have myself swept in with the crowd.

I can only imagine what happens inside. The humorists line up at the clocking-in machine before going off to change into their luminous orange boiler-suits. Then, as they enter the vast Word-Processing Hall, they pause beside a 40-gallon oil drum which is full of thousands of tiny slips cut from various newspapers. Each man closes his eyes, dips into the drum and takes one out.

"What have you got today, George?"

"*Dinosaurs May Not Be Extinct, Says Chinese Scientist.*"

"You're lucky, mate. I've copped *Rats Could Learn To Drive*. That's the fourth time this month."

The editor, who by tradition is allowed the first dip every day, is already three-quarters of the way through a powerful piece inspired by *Cockroaches Thought To Have A Strict Moral Code.*

Who is it that keeps the 40-gallon drum stocked with precious cuttings? I believe that in the basement of the office there is a large room occupied by people known as the Monitors. There are about fifty of them. Grave, grey, elderly men, and women who look like archdeacons' wives, read through the papers seeking out the raw material of humour. The place is as silent as a library. The Monitors have been trained to ignore reports of wars in the Middle East and of Mrs Thatcher's latest speech and to look only for the real stuff. From time to time the silence is disturbed by the faint rustle of newsprint and the snip of scissors as one of the grave gentlemen finds an item and cuts it out. *Buddhist Monks Form Jazz Band*, it says. An hour later the other Monitors look up irritably as one of the ladies moves from her desk and tiptoes to the supervisor who is seated on a raised platform at the end of the room. "A Mr Peach has become engaged to a Miss Victoria Plumb," she whispers. "Have we had that one before?"

My other theory is that these items, which I can never seem to find but which seem so plentiful in Tudor Street, have not actually appeared in *any* newspaper. It is all explained by one of those Old Spanish Customs of Fleet Street.

*"Twenty-four years and five children ago, I proposed to you – don't you think it's time you said yes?"*

*"I never realised they have red hearts just like us."*

For as long as anyone can remember one man has had the job of doing a tour of the printing departments of all the newspapers late every night and collecting the sweepings of unused fillers from the floor.

At about three o'clock in the morning he meets the editor of *Punch* in an all-night café down at dark alley off Fleet Street.

"What have you got for us tonight, Sid?"

"Over a thousand items, unsorted," Sid replies, indicating a bulky sack under the table. "A pony to you, squire."

"That last lot you sold us was a load of rubbish," the editor says. "Most of it was just miscellaneous misprints and a few Stock Exchange closing prices set in the wrong type."

"You'll find some real goodies in this lot, Mr Coren," Sid assures him. "In fact, one of the items actually inspired me to pen a few whimsical words on the back of my pay-slip. Perhaps you might like to consider it for publication."

The editor uses the contribution to wipe down the top of the café table and begins to rummage in the sack.

"There's a genuine *Fishermen Find Pop-up Toaster In Shark's Stomach* in there," Sid says. "I saw it with my own eyes. I said to myself, 'This one is sure to lead the boys into the wilder realms of speculation.' Those were my very words to myself."

The editor leans across the table, grips Sid's arm and says in a low, urgent voice: "What we are really looking for is a mint condition *Japanese Develop Talking Cigarette: Health Warning Spoken In Four Languages*. We would pay a good price for one of those."

"Don't worry about it, my old friend. I will put the word out."

Money changes hands and the editor makes his way back to the office carrying the sackful of items. One of these dark nights I may waylay him, hit him over the head, grab the sack and run off with it. In some derelict building I will go through it, pick out an item and dash off a witty piece. Then I will throw the sack and the remaining cuttings into the river.

Two days later one of the humorists will dip into the 40-gallon drum and take out a small cutting.

"Here's a good one, George. *Litter-lout Mugs Editor and Gets Sack.* That looks promising." ❧

*"They moved him to middle management."*

# CINEMA

**THE INNOCENT**   ANDREW HANLEY *as Tim*

**PRIZZI'S HONOUR**   JACK NICHOLSON *as Charley Partanna*   JOHN HUSTON
ANJELICA HUSTON *as Maerose Prizzi*   KATHLEEN TURNER *as Irene Walker*

# Michael ffolkes

**MAD MAX — BEYOND THE THUNDERDOME**   MEL GIBSON *as Mad Max*   TINA TURNER *as Aunty Entity*
ANGELO ROSSITO *as Master*   PAUL LARSSON *as Blaster*   ANGRY ANDERSON *as Ironbar*

**CLOCKWISE**   JOHN CLEESE *as Brian Stimpson*

# CHRISTOPHER MATTHEW

# MONOPOLY

VINE STREET £200

VINE STREET £200

MARLBOROUGH STREET £180

MARLBOROUGH STREET £180

COMMUNITY CHEST

BOW STREET £180

BOW STREET £180

MARYLEBONE STATION £200

MARYLEBONE STATION £200 BRITISH RAILWAYS

NORTHUMBER LAND AVENUE £160

NORTHUMBER LAND AVENUE £160

WHITEHALL £140

WHITEHALL £140

ELECTRIC COMPANY

£150

PALL MALL £140

PALL MALL £140

JUST VISITING

IN JAIL

PENTONVILLE ROAD £120

PENTONVILLE ROAD £120

EUSTON ROAD £100

EUSTON ROAD £100

CHANCE ?

**For years I have had a secret yearning to visit Atlantic City, New Jersey – not to shoot crap with high rollers from Detroit, crack witty with show-girls and rub shoulders with retired hit men – but simply to stroll along the Boardwalk and through Marvin Gardens, up Baltic Avenue and down St Charles Place and all those other streets whose names in 1930 brought back to Charles Darrow, an unemployed heating equipment salesman of Germanstown, Pennsylvania, happy memories of pre-Depression vacations with his wife and inspired him to invent the game of Monopoly.**

**I daresay it would all be a terrible disappointment, but possibly no more so than it would be to any American daft enough to try the same exercise in London.**

Given that the object of the game is the buying, renting and selling of houses and hotels, the final choice of London landmarks made by Waddingtons for the English version in 1935 is, on the face of it, pretty bizarre. Since when has anyone ever built a house in Bond Street or a hotel in Trafalgar Square? And what exactly is Mayfair?

Surely anyone launching the game today would plump for the likes of Eaton Terrace and Redington Road; Holland Villas Road and Ilchester Place; Redcliffe Road and Clapham Common West Side. Or would they?

To the upwardly-thrusting executive, a stunning period family house, decorated to the highest standard with taste and flair in Belgravia or Holland Park or Wandsworth, is understandably the *ne plus ultra* of successful urban living, but to the board-game-playing youth of Macclesfield or Moreton-in-the-Marsh could these addresses ever have the same magic as Pall Mall, Piccadilly, Leicester Square, The Strand, or even Fleet Street?

Monopoly, after all, is only a game. The names are just names and the prices just prices. There are a few figures that seem to bear some faint relation to the reality of fifty years ago: for example, given that the rent in the game is reckoned on an annual basis, £40 for a house in the Old Kent Road, including rates, would not have been too far off the mark in the Thirties; but on the whole, the sums of money involved are purely nominal.

The cost of building the Dorchester in 1930 would look like loose change compared with the £50 million (or is it £80 million? No one really knows) which the Sultan of Brunei paid Regent International for it last November, or indeed the £200,000 a room it could cost to build today; but £200 plus four houses in Park Lane would have seemed as dotty a figure then as it

does now. Monopoly money has always been Monopoly money and attempts to work out a neat formula for translating it into 1985 prices, though a moderately diverting pastime, are really quite pointless.

Even so, supposing one were to accept the game at face value, what would one find to buy or sell or rent or make a fortune with or be bankrupted by in the two dozen streets and squares and districts over which so many billions of silver top hats and shoes and irons have passed in the last half century?

Perennial rabbits, like me, tend to buy as much as they can, as quickly as they can and preferably at the highest possible price in the vague hope that their opponents will land on them and have to lash out crippling rents. Wiser

heads, however, have worked out which are the best properties to own, both in terms of percentage return on investment and the probability of people landing on them, and it may come as a surprise to many to learn that heading the list are the light blue and orange groups which contain, in reality, some of the least attractive sounding addresses in London.

Despite a spirited attempt by estate agents to create King's Cross Village in the side streets off the lower end, it would be hard to imagine a noisier, busier and more depressing place to live than **PENTONVILLE ROAD**. A string of office blocks and wholesalers between which commuters hurtle from King's Cross to the Angel, it does boast one nice clutch of big eighteenth-century terraced houses, which Holden Matthews reckon would go for around £90,000, undone – if ever they were to come on the market, that is. There's a reservoir close by, but since the **WATER WORKS** on its own is generally regarded by the experts as the feeblest investment on the board, its presence can hardly be considered a draw for even the most desperate punter.

(To own the **ELECTRIC COMPANY** as well is marginally more worth while, even though the CEGB are currently in the throes of hiving off one of their more distinguished properties, Battersea Power Station, for around £1.5 million to the Alton Towers people who earlier this year won a competition for the best development scheme with a London version of the Tivoli Gardens. So far, 90% of Wandsworth has given it the thumbs down, but even so, they're hoping for a favourable decision on their planning application early in the New Year.)

Although on the fringes of Bloomsbury, **EUSTON ROAD** has always been deeply unresidential and curiously unappealing. However, it does boast one outstanding building in the shape of Gilbert Scott's old Victorian Gothic hotel on the front of St Pancras Station. Worth anything upward of £5 million, it was put on the market by BR three years ago, looked at long and hard by Eagle Star, and then withdrawn. Since then, various other parties have expressed interest through Edward Erdman and proposals are being considered – possibly for a hotel.

The eponymous hostelry at **THE ANGEL, ISLINGTON**, has long since disappeared, but ever since Bruce Page and his *Sunday Times* Insight pals discovered the architectural delights and the cheap prices of Canonbury Square in the Sixties, the yuppies have been moving in and colonising the whole of Islington, including Highbury, Barnsbury and Canonbury, with undiminished zeal. The Angel, also known in the business as East Islington, comprises the area between Camden Passage and the City Road and is now reckoned to be one of the most desirable necks of this ever-improving wood. In fact, it's the only cheap square on the board that has really come up in 50 years. Roy Brooks have a 4-bed Georgian house in Duncan Terrace for £129,500 and Holden Matthews are offering a

big 5-floor 1820s house backing on to the Canal in Noel Road for £280,000.

Equally sought after in the game, though less so in real life, is the orange group. There has never been a stampede to live in **BOW STREET**, as far as I know; however, there have been a few recent developments and refurbishments in the Covent Garden area, notably in Bedford Street where agents E.A. Shaw have now sold all twelve flats in Bedford Court for between £45,000 and £100,000, and in Bassett Chambers in Bedfordbury where they have unloaded eight more in about the same range. There is a small hotel called the Broad Court round the back of the Bow Street nick, but otherwise Covent Garden is basically a world of offices, shops, restaurants and buskers.

**VINE STREET**, off Swallow Street, is so small as to be almost non-existent – except presumably to those unfortunates en route to the police station and tradesmen using the goods entrance to the Piccadilly Hotel. A Crown property, it was bought two years ago for £14.6 million by some Kuwaitis for whom Gleneagles, now taken over by Arthur Bell, who in turn are owned by Guinness, have done it up at a cost of £16 million and re-launched it as The New Piccadilly – "a paradise for those accustomed to five-star service". And which of us isn't, these days?

There isn't a police station actually in **MARLBOROUGH STREET** (it's 300 yards away on the corner of Lucan Street and Petyward Street), but there are a few houses at very silly prices crouching beneath the looming grey cliff face of the Sutton Dwellings council tenement blocks. Nos. 1-7 were built in the early Seventies. Described by one local agent as "damned ugly but practical", their 3 beds, 2 baths, 1/2 receps and integral garages sell for around a quarter of a million. Another half-

dozen or so are period and slightly larger. One was sold last January for £185,000; the owner spent £12,000 on it and re-sold it in June for a very silly £260,000.

Selling on the board at between £140 and £160, with percentage returns on investment in

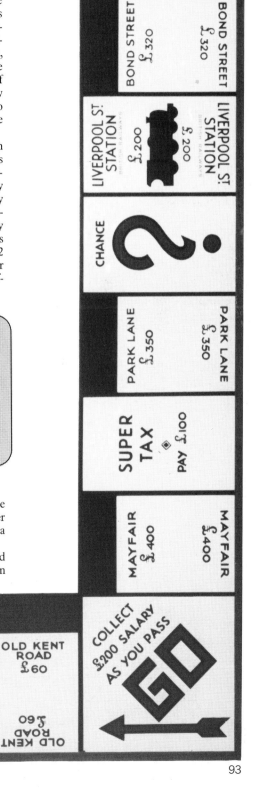

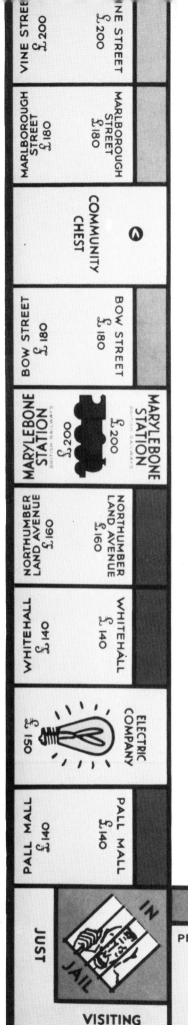

a hotel of up to 136.36, but in real life totally unavailable, are sites in the crimson group.

Being a schoolboy at heart rather than a prefect, I shall never know what it is like to grasp at political power, and the only way I could live in **WHITEHALL** would be by moving the family to the marble and mahogany splendour of Whitehall Court, where a 5-bed flat would cost us around half a million plus four grand a year in service charges. I did ask one top London agent how much he thought No. 10 Downing Street would fetch on the open market. He thought somewhere between eight and ten million. But presumably they'd have to do something about that poky little kitchen first.

---

### CHANCE
#### "DRUNK IN CHARGE" FINE £20

The Magistrates' Association's suggested penalty for driving with excess alcohol starts at £200 and carries automatic disqualification for a year. It is possible to be done for being whistled in charge of a horse, with cart or without, which is why a lot of country people contribute to a chauffeur-ridden "Get You Home from the Hunt" scheme.

---

**PALL MALL** is still essentially clubland. However, more and more clubs these days exist purely through the kindness of their landlords, and with several short-term leases about to expire and developers standing by to turn them into profitable offices and flats, as they did with the Junior Carlton, the suggestion that there will be only ten clubs left by the end of the century may not be as daft as it sounds.

The only people who ever seem to have inhabited the thoroughly gloomy **NORTH-UMBERLAND AVENUE** are those hard-faced desk-bound senior Intelligence wallahs one has met in countless SOE, M15 and 007 movies, sitting at a desk on the fifth floor with their backs to Trafalgar Square, ordering stars to their almost certain deaths – which, knowing the speed the traffic shifts round that particular corner, could well mean slap outside the front door.

Equally uninhabited and uninhabitable is most of the highly desirable red group. There have been a couple of mild flurries of excitement recently in **THE STRAND**, firstly when Intasun took the Charing Cross Hotel off BR's hands in a £37 million deal which included The Grosvenor in Victoria, and again when 13 flats in the East Wing of The Savoy – sold in 1980 to the Ladbroke Group – came on the market in July at between £280,000 and £950,000, and went.

Meanwhile, further east in **FLEET STREET** ("the stuffiest street in London", one agent called it), there has been a certain amount of small-scale activity – solicitors, accountants, insurance agents and other fringe City types moving in and out of small office suites mainly – but, apart from the apparently permanent scaffolding of the Higgs and Hill refurb. job for Scottish Mutual on the corner of Chancery Lane and the Mansell ironmongery next to Johnson's Court, little seems to disturb the reassuring roar of traffic and printing presses. The feeling amongst commercial agents is that it is only a matter of time before the newspaper industry moves out to dockland (or did I hear dreamland?); however, for anyone with his eye on an existing newspaper building, the going rate is around £18 a square foot. For what that's worth.

As for **TRAFALGAR SQUARE**, no one lives there except the pigeons and the protesters outside South Africa House.

Having all my life been prepared to kill in order to acquire that pair of dark blue beauties that sit so alluringly and expensively on either side of the "Super Tax: Pay £100" square, it has come as both a surprise and a relief to discover that they are not that bigger deal after all. They cost too much to develop and relatively few suckers land on them. Of course, when they do, it means fistfuls of grisbi all round, just like in real life.

**MAYFAIR** is a mass of contradictions. Despite the enormous amount of offices with which the area has long been riddled, and such massive undertakings as the Landsdowne House development in Berkeley Square, where Legal and General are busy knocking up 177,000 square feet of offices which are expected to bring in £5 million a year in rents and whose capital value won't fit on to most pocket calculators, the feeling is that the whole place –

---

### COMMUNITY CHEST
#### YOU INHERIT £100

Fifty years ago you could have treated yourself to a beautiful second-hand SS Jaguar, one careful chauffeur-driven owner plus enough petrol for a year's carefree motoring. These days, if you got change out of two top stalls for *Les Misérables*, two double Bell's in the interval and a couple of courses at the Interlude de Tabaillau afterwards, you'd reckon your luck had changed.

---

particularly the bit west of Bond Street – will gradually become more and more residential.

Many of the leases on houses requisitioned immediately after the war as offices are due to lapse in 1990 and the *on dit* is that Westminster City Council would like to see them lived in again. Not that there have ever been that many houses, even in **PARK LANE**, and those that do come up, can fetch fearsome prices.

John D. Wood, for example, are currently asking just the £3 million for No. 20 Hill Street. Mind you, it does have 5 receps, 15 beds, 13 baths, 24-carat gold-leafed plasterwork, Baccarat chandeliers, rosewood panelling, walk-in freezer, and for all I know, a reproduction of the Spanish Riding School in the basement.

On the other hand, there's no shortage of flats in Mayfair or Park Lane. Wood can sell you a

38-year lease on a 1-bed, 1-bath studio in Upper Brook Street for a mere £60,000, while a flat in Grosvenor Square could set you back a million or more. Not surprisingly, the rental business is brisk. You could let that studio for anything between £370 and £450 a week. Not bad value when a single room at The Dorchester costs £130 a night without breakfast.

In 1935 it would have been nearer £7 a week inclusive. Not that room prices seem to interest a lot of hotel owners these days as much as straight property dealing. Take The Londonderry in Old Park Lane. Built in 1969-70, it was sold in 1976 by the Barclay brothers to a Middle East consortium who traded for a while before closing it down for refurbishment. After two and a half years they had got nowhere. Earlier this year, the Barclays bought it back for £18 million. MacAlpines did it up for £6 million and now it's worth about £30 million.

Which brings me back to The New Piccadilly and the yellow group. Despite the distinguished presence at Hyde Park Corner of Wellington's old gaff, No. 1 London (once a semi: the east wall is false), **PICCADILLY** itself has never been the most flourishing residential street in central London. In fact, one big residential agent went so far as to suggest that if there were more than 50 flats in it, he'd eat something very indigestible indeed.

Obviously he wasn't counting Albany, sometime home of Edward Heath and many far more distinguished figures that no one has ever heard of. There are 69 sets of rooms altogether – 18 in the splendid eighteenth-century mansion facing Piccadilly and the rest off the early nineteenth-century Rope Walk behind. All are owned on freeholds and although one, nicely done up, did sell recently for £275,000, they almost never come on to the open market. Many are rented for anything upward of £500 a week for 2 receps, 1 small bed, 1 bath and a kit/dng rm. They're all on two floors, do not admit domestic pets or children under 13 and are, according to one long-standing resident, "not as grand as everyone supposes. In fact they're really rather primitive, with no central heating. A bit like living in an Oxford college."

Of the other two names in the yellow group – **COVENTRY STREET** and **LEICESTER SQUARE** – no agent I have spoken to has anything pertinent to say, except that when in 1935 Charles Forte paid £5,000 for a milk bar in Coventry Street, the entire estate agency world fell off its chair in stunned disbelief.

The brown group never topped anyone's residential list in 1935 and it still doesn't today – either on the board or in real life. Apart from Surrey Square and Glengall Terrace where in April Roy Brooks sold a classic Regency house with 3/4 beds, a double drawing-room, lots of stripped pine and a 70-foot garden for £66,000,

the **OLD KENT ROAD** is dominated by council blocks and traffic. The idea of banging up a hotel with views of the old Bricklayers Arms railway depot or the south-eastern gas works has yet to cross anyone's mind; ditto within a stone's throw of the London Hospital which constitutes the major feature of **WHITECHAPEL ROAD**.

Still, for those pioneering souls who are excited by the prospect of living in one of the last areas of true cockney London, surrounded by a permanent street market, jellied eel stalls and the faint odour of curry, there are one or two nice terraces of early nineteenth-century houses at very tasty prices. A year or two ago, Roy Brooks sold a Grade II listed Georgian house in Jubilee Street, a little further east, with 2 big receps, 3 beds, a splendid bathroom, 2 basement rooms and an 80-foot garden for around £73,000. Today he'd be asking between £90,000 and £100,000.

The second most expensive group on the Monopoly board, and yet curiously one of the least desirable, is that haven of greenery comprising **REGENT STREET, OXFORD STREET** and **BOND STREET**.

Apart from the odd flat and a few not very exciting hotels, like the ex-Max Joseph Stratford Court above Dolcis in Oxford Street and the 700-bed Mount Royal, sold two years ago to Mount Charlotte Investments in a £21 million package with another hotel behind Euston Station, there is almost nothing that bears any relation to the game, or ever did. The vast majority of property deals are concerned with shops, which are forever changing hands, are extraordinarily complicated to value and whose prices are geared almost entirely to the level of sterling and thus to the tourist industry.

Oddly enough, for all its zazzy foreign-based fashion companies, best Bond Street, like best Regent Street, rents for around £90 a square foot, whereas Oxford Street, with its bigger turnover, compares, at £160 a square foot, with the Brompton Road between Sloane Street and Harrods. So much for Bond Street being the most expensive site in the green group.

I have always been a keen railway station collector, which in the light of the massive Rosehaugh Stanhope development of the old Broad Street Station site and its funding of a refurbished **LIVERPOOL STREET STATION** may prove that I have more of a nose for business than I thought. The fact that BR's plans to close **MARYLEBONE STATION** and offer it as a valuable development site have become bogged down in procedural wranglings is just one of those unfortunate things that can happen to any would-be property developer.

On **KING'S CROSS** and **FENCHURCH STREET** I have nothing to report and neither, apparently, does anyone else. ✌

95

# On the Carpet

**A**FTER the dinner and the speeches and the obligatory debriefing in the Managing Director's suite ("I thought it went very well, liked your story about Prince Andrew, and call upon your customary generosity of spirit to forgive Whitmore throwing up over you in the bar"), I returned to my room in the Istanbul Sheraton Hotel on Sunday night to find that the floorman (women in Turkey are little in evidence in non-manual jobs) had placed by my bed a small, neat, white cardboard box, overprinted with the message: "*Gute Nacht*/ Good night." It contained a piece of yellow Turkish-delight.

It is difficult to imagine a less suitable confection on which to go to bed than the glob of icing-sugar-coated, lemon-extract-flavoured, hard rubber chew. I ate it. That is, I put it in my mouth, masticated, wondered why, spat it out and flushed it down the loo. It came back, lurking at the bottom of the bowl (good Turkish-delight floats) and I flushed again and it reappeared again, so I took it out and wrapped it in a piece of tissue, went on to my balcony and lobbed it towards the Bosporus; it sped like a bullet. Cannot argue with its genuine Turkishness; less sure about the delight part.

In Tunisia, where we went for the New Year, they had these plates of marzipan dates and marzipan walnuts and chocolate-coated marzipan and plain marzipan, which were taken to all the rooms nightly, at tipping time. It worked well; I tipped and my daughter, Em, ate. And there is a British hotel group, I forget exactly which group but it is not the one that provides a trouser-press, that leaves high-class filled chocs

on the pillow. Officially, this sort of "gift" (I use the inverted commas because if you pay £80 a night, gift without commas is naive) is for identification. They – the Saatchis of this world – reckon that when you return to Istanbul where each large international hotel is pretty much like each other large international hotel, you will recall the Turkish-delight and say, "Miss Wainscote, book me into the hotel that had the filled '*Gute Nacht*/Good night' box. I want to see

> **"I flushed again and it reappeared again, so I took it out and wrapped it in a piece of tissue, went on to my balcony and lobbed it towards the Bosporus."**

if the yellow blob won't flush all the way round the bend this time."

There is another British chain of hotels (another that does not provide trouser-presses) that dispenses chocolate-covered biscuits; up-market KitKats, wrapped in silver paper, the only unpowdered commodity on the tray by the kettle near the notice stating, "These things are provided for your convenience." They also give you a cloth for shining shoes, "for your convenience", when it is abundantly clear that the whole thing is being done for *their* convenience. For one's own convenience one used to leave shoes outside the door of the room and get them back nicely polished by the night porter. Now, all you leave out is a breakfast order-form, which pas-

sing drunks alter so that you are brought twelve buttered kipper fillets at 6.15 a.m. when you wanted a croissant at 8.30.

Everyone "gives" something, though no one, it seems, has thought about the offering with much care.

Why food? I mean, the hotels have spent the lifelong day trying to flog soup, fish, meat and sweet; sandwiches and snacks in the 24-hour a day, American-style coffee shop; room service – please see separate menu – and there is a mini-bar which invariably contains blocks of chocolate and salted nuts. If the chain of hotels that gives you a trouser-press also provided a Thermos flask of Ovaltine, I am pretty sure I would remember the name and Miss Waistband would be requested to book me in nowhere else. (If Ovaltine seems *vieux jeu*, the mini-bar quite often contains miniatures of liqueur and Tia Maria cheers up Ovaltine no end.)

But why not a book? One other than the Gideon Bible; I tried Deuteronomy the other evening in Harrogate – though I expect it is no different from Deuteronomy in Tunbridge Wells – and found it to be poor bedside reading. I expect Winston Churchill's bill has something to say about it. Hotels could do a deal with Jeffrey Archer and send mini-bar profits soaring. I understand that deals with J. Archer are currently not hard to obtain, though when he and I worked in the same place he had a reputation for being ornery.

Unfortunately, there is something not quite nice about cooking in a hotel room; you can shave in it, plug in an electric typewriter, a bedside vibrator, or a travelling smoothing-iron – but a hot plate is out. You have to bring your own, and an adaptor as well and a pan. Then you are in business.

Seldom do I stay in a foreign town where I do not see sausages that I would buy had I the means of sizzling them in local wine; and vegetables like aubergines and okra which need no more than a simmer in a pan lined with cream and chilli peppers. Beans and lentils could be soaked overnight and cooked and served with garlic and olive oil and Tabasco for elevenses. A non-stick pan heats up stale bread, warms Heinz tomato soup which benefits from a glug of mini-bar sherry, and if you are caught with it in your hand-baggage on the airport scanner, I am sure you can explain.

To return to Istanbul, which I don't think I would voluntarily, there is not much of what Americans call "action". It is hard to walk a dozen paces without being offered postcards, transparencies, Turkish carpets or a shoeshine. From the churches the mid-oriental wail that calls the faithful to prayer is recorded and goes out on the repeat button. Inside it is like Allied Carpets only they don't have sales, and you have to take your shoes off to go in, and bargain with a man trying to introduce a shoe-horn between you and your footwear when you leave.

What did we have for dinner in Istanbul, did I hear you ask?

Oxtail soup and beef Wellington. It is an international hotel.

*"Rare, medium, well done, great or small?"*

# ROAD TEST

## ERROL WELLINGTON tests the DATSUN LOGANBERRY 1.3 GL

Hum, wid de comin' of October, de crisp mornin' mist, leafs droppin' off of de trees, de wippy conditions under de back wheels, plus de nostalgic smell o' de burnin' videomarts driftin' over de autumn lanscape, which of us ain't feelin' de ole urge to leap into a spankin' new motor an' turn over de engine?

Also turn over de spankin' new motor, while we about it! Dis amazin' Datsun Loganberry not only holdin' four people comfortably, four people also holdin' dis amazin' Datsun Loganberry comfortably, git two on de offside door-sills plus one at each offside corner, and de Datsun Loganberry wizzin' over a treat. I an' I staggered by de astonishin' Jap technology – soon as de car landin' on he back, he wing-mirrors flyin' off, he boot-lid hurtlin' through he back windah, he wheels rollin' down de road, he horn startin' up, he lights gwine on an' off, man walk by, man reckon' he lookin' at Christmas up Selfridges, only thing lackin' is de famous Uncle Honky wid de lucky dip on he head an' de busted laigs stickin' out!

Lotta people enquirin' of I an' I concernin' de ignition problems o' de Loganberry, an' it certainly true dat de Datsun sufferin' f'om severe shortcomins in de past, it like tryin' to set light to a wet horse, but de Nips seems to be gittin' de trouble licked wid de new model, it ain't took I an' I but one milk bottle to git de test car going, we turnin' in de remarkable figure o' nought to 250 centigrade in 7.3 seconds!

Also bags o' room in de glove compartment for a 3-poun' chicken plus six potatoes, everythin' gittin' done to a turn by de time me co-driver Winston back wid de new colour tee vee an' de drop-flap dinin' suite.

Wot about road-holdin', I hear you enquirin'? *Fantastic*, is de only word! Me an Winston draggin' de Datsun across de worl'-famous Railton Road, an' *nothin'* gittin' past, de ole SPG Transit bouncin' off like he a dam' short-pitched number f'om de outstandin' Joel Garner, lotta brothers comin' up an' yellin': *"Wow, it Pearl Harbour all over again, man, it de incredible Jap secret weapon, how you like dem apples, honky, etc."*

My perfessional view is, everyone gonna want a Datsun Loganberry 1.3, but you gotta move dam' quick. Stocks look like dey runnin' out fast!

# MARIAGE À LA MARTIN

"What's the drill here? Do I spend eternity with my first wife or my second wife, my third wife or all three or what?"

"I've changed my mind. We'll stay home and pick at the turkey."

"It's all so exciting! Harry and I want to get married. His accountant is doing a cost analysis with ten-year projections."

"There, as you may have guessed, are Lunceford's booby prizes."

"Could I have her call you in the morning? She's just settled her brains for a long winter's nap."

# BOOKS

## JOHN CALDER

# Samuel Beckett—80 n.o.

Samuel Beckett, the only Nobel Prize winner in Wisden, is 80 on Sunday. John Calder, Beckett's London publisher and long-time friend, introduces new readers to the cosmic humorist's work.

SAMUEL BECKETT'S most auto-biographical play *Krapp's Last Tape*, written in 1960, depicts a writer on his 69th birthday, death looking over his shoulder, knowing he will never reach beyond the biblical 70. I had dinner with him shortly before that awesome date in his own life and he was surprised to be still around, depicting his future as more reclusive and with work as his company.

Samuel Beckett is 80 next week. Born in Foxrock, near Dublin, on Good Friday, April 13, 1906 (a date many consider significant), he came from a comfortable middle-class Pro-testant family, was sent to school in Ulster, and went on to Trinity College in Dublin, where he excelled not only academically but at sport as well. He is the only major writer listed in *Wisden*, the bible of cricket. Under an exchange agreement between the Sorbonne and Trinity, he taught for the year 1929-1930 in Paris, returned to Trinity for a year to lecture, then travelled, with some time in London and Germany, before settling in Paris. He was active in the Resistance until, with the Gestapo on his heels, he cycled to the Vaucluse in the South of France, where, in company with a Jewish painter, Henri Hayden, he hid until the war ended. The Vaucluse is the setting for *Waiting for Godot*, the play that brought him international fame in 1953 and it is no secret today that Estragon, the earthier of the two tramps in that play, is based on the character of Hayden, and Vladimir, the philosophical tramp, on Beckett himself.

After many years in France, Beck-ett was fluent in French and began to write in that language to escape the rich rhetoric so often found in Irish writing. After *Godot*, his novels and other plays were quickly recognised as the masterpieces they are and he has never stopped producing ever since. The Nobel Prize in 1969 crowned his achievement to that date, and described him as the writer who has done most in our time to recog-nise the plight of the downtrodden, the unsuccessful and the persecuted. While this statement is true, it is a rather simplistic view of what Beckett is really about.

His work falls into three periods. The early work owes much to his Irish predecessors, especially Joyce and reflects his studies of Dante, medieval philosophy, Descartes, and Goethe. *Murphy* (1938), his first novel, is on one level a very funny novel about a work-shy Irish writer in Lon-don, supported by a prostitute, whose

preoccupation with the body-mind relationship, a problem dear to many generations of philosophers, is the main subject of the book. But the war traumatised his view of humanity: he observed the brutalities and cruelties of the wartime occupation of France, and those occasional moments of kindness and affection which become more real at times of crisis. He also believed, at the end of the war, that a lump growing in his cheek left him with only a short time to live, so that what he had to say had to be written quickly; as a result, he shut himself up in the country for two years to write *Godot*, three important novels, and much else, the fruits of reflection and observation from his years of hiding.

These works, and others that fol-lowed during the sixties, make up the work of his middle period, upon which his reputation principally depends. He was once considered abstract and "difficult" because of his original, slightly archaic use of lan-guage and inclination to pick drop-outs for his heroes, men without ambition or interest in the comforts of middle-class existence, and women whose aims seldom went further than finding a man to care for. His novels are far removed from the situational, socially oriented literature of his contemporaries.

The very simplicity of Beckett's situations have put off some readers and literary enemies have accused

him of charlatanism, because Beckett cuts through all the social conven-tions and shows people as they really are, or would be if their pretensions were dropped. Those who are self-indulgent, self-pitying, bullying, uncaring about others, ponderous, and vain, are shown without self-disguise or shame (Pozzo in *Godot*, Hamm in *Endgame*, Moran in *Mol-loy*). Others who are totally unable to cope with life, who only want to lie prone all day and think and, if possi-ble, be looked after, are portrayed without any façade. How Beckett's characters got the way they are is unimportant: he describes them as he finds them and if audiences some-times feel uncomfortable, at a right-eous church-going pedant's casual admission that he masturbates in front of his cheval glass for instance, or the cruel enjoyment of another's misfortune, found without shame in many of his characters, it is because they are looking at their real as against their pretended selves.

The Beckett middle period is earthy, rich, abounding in humour, with many a time bomb to shake our complacency as we realise the full implication of the words. The novels of this period are mostly monologues, a voice telling its own story, the incapacitated remembering times of greater mobility, the matter-of-fact relation of everyday misfortune.

At best life is interesting for those with the ability to get interested. Life

is habit to most of us, going through the same rituals of work and leisure, shutting out thought. There are signi-ficant moments, of love, sexual suc-cess or failure, short-lived achieve-ment or disappointment; but it all comes to the same in the end; Beckett repeatedly shows how masters and servants, the successful and the unsuccessful, are simply different sides of the same coin and frequently interchangeable.

Beckett's first post-war novel, the last written in English, was *Watt*, com-pleted in 1945. Like *Murphy* it is a philosophical investigation of a prob-lem, in this case the nature of reality and illusion, seen through the adven-tures of Watt, who enters the employ-ment of a mysterious Mr Knott as a servant and is constantly confronted with the need to doubt what he observes or hears. This was followed by four novellas written in French, later translated by the author into English: *First Love, The Expelled, The Calmative*, and *The End*, all of them concerned with similar anti-heroes, thrown out of their lodgings and trying to survive in a hard world that has no place for non-conformists. After this he wrote the great series of novels that we know as the "trilogy," *Molloy, Malone Dies*, and *The Unnameable*, and concurrently *Wait-ing for Godot* and *The Texts for Nothing*, the latter a series of short savage outbursts of protest.

The trilogy is not one continuous work, although the protagonist of each, telling his own story, is aware of the earlier protagonists and their stories, as if each were the author of the earlier work. In each case the nar-rator is waiting to die. Molloy tells his story from his mother's bed, his mother presumably being dead, and although we hear of his wanderings and experiences up to the time when, within sight of a town after many days and months crawling through a forest, he collapses waiting for help to come, we do not know how he got there. Molloy's narrative is followed by Moran's in the same novel.

Moran is a private detective, as conformist as Molloy is not, and Beckett contrasts two dissimilar char-acters, one in search of the other, whose experiences become a com-mon one, reiterating a favourite Beck-ett theme, that decline is the common lot of saint and sinner and that he who understands what is happening to him is probably better off than he who does not. If life is a long waiting – the theme of *Godot* – we have to invent ways to fill the time; and the cosmic loneliness of man without belief can be alleviated a little by human warmth and companionship, by boredom and misery shared.

But the central theme of *Waiting for Godot* is not anguish in the face of death. There is no real fear of death in Beckett, providing death is release and oblivion. The central theme is the sense of waste and our fear of anonymity, of being born, suffering through our small span of years, dying and being forgotten, so that in a short time the record of our passing through the world is extinguished. All that effort for nothing! Beckett is keenly aware that each of us is the centre of his own universe, each an *I* aware of a *me*. Belief in an afterlife is confidence in the continuity of identity, but for the thinking, agnostic mentality of today, the anguish lies in an awareness that life – for some at least – can be pleasant, but that the shortness of the good years makes nonsense of the whole life experience: the real struggle of man to avoid being forgotten is to leave something behind him by which he can be remembered.

There are two opposing views of Beckett's influence on our religious thinking. Some see him as contributing to the decline in religious faith, although he never declares himself: indeed his characters often speculate metaphysically. But many detect in his aestheticism and anti-materialism a strong religious sense, and certainly he is widely read by many with an interest in religious philosophy.

It is often in his poetry that Beckett, most economical of writers, uses the greatest economy in expressing this thoughts. The shortness of life, the anguish of love, or the agony of man trapped between a reluctant birth and an unknown end are all expressed in lines such as these:

and live the space of a door
that opens and shuts

…a last even of last times of saying
if you do not love me I shall not be
loved
if I do not love you I shall not love …

… Down in the grave, lingeringly, the gravedigger puts on the forceps

The impact of Beckett's language, the most nakedly romantic of any writer since Elizabethan times, once the reader has tuned his ear to the grandeur of its music and the visual images in which it abounds, is tremendous. Beckett is addictive: unforgettable lines, the sharp wit of his humorous asides, his extraordinary insights into human nature and clear-sighted honesty, above all the shape of his language, put him above any other writer living. One does not go to him for cheer, but one does for comfort. We all have our sorrows and deprivations, but Beckett makes us realise how hollow are the things we are persuaded or expected to want, and what matters are the riches we put into our heads rather than our pockets; it is good to have less. *Endgame*, the play that follows *Godot*, depicts the last moments of a man's life. One by one Hamm, the curmudgeonly protagonist (the *hammer* of the three *nails* in the play *Nagg*, *Nell* and *Clob*) discards his props and possessions until he is ready to face the inevitable. I have always found it comforting as well as moving, because it says something positive about human dignity and courage, and the real priorities of existence.

Beckett's reputation would hardly be less had he written nothing during the last twenty years, but his third period moves away from the poetic savagery of *Molloy* and the dialogue on human destiny that is characteristic of *Godot*. A new reflective calm comes into the later work, mostly disembodied, highly concentrated texts – it makes little difference whether he calls them plays or fictions – where he observes the beauties and the tragedies of the world anew, reframes the questions he has put before, and finds fresh forms for old preoccupations.

In *Catastrophe*, he makes a clear unambiguous statement about totalitarianism. Written to depict the plight of Vaclav Havel, the Czech dissident, he creates a human sculpture on stage, a depiction of human suffering at its most impotent, the reduction of man by the power of the State; this is committed theatre at its finest, but, as with all Beckett's work, it has many other things to say as well. In his more recent work, Beckett has made much use of phantoms, ghosts that the mind creates to outlive mortal life and remember us after we are gone, a new twist on our fear of anonymity and being forgotten.

*Ohio Impromptu*, and the earlier *Footfalls*, both featuring ghosts conjured up to remember the living, and his penultimate prose text, the haunting and beautiful novella *Ill Seen Ill Said*, bring a metaphysic of the private mind (more accurately of the will), into existence. Man creates what he wants to believe in, even beyond his own life span. He has succeeded at last in dividing mind and body, or of making the body so subservient to the mind that the former does not matter any more. The short texts that he has written since the middle sixties depict the life of the mind inside the skull, minds that remember, minds that reflect, understand their condition, that the author can appear to project into outer space or in which he can create a whole new universe, minds of victim or torturer, and capable of creating ghost stories as haunting as any in our literature. ❧

*"I guess he must have lost some of the boyish charm somewhere between his fifth and sixth wife!"*

# WHO DARES LOSES

**The Man Who Drew Tomorrow
How Frank Hampson Created Dan Dare**
Alastair Crompton
*Who Dares Publishing* £9.95

I FIRST MET the Reverend Marcus Morris through an old college friend, John Metcalf, who was engaged at the time in becoming a legend of the advertising business. Metcalf had obtained an important account, that of the Hulton Press, for his company. Specifically they were commissioned to spend £30,000 (a lot of money in 1950), on newspaper advertising to create a favourable atmosphere in which Britain's first Christian comic, *Eagle*, could be launched.

It was infinitely entertaining to observe this curious alliance of brilliant and ambitious men struggling with the problem of projecting Dan Dare (in association with St. Paul), into the boys' schools of Britain. In the heady atmosphere of a Fleet Street just beginning to feel its oats after a long dreary post-war, all things were possible. Would-be press barons easily imagined themselves to be potential newsprint titans. The example of Lord Beaverbrook, optimistic and piratical, was still actively present. And into this fetid world of flesh-eaters enters an innocent Daniel from an obscure parish, unusually well-dressed for a poor vicar, the aforementioned Rev. M. Morris.

In 1948 the *Liverpool Post* summed up the career of Morris to date. "A Birkdale vicar has been responsible for forming a new church society whose aim is to capture the popular

reading public who seldom see religious periodicals. Styled The Society for Christian Publicity, the new organisation will endeavour to tap a hitherto unexplored field by producing magazines and other periodicals with appeal to all levels of public opinion among non-church-goers. Morris consolidated his campaign in a Sunday newspaper under the headline *Comics that bring Horror to the Nursery*. "Horror has crept into the British nursery," thundered the Savonarola of the smelly, grubby *Dandy* and *Beano*-dominated school-rooms. "Morals of little girls in plaits and boys with marbles bulging in their pockets are being corrupted by a torrent of indecent coloured magazines that are flooding the bookstores and newsagents." He gave examples of the gross indecencies comically perpetrated. "A character murders a group of six policemen with a machine gun, chortling, 'Dis is fun.' And 'Two little boys thump each other's noses and brandish pistols through seven drawings, to end with 'Now yer know who's the toughest guy around here.'"

Morris dizzily claimed that such material led children to commit crimes of violence; had actually resulted in a boy losing both legs; had actually produced murder. And then he perorated himself into the orbit which *Eagle* would eventually take over, the high-flight atmosphere of the Christian comic: "I shall not feel I have done my duty as a parson and a father of children until I have seen on the market a genuinely popular children's comic where adventure is once more the clean and exciting business I remember in my own schooldays, not abysmally long ago (*Marcus was 33 at the time*). Surely, there is adventure enough for any boy or girl in the lives of men like Grenville of Labrador? And some of the daily dangers St. Paul met would make even Dick Barton look like a sissy. There is a healthy humour that does not involve a bang on the head with a blunt instrument. Children are born hero-worshippers, not born ghouls. They will admire what they are given to admire. It is up to us – whether or not we go to Church every Sunday – to see they get a glimpse of what really brave men have done in this world, and share laughter that comes from the heart, not from the gutter."

Enter the hero of Alastair Crompton's (slightly fourth form) biography, *The Man Who Drew Tomorrow*. Frank Hampson, a commercial artist whose love of comics was life-long, came from a totally un-Bohemian, uncosmopolitan, unartistic, thoroughly Anglo-Saxon background, son and scion of honest railwaymen and police officers. He was, therefore, decent, patriotic, unsophisticated, demanding, obsessive, and dutiful. Hampson had studied the great American masters of the comic strip and could out-draw any of them, even if his imagination was somewhat more stilted than theirs. He admired *Prince Valiant* (for morality and naturalism), *Rip Kirby* the detective (for tireless pursuit of the truth), and *Terry and the Pirates*, whose author Milton Caniff had brought the techniques of cinema to the comic-strip. He had fought an honourable war, rising from the ranks to the lower reaches of the officer-class, greatly pleasing to his father who retired from the police with the rank of detective-inspector. At the war's end, married and penniless, Hampson had little time or patience for the absurdities of art college: he had to make a living. It was not long before he met in Southport (the setting for this Christian comic revolution), John Marcus Harston Morris, Exhibitioner of Brasenose College, Oxford. The Reverend soon found that he had a staunch ally in the battle against the pornographic, sadistic, and necrophilous American comics which threatened the sanity of British schoolboys. Hampson's influences might not have been quite as Christian as Morris's, but they were in the

*"I want the same trip as last year – I've got new glasses."*

*"Tell me, am I a puppet or a pot-holder?"*

# TOM SHARPE

▶ WOLF MANKOWITZ

Tom Sharpe, Britain's most popular comic novelist, thinks maybe he has discovered an amazing truth behind the works of The Master, P. G. Wodehouse. Or, maybe he hasn't. At least he's discovered the Colonel (*right*). Now read on.

central Anglo-Saxon tradition of decency, honour, and patriotic self-sacrifice. He loved the techniques of the Americans, but along with that great oracle of the post-war years, J. B. Priestley, the rasping voice of Britain, detested Yankee "scenes of mutilation, gouging, eye-pricking, face-treading, flogging and preparations for rape. The heroines' skirts were usually riding up their thighs and all had pumpkin breasts." Priestley, of course, well-knew a pumpkin breast when he saw one. Now with rumbling rhetoric he added his powerhouse to Morris's persistent little droning lawnmower. "This new violence, with its sadistic overtones, is not simply coarse, brutal from a want of refinement and nerves, but genuinely corrupt, fundamentally unhealthy and evil. It does not suggest the fairground, the cattle market, the boxing booth, the horseplay of exuberant young males. It smells of concentration camps and the basements of secret police. There are screaming nerves in it. Its father is not an animal maleness but some sort of diseased manhood, perverted and rotten." And Jack certainly knew about animal maleness.

So, apparently, did Morris and Hampson, because Britain's boy animal males swallowed Dan Dare whole; the *Eagle* rapidly ascended to nearly a million. Frank ascended to a giddy £4,000 a year, more than any of his decent progenitors had ever earned. But then, as Mephistopheles and Morris both knew, in Fleet Street, as in the world, nothing is for nothing. All this happy success had to be paid for, and the price was the copyrights of Dan Dare and the *Eagle* which,

without much thought from either of their devisors, had been transferred to the generous publisher. Hampson didn't care, it seemed, so long as he had his perfect studio and could fulfil his dream, which was to be acknowledged eventually by his peers, as being one of the world's great comic-strip artists; and Morris always had a great career in view.

So there we were then. For the next ten years, to the tune of *Onward Christian Soldiers*, reputations and fortunes were made until, as the Sixties locked away the preceding tearaway halcyon decade, Teddy Hulton sold out and was once more as rich as his follies and Lady Hulton required him to be; Marcus Morris was Lord of the Magazines, having graduated from children's comics to the infinitely more comic editorial mast-head of the women's press; Metcalf, his brilliance as a promoter confirmed, was the advertising industry's newest Prince of Lightness; and Frank Hampson, the principal begetter and creator of the brilliant futuristic realism which had lifted the Hultons and everybody else into the heady stratosphere of hefty profits, Hampson, the boy scout of outer space, was unemployed, broke, and more than a little disordered by overwork, his own obsessionalism, and the shocking discovery that reality is not a beautifully coloured and extraordinarily well-drawn comic-strip in which Good conquers Evil and men are essentially decent.

An astounding adventure story of Fleet Street in the fantastic Fifties – as incredible as any of Dan Dare's though, sadly, not quite as decently Christian. 🍃

ONE OF THE GREATEST pleasures I know is to meet an astonishing person. Such an experience came my way last year when I met Colonel Norman Murphy, the author of *In Search of Blandings*, at Hunstanton Hall in Norfolk. We had arranged to "rendez-vous" there (my phrase, almost certainly, because in my Marine days Colonels always rendez-voused) to look for the Octagon which plays such an important part in "Jeeves and The Impending Doom", he was to find it and I was to photograph it. Of course at the time I didn't really believe him; I knew Wodehouse had lived at the Hall on and off during the late Twenties and early Thirties but I'd always toed the accepted line that P.G.W. was the creator of an idyllic world, not its meticulous recorder.

Colonel Murphy KNEW the Octagon was at Hunstanton and obviously regarded me as a heretic.

"We'll find it over there," he said with daunting authority as I tried to lead him in the direction of the moat, "over there" being in the opposite direction. I have an idea he even told me how far it was from the house.

Sure enough, behind a gate, across a bridge over a muddy pond and surrounded by shoulder high stinging nettles, was the Octagon just as Plum, through Bertram Wooster, had described it. It wasn't what I had

expected. In my mind's eye it should have been on an island in the middle of a large ornamental lake instead of on a small island in a pond but there was no doubting its existence.

I came away from it with sneaking suspicion (why do suspicions always "sneak"? They should be more forthright) that I was in the presence of some ghastly guru who walked – loped would be better – at 25 miles an hour, never stopped talking and who KNEW with a fearful infallibility everything there was to be known about dear Plum and was about to destroy his idyllic world in a welter of disappointing facts. It was almost as though I had agreed to meet some galloping serpent in the Garden of Eden and was being given a very exact lecture on the constituents of apples and what Eve was wearing.

For another hour we shot into courtyards, and out of them, invaded what looked like private gardens while the Colonel questiond anyone foolish enough to ask what we were doing. In the end, on the far side of the moat, we came across some broken down outhouses. Among them was an abandoned chicken run which backed onto a brick shed with a square iron door about two feet high.

In an attempt to introduce some levity into the proceedings, I remarked that we were now standing in the presence of The Empress Of

*"Right, now it's our turn. Have you got Mr Bun, the Baker?"*

# The Wodehouse Man

Hitherto the figure of Roderick Spode, leader of the Black Shorts (yes, shorts, not shirts) and based on Sir Oswald Mosley, was thought to be the only character in Wodehouse to have come from real life. *The Code of the Woosters* cover by Ionicus.

Blandings' famous pigstye. It was a flippant remark – at least I thought so at the time; no prizewinning pig could possibly have squeezed through that small iron doorway. But the Colonel seized on it with all the enthusiasm of a fanatic. I can't remember what he said but I do remember wandering away with Mrs Murphy and muttering something disparaging about weaners. Behind us the Colonel was scrambling in and out of more stinging nettles and, having proved the obvious, that only the infant Empress could have lived in the stye, had turned his attention to some crumbling brick walls. I won't go on. You will find how astonishing

Colonel Murphy and his methods are in *In Search of Blandings* to be published by Martin Secker & Warburg later this year.

Instead let me turn to the man Murphy himself. He is of course an eccentric, one of that special breed whom all men of good sense treat, as the Muslims do village idiots, with the highest regard and as such to be protected. Colonel Murphy needs no protection. Armed with a seemingly infallible memory, the capacity to walk most people off their feet and to provide information with an unstoppability that makes the Ancient Mariner look like an amateur, he is one of Britain's great obsessives. For

40 years he has made a study of London and acquired a mass of information that is, I suspect, more encyclopaedic than that of anyone else in the world. Streets are his speciality. From his office in the Ministry of Defence he strode forth during his lunch hours and made the remarkable discovery that every source of information he needed was within a mile. I should add here that a Murphy mile is two and a half times longer than that of any normal biped. In nine minutes he could cover the one and half miles to the British Museum Library; in less he could hit Somerset House and the same time took him to St Catherine's House where wills are kept. Only Kelly's Directories defeated him, being out at Hampton Wick. He went there at weekends.

So year after year and lunchtime after lunchtime the strange, thin figure of this obsessive ex-schoolmaster-cum-lawyer-cum-IBM-employee-now-soldier stalked the streets of London seeking what interesting facts it could devour until one day, one weird and wonderful day in 1972, it entered a bookshop and picked *A Pink 'Un and A Pelican* by A. Binstead off the shelves and a new and astonishing P.G.W. expert was turned loose on the world.

Presumably the idyllic world of Blandings and Brinkley Court had entered our desk Colonel's imagination as a schoolboy, but now it seized him.

The streets of London he knew so well were peopled with the ghosts of Galahad, Lord Uffenham, Uncle Fred, Bertie Wooster, Jeeves, Aunt Dahlia and a host of others. Fiction had turned to fact. At least in Colonel Murphy's mind.

From that sublime revelation his forced marches to Somerset House and the British Library took on a new meaning. Where before he had con-

centrated his attention on the hidden life of old London, he now delved into birth certificates and wills and Kelly's Street Directories. There he unearthed facts about Wodehouse aunts and uncles and numerous relatives and at the same time applied his infallible memory to characters and places in Plum's novels and linked real people and real places to their fictitious counterparts.

He visited every house Wodehouse had lived in, and during his weekends and holidays followed clues to Kent, Sussex, Shropshire and anywhere else in the country that might have provided The Master with inspiration.

I have no idea how many quiet householders have suddenly learnt they were living in part of the idyll and this by a man in a bowler hat and carrying an umbrella. So for nine years this astonishing man unearthed the material, the prima materia, from which P.G.W. distilled his magical stories. When he had finished and the book was written he sent it to five publishers and wrote to a further ten. In each case it was rejected. The Colonel was not to be defeated.

Rightly determined to prove their judgment wrong, he had the book printed and published himself and sold it so successfully that it has become a collector's item and the publishing world has woken up to the fact that it once rejected the most important work on Sir Pelham Grenville Wodehouse since Richard Usborne's *Wodehouse At Work To The End*. Certainly the two biographies add little to our knowledge. *In Search Of Blandings* tells us much more and, while scholars may dispute his findings, I am convinced.

But then I was there when this astonishing man saw the first glimmer of light that led him to reveal the splendid origins of the Empress of Blandings.

*"Mind you, we don't claim to work miracles."*

# MUSE HEADLINES

## BUD GRACE

"It's that half-wit cartoonist."

"He says it's his muse,
but *I* think it's Edith Husselmeyer
with a fake nose and a fright wig."

"Well, one of us better sober up."

Her brassiere strained under the weight of her heavy breasts...

"Strictly speaking, it's not my muse. It's my ex-wife's dead mother."

# DOC BRIEF

Well, this week I thought I'd go back to my origins.
And I don't mean looking back a couple of generations to show that my father
was the Kunta Kinte of the Mile End Road. I'm talking about the real business of *genetics* — that
mysterious process which decides what you are going to grow up into (though without
telling you how or paying for it). Here's a little unravelling of the most
fundamental riddle of life itself.

## UNDERSTANDING DNA

DNA is a huge, complex molecule containing protein, sugars and amino acids, and most scientists say it is the most fascinating mixture of these materials in the whole world, though personally I prefer Marmite.

Anyway, what's really important about DNA is that it can reproduce itself which, on the whole, Marmite can't. Now you might be saying to yourself: what is so clever about being able to reproduce yourself? Even rabbits can do that, as can lizards, slime-moulds, Conservatives etc. Well, of course, the answer is that all living things are able to reproduce themselves *because* they have DNA in every cell of their bodies (and *if* their wives agree).

In other words, the possession of DNA is precisely what distinguishes living matter (e.g. animals, plants, viruses, hell's angels etc) from all non-living matter (e.g. rocks, ink, Marmite, snot, receptionists etc). The initials DNA actually stand for "DeoxyriboNucleic Acids", though I must say I have never been able to understand how all living organisms can manage with so much acid inside them when you think what happens when you leave a car battery on the living-room carpet.

Now, as I'm sure you all know, the structure of DNA is a double helix. For those few of you who don't really quite understand what that means,

the best way to think of it is to imagine a helix and then just double it. OK? Now, as you probably know, there was tremendous competition in the world of biochemistry to discover this structure. It was in Britain that Crick, Watson and Wilkins worked out the correct answer first, while Linus Pauling had imagined DNA as a triple helix, Horn and Hardart thought of it as a sinusoidal parallelogram, Grune and Stratton thought it was the same but yellow, whereas Oppenheimer and Fermi didn't care what it looked like so long as they could blow up a desert island with it.

Once the true structure of the molecule was unravelled, the mystery of how something could reproduce itself was instantly solved. Because it was now obvious that the double helix reproduced itself by first unzipping and thus becoming *two single helices*, each of which simply reproduced itself and Bob's your uncle. Or rather Bob and Bob are your two uncles.

Anyway, this knowledge burst upon a waiting world with stunning results. For now that everybody could understand the secret of reproduction, there remained only one further question for the biochemists to answer, namely: once you have successfully reproduced, how can you afford to pay for your kids' education? More research is needed into this complex issue.

## CHROMOSOMES

Chromosomes are the genetic equivalent of a washing-line. Sort of. What I mean is that inside each nucleus of every cell is all the information about that particular individual. Everything is there — hair colour, eye colour, recommended lipstick, blood group, height, fingerprints, bowel habits, hat size, IQ and phone number of your solicitor.

So how do chromosomes manage to hold this vast amount of information? Well, one answer is that they don't waste time watching television. Another answer is that they are like washing-lines in that all the genetic material (to which I have already alluded, above) is strung up on, along. But there is even more to it than that, i.e. sex.

You see there are 23 pairs of ordinary chromosomes, which were named by their imaginative discoverers with names like Chromosome 1, Chromosome 2, Chromosome 3 (do stop me when you've got the hang of it) etc. And then there are the sex chromosomes. These are called X and Y because they didn't want anyone to know their real names.

If you have two Xs then you are a woman, whereas if you have an X and a Y you are a man. If you have a single X then you either have Turner's Syndrome or else you are an adult movie and might turn into a PG after surgery. If you

# ROBERT BUCKMAN

have two Xs and a Y then you are a Swedish arsonist wanted in five countries and unless you leave the money in the usual place your chromosomes will send all the information they have on you to *Private Eye*.

Now that you understand the role of the sex chromosomes, you might be wondering how sex is actually decided. Well, usually it depends on how things go during dinner, but the true facts of the matter are that the sex of the child is decided by the father. You see, all the sperm cells — oh, sorry, that's a very sexist thing to say — I mean all the sperm-person cells carry either an X or a Y, whereas all the egg-person cells carry an X only in a non-discriminatory, positively-affirmative way.

Thus, when an X-sperm-person cell meets and X-egg-person cell (within the context of a caring, sensitive, mutually respectful Fallopian tube, of course) then the resultant embryo will be XX and will produce all the hormones necessary to develop breasts, ovaries, dolls' houses, headaches, dressing in women's clothing, desire to rule Britain etc.

On the other hand, a male father's Y cell will produce an XY embryo which will develop testicles, a beard, haemorrhoids, an overdraft, dressing in women's clothing (oh, come on, let's not have value judgments), desire to have your own chat show etc. An easy way to remember this rule is that the Y chromosome is a major cause of the Y-front. Or not, if you prefer.

## GENES

As was stated above, genes are the packets of genetic information strung out along the chromosomes, which thus give rise to the oldest joke in the entire history of cytogenetics, viz:

*Q:* How do you tell the sex of a chromosome?
*A:* Pull down its genes.

(It's a sort of play on words, really — "genes" could be mistaken for "jeans", the item of clothing which, when pulled down, would reveal — oh, for heaven's sake, I haven't got all day you know.)

Anyway, what I have stated above should explain to you that you get half of all your genetic determinants from your father, half from your mother and half from the DHSS, if you get your application in early enough. This explains why

children seem to be a mixture of their parents. For instance, if your father is very tall and your mother very short, you will be in between. Similarly, if your father is very athletic and your mother very sedentary, you will be in between (and doing all the shopping). By the same token, if your father is very stupid and your mother very rich, you will be a bit of both i.e. a merchant banker, whereas if your father is very stupid and your mother even more stupid, you will be an estate agent.

One theory of genetics proposed by a man called Lamarck (congenitally French) suggested that if you developed certain features like muscular strength during life, these could be passed on to your children by what he called "the inheritance of acquired characteristics". Naturally, this was complete nonsense (be-

cause if it were true all Jewish boys would be born circumcised) and was regarded as totally ridiculous until the present Government adopted it as the model for their tax laws, which might seem less painful than circumcision, but aren't.

### THE DOCTOR ANSWERS YOUR QUESTIONS

**Q:** As an employee of an American company, I have had to have so many face-lifts that my facial skin has become very tight, so that now every time I bend forward I smile. What should I do?
**A:** Get a job as a waiter in a Japanese restaurant.

SPLICE
of
LIFE

"I pronounce you man and wife. You may now let your bodies go to pot."

"Maybe you're trying _too_ hard to understand me, Margaret."

"There must be more to wondering whether there is more to life than just wondering whether there is more to life."

"Hey! It's a great new wife-swapping idea from Reader's Digest."

"Did we have some children that grew up and went away?"

# BASIL BOOTHROYD
## What, Already?

There's less and less delay
Between the shortest and the longest day,
Or so it increasingly seems
After seeing lots of both extremes.

And I'll have seen plenty
By March Twenty,
The date
When winter is deemed to abate
And it's suddenly spring.

Ding-a-ding.

The last ashes riddled,
The calendar more or less middled,
The attention focuses
On crocuses
But with no hurry as yet
To keep rushing in the garden umbrella
                    out of the wet.

Though summer,
That unreliable incomer,
Also comes in pretty quick.

I used to have a trick:
When I first spotted how fast
Life was going past
I could make it last
By thinking what eons separated the snow
From the primroses starting to show.
It kidded me that time was slow.

Now it doesn't work for some reason.
Every couple of weeks there's the next season,
And it may surprise you to hear
That this year
Only ten days after we've discarded
                    our thicker socks
In celebration of the vernal equinox
The powers that be
Are hustling us into BST.
What?
It's the truth, believe it or not.
At this rate, whether or not you believe,
By about Wednesday it could be New Year's Eve.

The acceleration
Doesn't worry the younger generation:
At ten or eleven
It's a thousand years to 1987.
While the older lady and gent
Will soon be asking where 1986 went,
Having failed to catch spring
On the wing
When it came round again in five minutes flat.

Not that I mind that –
I mean the speed of it.
I feel the need of it.
I wouldn't want to miss one,
Particularly this one,
Being in serious arrears
In recent years
With all the things
I meant to get ready and shipshape for
                    previous springs,
If only they hadn't materialised
Quicker than I'd realised.

All that gear
I planned to sort out in good time last year,
Oh, dear,
But kept getting
The peasticks enmeshed in the fruit netting
As I looked for the secateurs
Supposed to be his 'n' hers
But more hers than his, quite frankly,
As he tends to stare at them blankly
While she's the one to wonder
Why nobody's pruned the floribunda.

We're short of space
In this place.
We lack, as she's often said,
A decent shed.

It's tough
Having nowhere to keep all the stuff.
As things are
You can't get at it without moving the car.
Even then, for people passing the garage,
It sounds like the Alamein barrage.
I can hardly stand it myself
As the paint cans come bombing off the shelf,
Rolling and spilling,
Though in the ordinary way unwilling
To budge a lid,
Which I remember trying last time, but never did.

Don't worry, I'm not Saint anything.
I wasn't going to paint anything,
Except, as before,
Parts of the garage floor.
It's just that I go into this spin,
The speed spring keeps coming in.
You can plan to beat it to it,
But you'll never do it,
And the more speed the less haste, they say.

I think I've got that round the wrong way,
Like those tubes of shining tin
I can never fit in
Where they belong
Amid the floral plastic and droopy perished
        elastic of what the catalogue called our
                    luxury patio *chaise-longue.*

There's a special way of holding it
For unfolding it
But if I ever knew how
I've forgotten again now
So it just lurches about
Letting colonies of colossal spiders run out.

And all that after
Humping it down from a rafter.
The heck with it.
You could break your neck with it.

Admittedly it's not required
Till spring has expired,
But people sent up in the garage roof
On behoof
Of locating wintering geraniums
(Where craniums
Suffer from lack of headroom,
And anyway the pots finally turn up under the
                    bed in the back bedroom)
Automatically cast an eye
Over various nuisances not wanted before July,
And in fact I was soft
Up in that loft
Not to extend my explorations
To the whereabouts of the Christmas decorations.

Because that's another season already on its way.

There's less and less delay
Between the longest and the shortest day,
Or so it increasingly seems
After a long and on the whole unvarying
                    experience of both extremes.

Spring's nice.
I could do with it twice.
It's just that when you're never ready, and
                    not all that efficient,
Once, on the whole, is sufficient.

# DAVID TAYLOR TALKS

SPIKE MILLIGAN HURTS. A graffito. *Graffito, ergo sum.* To be sprayed in letters six feet high, This Side Up, the other side down. Possibly it's a neon sign, or illuminated, knee-on prayer stool. It could be a book. Spike writes something beginning with B, nearly 3 million paperbacks sold to date. Is that why I've come to see him? If only he were a scholar, if only he could spell. If only his tomatoes weren't green.

We're all a bit strange. His son is a bricklayer, did I know that? Maintains Spike's house and says he's a happy man. But how *can* they govern China? What, when we can't any longer all fit on to an area the size of the Isle of Wight?

*Hitlergram Nummer Zwei!*

HITLER: If only I had known.

GOEBBELS: If only you had known vat?

HITLER: *That's* vat I don't know.

Publish and be drubbed. Bring tea! Fetch cake! It's life that's probably to blame. He was born in India, once, now it's standing room only. Terence Alan Milligan, son of late Capt. L.A. Milligan, MSM, RA retd. Perhaps it was the heat.

The graffito might do on a tombstone one day, tombstone as big as The Ritz. SPIKE MILLIGAN HURT, or HURTED. Certainly his head hurts and, by the look of him now, there may be bodily hurts besides. They recently improved his eyesight, making it worse than it was and harder to paint. For him to paint. Not for them to paint his eyesight. Who'd want to paint that? Van Gogh's eye. Choice of blue or brown, please state when ordering, tick box if colour-blind.

It hurts when he laughs. It hurts when he cries. Spike, as ever, might well do either and very likely both, apparently on whim. Read *Guardian Whim*, every Tuesday.

Still, back meanwhile in reality, cut, zoom, SFX, I found it, then: the way to Hadley Common. And the stars. When he moved here, to a turreted suburban château in much sought-after area, near school and Barnet, own flush toilet, a neighbour didn't know him from Adam, and he didn't know Adam either. Till one fine day, with a *rat-a-tat-tat*, the neighbour is standing at the door.

"Mr Milligan," says he, "I've just seen you. On the television."

That seemed to be that. Right he was, said Spike.

Moments later, the scene changes to the neighbour's door, with a *rat-a-tat-tat*, Spike standing without.

"Mr Neighbour," says he, "I've just seen you. In the garden."

Quiet, please, let's have some hush. When you're ready, Spike, go on a green. Drum-roll. And the next object is – a Qantas hello-person. A Qantas hello-person.

Spike calls up.

G'day, Qantas, would he hold a moment, please? ... *Tum-ti-tum-ti-tum, tum-ti-tum-ti-tum* ...

Sorry to keep him waiting ... *tum-ti-tum-ti-tum, tum-ti-tum-ti-tum* ...

AAARGH! The dreaded, accursed piped music strikes again!

Eventually, Spike's connected. Could they help him?

Just a moment, says Spike, would they hold on just a moment? *Yesterday, all our troubles seemed so far away* ...

Hello? Hello? This is Qantas, could they help him please?

Sorry to keep them waiting, answers Spike, one moment please ... *now it seems as though they're here to stay* ...

Click-brrrr.

Christ almighty, the stuff is everywhere: de-humanising wallpaper music, supposedly to soothe, but in his case making Spike seethe.

As so much does: like cruelty, rapacity, environmental rape. Like smoking, Mrs Thatcher or neglecting cats. Like hype and insincerity, war, the Japanese, and fluoride in the water. Getting asked about The Goons. Getting asked if he's off his chump.

All can be in a day's work for manic, stinging letter-writing Spike. You have to protest, and laugh, and maybe cry. The abject helplessness hurts just the same. The dinosaurs have perished. More tea! Extra cakes! Australia here he comes. Hello, mum! Ninety-two and an Aussie at last. The BBC want him out there next month, for a documentary, and he'd stay if it weren't for his kids. To be followed by a pantomime. It's best when there's no control.

Spike's First Law Of Physics says: If anything can happen, it will. He'd like to have met Churchill, Van Gogh and Jesus Christ. But this constantly nagging ultra-sensitivity hurts, whatever the Snap-Out-Of-It, Have-An-Aspirin brigade may say. There's just bugger-all you can do about it. Quasimodo was stuck with his bump.

Spike used to think psychiatrists would make it all better, take these pills, he'd become Eric James. Sid James. People always want to talk about that – his depressions, mental anguish, underlying gloom. No one ever writes up his bronchitis, though, to which he's been a martyr time and again. *The cough beneath the clown – by Spike as told to Our Pulmonary Staff.* Who listens to clowns? Journalists very often can't. He'll put a paper bag on his head and shout Go Away! Eff off! Alas, they seldom do. More tea!

The other thing they always ask is when will Spike retire? To which the answer is of course bedtime, same as usual. He was 67 in April, but just made it in to the new tax year, which he's started so he'll fin...

PROCLAMATION All persons should be made to wear a ... with their overdraft written on the front ..., initialled by the Queen. It'd help decide whose round it is.

Heavens! Look at the time. Bong! Bitter-sweet comic Spike Milligan was interviewed for Punch today. Bong! Twenty minutes into an earnest chat, no one had mentioned The Goons. In Part Two, Spike learns to walk and is packed off to school at the Convent of Jesus and Mary, Poona; Brothers de La Salle, Rangoon, and SE London Polytechnic, Lewisham. Bong! Later on, war breaks out.

And nostalgia grips. It doesn't take much. The well-stuffed diaries are to hand, fat albums of his life in photographs banked. The past is secure and peculiarly vivid, perhaps because of that. Craziness is permanent. Like jet-lag that's lasted sixty years. Shut your eyes and transfer, say, to the Italian front – forty years on you can still remember what the weather was like (not bad for the time of year). Look Milligan, says Major Startling Grope. The Sergeant says you aren't very good at your job. He's a liar, sir. I'm bloody useless at my job. I could lose us the war.

How did he ever get into this mess? To think he used to be a semi-skilled fitter, Woolwich Arsenal. The semi-skill was in taking two lengths of wire, straightening them out, linking them together and passing them on to the next bloke. They then disappeared for good. Spike at his best did fifty bits an hour. Call that a day's work? they'd ask. No, he'd reply, he thought he'd call it Rosalind.

Gags like that sustained The Goons (AT LAST! *New Readers and The Prince of Wales start here*). The Goons made him famous and wretched. The Goons could have lost him his sanity, his marriage, little things like that. It didn't make him *quite* so famous as some, at the time, when he did mind a bit. Now Sir Harry is retired and Peter is dead, Bentine is around here somewhere, try the teapot perhaps. And the weather's still not bad for the time of year. He's seen too many good things come to an agonising end. Especially life with his second wife Paddy, who died of cancer aged 43. Next person to wonder why Spike can't be funny all the time, please step this way.

Bong! Dateline Rome, 23 February 1945. Gunner Milligan, Offspring of an Irish King, D Battery, 56th Heavy Regiment, has hung up his trumpet. A grateful nation gives thanks ...

*It started with pains in my chest. I knew I had piles, but they had never reached this far up before. The Medical Officer made me strip.*

*"How long has it been like that?" he said.*

*"That's as long as it's ever been," I replied.*

*He ran his stethoscope over my magnificent nine-stone body. "Yes," he concluded, "you've definitely got pains in your chest. I can hear them quite clearly."*

*"What do you think it is, sir?"*

*"It could be anything."*

*Anything? A broken leg? Zeppelin Fever? Cow Pox? La Grippe? Lurgi?*

*"You play that wretched darkie music on your*

# SPIKE MILLIGAN

"It hurts when he laughs. It hurts when he cries. Spike will very likely do both…Who listens to clowns? Journalists very often can't. He'll put a paper bag on his head and shout Go Away! Eff off!"

*bugle, don't you?"*

*"Yes, sir."*

*"You must give it up."*

*"Why?"*

*"I hate it." He goes on to say, "It's straining your heart."*

*Bloody idiot. It's 1985, I'm a hundred and nine, and I'm still playing the trumpet. He's dead.*

Much the same must be said about the peaches he's now spotted laid to rest round the bottom of that tree, in the garden (perfect spot for a tree) round the house which is huge and now managed by the new Mrs Milligan, formerly Shelagh Sinclair of The British Broadcasting Corporation, which God preserve, if for no other reason besides Radio 3, last outpost of civilised culture. Spike's chaotic London office has been managed more or less since time began by Yorkshire's redoubtable Norma Farnes. Give us the facts, Mr Punch.

The reason, or part of the reason, for Spike's vast house, by the way, is that he did well from the sale of his erstwhile more modest suburban semi, out of which he was bought because all the local drains met under it and they wanted to install a new system. End of Aside One. More tea, Sookey! If people are to follow this in detail, they must have tea. Quick-brew, though, drink up. *Thames At Six* are coming at five. There isn't a moment to lose! Hark! Horses approach! Tea for the crew – that's 57 with, 122 without sugar and no cakes without consultation. Cut!

That'll have to do. No time, perhaps as well, to tell you his favourite racialist jokes or The 101 Best and Only Limericks of Spike Milligan. No time to save the whales. No time to turn bleak about pain and death and pointlessness or even to have a go in his new little snow-white Rover, here Rover, made from a million million Japanese bits. More bits!

Time to go home, time to go home, Spike now is tired, it's time to go home. But wait! Bong! Darling, I am home! Bong! Any chance of a cup of tea? Spike Milligan, Fused Again, Hadley Common. Shuffles papers. Pockets biro. Dims lights. Get up and walks into wall. Cut.

JEREMY, MEET ALICE. ALICE, JEREMY — I'M SURE YOU TWO HAVE LOTS IN COMMON...

...8,971,628,421,013, 8,971,628,421,014, 8,971,628,421,015, 8,971,628,421,016, 8,971,628.....

IT GIVES ME GREAT PLEASURE TO BURY THIS TIME CAPSULE CONTAINING THE FALSE TEETH OF ERNEST J. PEABODY, IN THE HOPE THAT FUTURE GENERATIONS.....

WELL, OLD FRIEND — I'VE EATEN THE LAST OF THE PALM TREE, SO I GUESS THIS IS IT...

# Channel Crossings

British television viewers are becoming increasingly fond of "zapping", the habit of switching channels by remote controls.

Broadcasting research figures show that a family with a remote control set may change channel for as little as three seconds, more than 20 times a day. *The Times*

| | |
|---|---|
| **Smiling Child-oriented Woman:** | Through the. . . *round* window. |
| **Brough Scott at Epsom:** | *(To nervous-looking man)* A question I really have to ask you is about the horse's nerves. Will you be sticking cotton-wool in his ears? *(Picture of foetus)* |
| **Voice-over:** | This is the foetus at three months. |
| **Strangely Reverential Whispering Voice:** | That's his fifteenth on-side single this competition. *(Desultory applause from almost deserted cricket stand)* |
| **Smiling Child-oriented Woman:** | And you can find out what happened to-morr- |
| **Cockney Voice:** | Amazin. |
| **Another voice:** | Naow. Amazda. |
| **Strangely Reverential Whispering Voice:** | That's the seventy-third time he's left the ball alone this innings, John. *(Shot of cricketers standing about aimlessly)* |
| **Voice-over:** | From now on the growth of the foetus will be swift. *(Shot of cat)* This cat is having kittens. This one is coming out of the vagina. It's born in a sort of bag. |
| **Richard Whitmore:** | and welcome to newstravelandweather with this week's edition of disaster special. We have reports from Bhopal and news of further deaths. Bradford: could it have been avoided? Brussels: Britain's shame. Chatila: will it happen |

again? Beirut: the last building left standing. Famines: all the world famines, plus more on the way, say met-men. A special disaster extra: coach crash round-up. Good evening. But first here is some good news –

| | |
|---|---|
| **Judith Chalmers:** | wonderful white spray effect. But here's Nigel. |
| **Smiling Nigel Dempster:** | Hello, Judith. Lovely to – |
| **Reverential Voice:** | An extra bit of bounce there from Frank Tremblet. But here's – |
| **Voice of John Hurt:** | *(Picture of fast car)* I'm convinced that doing this advertisement is a significant contribution to my bank bal- |
| **Voice-over:** | This woman is pregnant. She is going to give birth. *(Shots of woman giving bir –)* |
| **Voice of Frank Finlay:** | An outstanding expression of power and performance. |
| **Cockney Voice:** | Amazin. |
| **Another Voice:** | Naow. Amaz- |
| **Richard Whitmore:** | Underwater robots will man the whole venture. |
| **Brough Scott:** | The amount of wins this horse has had could be counted on the fingers of a one-toed sloth. But here's the Queen. |
| **Alan Coren:** | Clement has QWERTYUZ. Come on, Clement. Get your cursor out. |
| **Edna O'Brien:** | Oi loik the qwertyui tings in loif. Sun |

loit shoinin on a shtream, the dappled gleams of de sun's rays in the golden hair of young men. Men loik Harold Evans bedad. Tings like de Gaudanir, eggs, sunloit light wine. De good tings in loif, bedad and bejaysus, without a word of a lie.

**Robert Robinson:** *(Hitting a bell)* Our next word is. . . there it is. QWERTYUIOP. Come on, Frank, pull out the big one.

**Sarcastic Teenager:** You mix it, Sharon Watts, I'll kill yer.

**Another Sarcastic Teenager:** You couldn't hit a one-toed sloth with one arm tied behind its back and blindfolded. *(Cut to middle-aged woman talking to man in pub)*

**Woman:** I doan wanna share yer luv.

**Man:** You make me sound like the bleedin' Co-op.

**Judith Chalmers:** Her simple grace and beauty always delight the –

**David Attenborough:** The butterflies are attracted by a festering pile of rotten prawns which is added to the pool of urine.

**Voice-over:** There's another visit to Albert Square at 7 o'clock on Thursday. But now it's time for –

**Una Stubbs:** *(Excitedly, to miming actor)* "Sexual Behaviour of the Human Female"? *(Miming actor shakes and then nods head)* "Sexual Behaviour of the Human Female"?

**Male Voice:** "Fear and Loathing in Las Veg-

**David Attenborough:** Unappetising fare for humans maybe, but –

**A Policeman:** I'll come straight to the point.

**Hectic Voice-over:** *(To shots of cardboard packets of frozen prawns)* Mm! Menumaster prawns –

**Voice-over:** *(To pictures by Degas of prostitutes)* Degas then moved into his next phase. Brothels and their inmates became his life-long obsession. He painted literally hundreds of them. Many were burnt by his brother but many still survive. These, for example. . . and these. . . and these. . . and these. . . and these. . . Degas was fascinated by the configurations of the inside leg and its unique chiaroscuro. Indeed, it was from Degas's work on the human buttock that the post-impressionists learnt much about contour ratios. "The great achievement of Degas," said one post-impressionist, "was that he turned the other chee-

**A Policeman:** You'll have to do better than that, missus.

**Voice-over:** *(On a blank screen)* That's straight after this.

**Leo McKern:** I'm absolutely convinced that the slogan "the action bank" is much, much better than the "deaf bank" *(Winks roguishly at camera)*

**Cockney Voice:** Amazin.

**Another Voice:** Naow. Am –

**Woman:** *(To policeman)* You haven't brought me all this way just to talk about EEC prawn quotas, have you, inspector? And what about Roche? And the German I saw leaving Trebnitz's flat at two o'clock this morning? Where does he fit into all this ? I can have one phone call.

**Midwife:** Push! Push! Pu –

**Big Ben:** Bong!

**Pamela Armstrong:** *(Beaming and raising her eye-brows. She talks as to a retarded and difficult child)* Three *passengers* have been *killed* and others have been taken to *hospital* after a coach crash outside *Lowestoft*.

**A Woman with a Bloody Face:** It were terrible. It came out of nowhere. It were awful. I can't describe it. I just can't put it into words.

**Pamela Armstrong:** *(Beaming)* And we'll be bringing you more pictures of the dead and dying after the break.

**Policeman:** I think you'll find you won't be disturbed in here, madam.

**Drooling Voice:** Mm, Diet Pepsi.

**Midwife:** *(Holding up newly born baby to mother)* It's a boy!

**Australian Cricketer:** Which one of you bastards called this bastard a bastard?

**Norman Fowler:** I think that's a fundamentally important point.

**Robin Day:** *(Pointing)* Manwiththebeard.

**Voice-over:** But first the baby is washed.

**Robin Day:** *(Pointing)* Womanintheluridhat. Spit it out. Come on. Oh, all right. You sir. Yes, you sir. In the front row.

**Voice-over:** *(To football game)* Wilkins now looking for Boon. . . Wright's in there too, and it's –

**Pamela Armstrong:** *(Smiling and nodding)* Further *deaths* have been reported from *Bhopal* and the city in India where –

**Policeman:** I wasn't born yesterday, you know, madam.

**Midwife:** *(Making a note)* Just before midnight.

**Kenneth Clarke:** Let me say there never was a 3% ceiling, as you call it. Look. People who go on strike in our society can expect a lump of concrete on the head. Nurses are responsible people. I'll say it again. This is not outflanking. Nor is it.

**Robin Day:** Our next question comes from Mrs. . . Mrs er. . . Mrs er. . .

**Cockney Voice:** Amazin.

**Another Voice:** –

**Australian Cricketer:** If they go in first they're called rabbits. If they go in last they're called ferrets because the ferrets go in after the rabbits.

**John Hurt:** With a grip that gets stuck in.

**Francis Bacon:** I just happen to be a painter, that's all.

**Melvyn Bragg:** But why is that, Francis? Why? Go on, tell me.

**Francis Bacon:** I'm interested in fundamentally important questions. Like Degas. Have a drink. Cheers. Actually, I'm just an ordinary bloke, staggering from one bar to the next. Life? Don't talk to me ab –

**A Vicar:** The meaning of life, you know, is –

**Cockney Voice:** Amaz-

**Screen:** eeeeeeeeeeeeeeeeeeeeeeee...........

# W. Scully

"I think we'll soft-pedal 'designed by an architect for his own occupation'."

"Don't let a fully stocked deep-freeze kid you. They're just as insecure as we are."

"I must admit, Cynthia, I'm not fit to breathe the same air – polluted as it is."

"You're looking pretty glum. Have I taken you from the box or something?"

"Good grief! Are we only on the foundation?"

# The Washington Post

TUESDAY, NOVEMBER 12, 1985     40 cents

# Sodov Stays, But Khokup Compelled To Drop Dreck For Dingbat Deal As Farfel Flees And Firkett Finks In Fag Fiasco!

*Washington, Tuesday*

**In a dramatic eleventh hour development here in Washington DC last night, KGB top banana Mikhail Sodov ran from the VIP departure lounge at Dulles minutes before callover for his Aeroflot flight to Moscow, and sought political asylum in the airport men's room.**

**"These days, I always keep two, maybe three, cubicles vacant just in case any red wishes to ditch," washroom attendant James Earl Carter Jr, 61, told your reporter today, "also a .357 in a secret compartment in my washbucket, due to I do not want to be caught out if some commie shithead wishes to negotiate from strength, call it strategic defence initiative, men's room policy here at Dulles is shaft the bastard before he shafts you."**

### GUM Girl Scam

Sodov's re-redefection is a major coup for the US on the eve of the Summit, especially as he had earlier fingered his entire espionage staff to the FBI after tunnelling out of the Russian Embassy, subsequently changing his mind on the grounds that the Palm Springs ranch that went with the deal had inadequate stabling, climbing out of FBI HQ and, in a heavy on-knees session, informing his Kremlin paymasters that he feared he would miss the wind blowing off the steppes and the girls behind the GUM lunch-counter.

### Loose And Topless Move

But in a snap press conference on the White House lawn this a.m. Sodov confessed that he had been thinking about it, and the girls were not so hot after all, especially in view of the fact that the FBI had decided to throw in not only six loose-boxes but also two topless stable-girls.

Not that this has not proved slightly embarrassing for the US Administration, who, prior to Sodov's re-redefection had negotiated a fast face-saver with Antonin Khokup, KGB number 7 in Washington who had been persuaded, in return for 20% of *Superman IV,* to plant Dieter Dreck, turned-round East Germany treble-agent, in the Budapest office of the RMVD, so that the Hungarians could subsequently exchange him for Lemuel Dingbat, CIA number 3 currently held by the Polish FKVD, to whom he was forced to reveal details of Beulah Farfel's network of Ukrainian moles, which resulted in Farfel's exposure as a plant following her fake defection to the Russians.

### Mole Nix In Gay Gab

So far, so simple, but all five sides involved reckoned without the curve ball pitched Monday p.m. by British transexual Sir Eric "Brenda" Firkett, 49, lynch-pin of MI5's Carpathian operation, who, furious at being disinformed vis-a-vis what he termed the Dyke-Dreck-Dingbat fit-up, immediately sought asylum in the Cedok office in Brno, offering to blow the whistle on his entire Transylvanian network in return for a £3 Intasun fortnight for two on the sun-drenched Black Sea riviera plus immunity from Czech prosecution for running an illicit KY jelly operation throughout the Warsaw *(cont. on p. 7).*

117

# ON THE HOUSE

## "My concern was aroused when I learned that he has the initials MRDH woven in wrought-iron on the gates of the Palladian mansion."

IT must be something to do with the ephemeral nature of their trade, but as a breed, Tory politicians are very keen on collecting things. Some of them pursue quite commonplace collections; others seek the more bizarre. A few make do with women, or scandals, or scalps; but many set out on a positive search for acquisitions.

Thus we have Julian Critchley, who rejoices in the twin virtues of wit and relative sanity, collecting some sort of china – a refreshingly straightforward occupation which need not detain our resident psychiatrist. Tristan Garel-Jones, a Government Whip, is collecting all the books written by MPs during his own tenancy at Watford – which at least saves him the trouble of writing one. Norman St John-Stevas collects all sorts of wild and wonderful things and is particularly attached to artefacts relating to Pope Pius IX. And Michael Heseltine? He collects cartoons of Michael Heseltine.

Or he used to do so. All his political life he has taken the time and trouble to get hold of all the cartoons of himself that he can find. The problem now, though, is that all the newspapers are so stuffed with caricatures of Tarzan swinging from the trees and Goldilocks with the mace tucked under his arm, that he has been quite unable to keep up. He is even wondering whether he wants them all – a dreadful fate indeed for any self-respecting egotist.

I do not mean to be unjust or unkind. But my concern was aroused when I learned that he has the initials MRDH woven in wrought-iron on the gates of the Palladian mansion. "Terribly nouveau, that," said one very aristocratic Tory whose opinion I sought.

My source was a man of impeccable lineage and a graduate of the Alec Douglas-Home School of Social Behaviour. "Alec once explained to me the secret of studied inelegance," he went on. "You have to get a good suit, but make sure that it doesn't quite fit. Michael would never understand that.

"It all comes back to that simple rule," he said, " 'If you matter, you don't mind and if you mind, you don't matter.' "

Yet there is worse evidence still. It comes from the very doorstep of the aforementioned mansion. During the journalistic stake-out for the daily photo-call during the Westlands War, the Heseltines were besieged with hacks at home. Most of these were the hard men and women of the Street of Adventure who do not expect to be invited inside.

But the same is not always true of our brothers and sisters from the world of television – particularly not when they arrive by arrangement to record an interview. So there was particular ill-feeling in the case of one Granada crew, who were all kept outside in the filthy wet and cold until our hero was ready to receive them.

When they were eventually allowed inside, their dignity was further offended. They were all requested to take their shoes off – for the sake of the carpets.

**A man who does** know how to behave perfectly on all occasions is Francis Pym. This is beautifully illustrated by one incident when he was out shooting ptarmigan, or some such. He was accompanied by the detective assigned to him for security reasons, a man less well schooled in field sports. Francis took a shot at a bird, brought it down, but failed to kill it. He turned to the dick and asked him to do the necessary. Imagine his horror when the policeman pulled out his official-issue pistol and blasted the bird to bits.

**A potential tragedy** in which MPs could have blasted each other to kingdom come was once only narrowly averted through sheer luck. It came about when a Bill was introduced to outlaw replica weapons because of their use by terrorists in Northern Ireland. A committee of MPs, including some of the leading politicians from the province, were examining the Bill, clause by clause. They needed some practical help and sent for examples of replica guns from the Home Office.

*"Are we to leak how many valentines she's received from this Cabinet?"*

These were duly provided, along with some samples of the real thing, in order to demonstrate how good the dummy models can be. It was only after the MPs had examined and handled the guns that the Home Office discovered that one of the real ones had been loaded. Fortunately neither Gerry Fitt, nor Ian Paisley, had thought to pull the trigger.

**One little item** of happy family news emerged from the Government shake-up. Leon Brittan may have lost his job, but the new Scottish Secretary, Malcolm Rifkind, whose feet are now beneath the Cabinet table, turns out to be his cousin. Well, just. Rifkind's father and Brittan's mother are second cousins – although the Rifkind family arrived from Lithuania some time before the other branch.

Fascinating news for everyone else – but it presumably doesn't make Leon feel much better about being put out of Government. He was not getting much Jewish solidarity or sympathy from the Labour benches in the Commons, either. Gerald Kaufman was asked whether he was moved by Leon's troubles and had a ready answer.

"Poles have always loathed Lithuanians," he said.

**It is difficult** for me to report this, but I have to record that the Archbishop of Canterbury is carrying an extra new responsibility. It is his fault that the Government's sacrilegious Shops Bill to allow Sunday opening was not beaten in the House of Lords the other night. Dr Runcie himself was actually tucked up in hospital after his recent operation, when the Government scraped through a division with a tiny majority. But what caused comment and surprise was that not a single Bishop had been present or taken part in the vote. Inquiries were made. It was discovered that they had trooped off on a mass outing to inspect the Archbishop's hernia.

The rest of this week's Church News is more cheerful. It comes from the Rector's newsletter for St Margaret's, Westminster, the parish church of the House of Commons. The Rector recalls that shortly before Christmas the extremely silly MP for Leicester East, Peter Bruinvels, called on Christians to express their disagreement with the controversial Church of England report, *Faith in the City*. They should do this by reducing their contributions to church collections over Christmas, suggested Bruinvels.

The Rector is delighted to be able to tell his parishioners that all his takings for the Christmas period were up £390 on last year, and the collection at each individual service was increased.

"In the light of this experience, we hope that Mr Bruinvels will make an annual statement along these lines," he comments sweetly.

# FIRST DRAFTS OF WINTER

A handful of writers reveal the books they feel sure they'll find
time to polish off between now and next spring...

# STANLEY REYNOLDS

**Oct 22**

Dear Diary,

This is it. This is finally and definitely it. This winter I'm finally and definitely giving up going out each and every night to pubs. Am definitely and finally going to write that novel. The big one. First thing. Without any further delay. Tomorrow.

**Oct 23**

This is it. *Chapter One*

**Oct 24**

God, this can't go on. Went to six pubs in Islington. She didn't show up. Lucky break, her not showing up. Wrote dandy first sentence for the novel on a beer mat. Brilliant opening. Sent coat to dry cleaners. Beer mat in pocket. It was an absolute classic. The opening sentence, that is.

**Oct 25**

She didn't turn up again. Waited six hours in the Crown.

Thought I almost remembered that opening sentence for the novel. If can read handwriting on last night's beer mat it goes:

*All meaningful relationships are happy in their own way, but traumatised relationships are traumatised in their own way.* Something wrong there.

**Oct 26**

Waited two hours in the Coach & Horses. Woman walked in, thought it was her. Said, "Where the bloody hell you've been?" Boyfriend got shirty. Manager said to me, "I've had my eye on you all night, mate, don't want your sort in here." Went to the Queen's Head, saw three women could have been her. Have decided she is a common type. Have decided best under the circumstances to start the novel with a last paragraph. Work my way up to it.

*"And so," Maloof said, giving the fatman a steely glance. "You thought because McGurk saw Kincaide going into Sorley's I'd think Culpepper had got the (plans) (diamonds) (drugs) (Rembrandt) from Sheila Van Warren's penthouse where the naked body of Trixie LaTour was found. Well," Maloof said, "you thought wrong, fatman."*

**Oct 27**

Strangest thing happened in Crown last night. Fellow walked in, complete stranger. Said, "I'm not her husband, but I'm authorised to speak for her husband and he says, 'Lay off Bernice.'" Amazing, eh? I mean to say. Stood there puzzled for some time. Then got great idea for opening sentence.

*In the city of L. in the month of N. in the year 19— a (student) (axe murderer) (young man) (K) (a blonde with big tits) walked along P. Street one evening.*

Barman got shirty. "Think we're made of beer mats?" he said in a most nasty fashion. Most annoying that. Not as worrying as about "Bernice". I don't know any Bernice. Never have known anyone named Bernice. Do you suppose Doris is really named Bernice? Doris is, I suppose, the sort of name someone called Bernice would make up for a name. Do you suppose Doris is Bernice and Bernice is married?

**Oct 28**

Maybe I should forget about writing a novel. Maybe I should forget about Doris or Bernice. Probably should write a book about rural England. Write something nice. Something wholesome. Got the idea in the King's Head last night. Thought of terrifically simple opening sentence. *The thatched roofs of the shires of England represent...* Well, they represent plenty if you think about it. I'll have to think about it.

**Oct 29**

People get the sort of crap books they deserve. Forget trying to write something important that would defend the thatched cottages of England and all they represent. Wouldn't appreciate it. Came to that conclusion in the Crown last night. Thought of great idea for novel. Ought to make a fortune. Just the sort of crap they like. Scribbled down the opening. A real grabber. *"Now that you're finished," the Countess said, "you can get the..."* Handwriting pretty illegible. Trouble was some fellow just walked up to me and said, "You been warned twice now, lay off Bernice." Then he said something strange: "What's a man your age doin' playin' round wif a 23-year-old?" Doris is never 23. From the look of her Doris has never ever been 23. Not in this life time anyway.

**Oct 30**

This is it. Forget the serious novel. Forget the defence of rural England. Going to write the show biz blockbuster. Got a great idea standing in the Empress of Lithuania last night just before closing. Wrote it down right there, that's what Kafka would have done if he got an idea. It's here somewhere, the beer mat. *I'm not one to kiss and tell but Rock and I.* No, that's not it. That was a first draft beer mat I wrote before that fellow came up to me and said, "Just being a Member of Parliament ain't goin' to save you, mate." Obviously a complete case of mistaken identity. Doris is obviously not Bernice. Just found the missing beer mat of the show biz blockbuster. *Dirty Edna tossed shame out of the window like an old brassiere and was off on a great career.*

**Oct 31**

I think I may be too literary for writing a blockbuster. I mean, having read 8,000 books doesn't necessarily mean you can write one. In fact, looking at Jeffrey Archer you might say the exact opposite is probably true. Trouble with us literary gents is we've never lived. I mean, not really lived. Never really go anywhere, see anything, except down to the cottage at weekends, out to a pub or two of an evening. Must stop going to the pub. That fellow came in again last night. Said, "Well, mate, you done for Bernice all right, you have, you was warned but you wouldn't be told. Read about it in the *Standard* have you?" Then he walked away. I mean, you get some real head cases in Islington these days. Looked at the *Standard*. "Blonde Mystery Corpse" found floating in the Regent's Canal. About time something happened in Islington. Nothing ever happens in Islington. And Jesus, Diary, did you see who won the Booker???? Come the New Year. Definitely going to.

*"I wandered lonely as a cloud..."*

# JILLY COOPER

WHEN I was young, publishers made amorous advances to me. Now I am middle-aged, they offer financial advances for other services. Such is my alacrity in grabbing these proffered sums of money, that I have got myself into rather a pickle this winter – having agreed to deliver far too many books by April next year.

What with six weeks revving up for Christmas, and at least six weeks afterwards recovering from excess and frightful fights with relations, this only leaves about six weeks to write – and no doubt even then power cuts will continually put my typewriter out of action.

Since we moved to Gloucestershire, everyone has been very keen for me to write about wildlife. *The Secret Diary of a Gloucester Mole – Aged 13¾* must, alas, remain a secret, because the little sod's gone into hibernation for the winter, and refuses to be interviewed. Equally, *Gloucestershire Summer Blooms* is a non-starter because they all stopped flowering in July.

*The English Woman's Coalshed (with a foreword by Hutch)* has ground to a halt since the miners' strike rocketed coal prices, and everyone switched to logs. Instantly I switched to *Tree Felling for the Older Woman*, but unfortunately squashed the vicar and three sheep flat trying to get practical experience.

Having convinced my publishers there is infinitely more sexual junketing in the country, I had hoped to score with *Come into the Garden, Lord*, Gloucestershire's torrid answer to *Hollywood Wives*, and *Wimps and Shepherds*, a thought-provoking exposé of the Cotswold Gay Set. But sadly my children will be having concurrent very long weekends home, when I should be writing both books.

*Royal Underwear – a Corgi's Eyeview* seemed a winner, too, but sadly, despite constant bribes of Kennomeat, the Corgies wouldn't bark. Even worse, *The Complete Flora*, a lovingly researched study of Sara Keays's baby, has been pre-empted by the national press, and Miss Keays herself.

I fully intended to rattle off my ten-volume guide to the First World War, entitled *Somme People*, this afternoon, but got sidetracked making the Christmas cake and planting the indoor bulbs.

I have accepted a fat fee to ghost *The Lord Goodman Book of Health and Beauty*, but am more attracted to the idea of *The Faminist's Cookbook*, a slim volume for the liberated anorexic.

My sure-fire potboiler, *Madonna e Mobile*, came unstuck when the wretched girl got married and turned respectable, and we're running into such a fearful legal trouble with my frank-kiss-and-tell autobiography, *Somewhere Under the Rambo*, that I doubt if that's going to see the light of day either.

If I can actually finish: *How To Trade Your First Wife In for A Younger Lusher Model and Still Remain a Jolly Good Fellow*, a special study of Harvey Smith and Andrew Lloyd Webber, it seems a cert. Alas, the berries are so thick this autumn, it's obviously going to be a hard winter, and we'll get snowed up, and the trains will go on strike, so I won't get out of the Cotswolds to interview either Mr Smith or Mr Webber. I prefer to stick with *Around Clare Francis in Forty Drinks*, a study of publishers' cocktail parties.

The Americans have paid me an embarrassingly large advance for *Ewing and Non Ewing*, a guide to the American class system, but I haven't had a moment to research that yet either. And the same goes for *Hullo Young Lover*, hints on how to trap and keep your own Toyboy.

As none of these books is likely to be anywhere near finished by April, I'm going to have to fall back on fiction. Just this morning I accepted a six-figure sum to write *Warhead Revisited*, a sensitive account of an Islington lesbian's return to Greenham Common and true love. *The Guardian* will serialise, Channel 4 will dramatise in 36 episodes, delivery date May 1st without fail. Or it will be, if nothing more interesting and lucrative turns up in the meantime – like *Lice*, a blockbuster novel about a young louse trying to find out which of four female lice laid her. Film rights sold. ❧

# RICHARD GORDON

AUTHORS are incessantly writing about other authors or themselves, never about their readers.

They are a difficult lot to know. Actors glimpse their audience gawping from the stalls, artists can lurk round the Royal Academy all summer, if they have the time. The author is the invisible striking at the unseen, like a cruise missile.

Letters and literary lunches make for clumsy fingertip-touching. "I wrote inviting authors to meet their readers," Christina Foyle remembered about opening the cultural canteen of the Dorchester. "H. G. Wells wrote that, from the letters he received, he did not wish to meet his readers."

The reader's psychology is essential intelligence for all aspiring authors, and should be assiduously taught by university departments of creative writing and writers-in-residence everywhere.

The British public is not in the slightest interested in books. These are dreary items. You have to *read* them. Not even pictures, as Alice noticed.

They are intemperately interested in the races. Thus the Booker Prize glitters among the glories of English Literature. Television presentation of the hopeful heaving bosoms of tarted-up lady authors and the frilly dress-shirtfronts of the publishers combines the genteel culture of the Sunday papers with the raucous excitement of the Grand National.

Champagne pops, and the sales of the winning novel hit intoxicatingly the empty stomach of the book trade. Readers never read the books they buy. To take the prize home makes them feel intellectual, as selecting from the shop's dominating shelves a book on dieting makes them feel slim, cookery books make them feel gourmets, and sex guides make them feel sexy.

If everyone read our annual output of books, we should be a nation of cultured, emaciated, randy Escoffiers.

Readers never buy the books they read. They are all women. With celebrated female self-sacrifice they endure the fag of visiting the public library, the irksomeness of squinting along the shelves, the tedium of the waiting-list, the snootiness of the librarians, the risk of fines, to share at last with the author the printed page with the sighing voluptuousness of the marriage bed, for which he gets 0.92p a go.

One day I shall put all this in my book *Readers Digested*, though luckily no one will read it. ❧

# VALERIE GROVE

**"18 May, Gloucestershire.**

"Return drenched and frozen from walking the dogs through the fields before breakfast. Find letter from Constable, the publishers, asking whether I would like to go to Mexico for a fortnight and write a book ... I accept with alacrity."

A fortnight, a book! I should think alacrity is what you would accept with. The above paragraph is how Jilly Cooper's new book (*Hotfoot to Zabriskie Point*) opens and to me it represents the ideal publisher's proposal, a real incentive to get on with it.

Getting started on a book being the hard bit, the diary format eases the way, as so many have realised. You don't have to keep it up all that long. Lord Longford kept a diary for a year and Lord Weidenfeld published it:

"1st January 1981. I have resolved to keep a diary for a year so here it begins. What is my prime objective for 1981? To finish a better man

than I am at the moment, though I shall never in this life know whether I have attained that end."

This is the beauty of a diary. Straight in, and no wrestling with arresting openings, "Hell!" said the duchess, or it is a truth universally acknowledged ... John Julius Norwich once recalled his first diary entry: "January 1st, 1937. Hung about." Mrs Woolf never hung about. "Friday 3 Jan 1936. Headache, head bursting, head so full, racing with ideas and the rain pouring." Ah yes.

I, too, was a teenage diarist in the Mole mould. It began on a Friday the thirteenth, in a cunning code (French): "C'est vendredi le treizième!!!" and I was, I now realise, good heavens! *exactly* 13¾.

Five or six times since then, in maturity and in English, have I taken up a crisp clean volume with a mental vision of E.M. Delafield's *Diary of a Provincial Lady* ("November 7th. Plant the indoor bulbs. Just as I am in the middle of them, Lady Boxe calls...."). It is quite easy to embark on such a volume in studied self-Pooterisation – "We settle down in our new home, and I resolve to keep a diary" – but even Mrs Pooter has been done in hard covers, brilliantly, by Keith Waterhouse, blast.

A book, this winter, there has to be. I was in-

terviewing John Braine the other day and after a large brandy he pointed a stubby, mocking finger at my humble reporter's notebook. "You've got to write bewks! Take my advice, stick to bewks! Your words are writ upon *sand*! Articles don't get *royalties*!"

He is right. I have pondered various possibilities. A children's book, long on title and short on plot (*Oliver Goes to the Dentist, Nancy Qualifies to Be a Librarian*)? A dynastic saga, three generations of a suburban family? I read in the *Daily Express* that my old friend Sally Beauman is getting a million dollars from Bantam Books for a novel "about poverty and wealth over three decades" called Destiny. It is not even written yet. "I'm ecstatic," she purrs.

When I sat down to write this I was quite ready to all alone bemoan my bookless state but it has been rather cheering. No calls yet from Constable to do a fortnight's bookmaking in Mexico but while unearthing diaries I found a small volume I kept in 1983-4 expressly for jottings in the Kids Say The Darnedest Things category. My favourite that year was Emma, then four: "If I was a daddy, and had a willy, *I* wouldn't hide it in my underpants!" Now there's a book that will keep us on a roar in years to come. ❦

*"I can't put my finger on it, bosun, but there's something aboard that's not quite ship-shape."*

# OVERCOMING FRIGIDITY

Cruel winter, unlike many people, will visit New York City this year, again... or so supposes ARNOLD ROTH

# MOTHER'S DAY

EVERY Wednesday I take Alison to the swimming baths with a friend and her four-year-old daughter. The pool is one of these new-fangled jobs with its sides punched in and a palm tree gamely lurching out of a central island, looking as if it would rather be somewhere else. We stand in the shallow end with water lapping round our ankles while the girls paddle about trying to keep their faces dry. We do it on the assumption that, if they are exposed to water over a long enough period, they will learn to swim by osmosis, and that one day they will turn, give a cheery wave, and backstroke off to the deep end.

Last Wednesday, we nearly didn't make the five-mile journey to the pool. We were about halfway there when my friend noticed that the temperature gauge in my car was registering intense heat. It had disdained hot, having left the last red mark behind, and was pressing against the side of its case to denote immeasurable degrees of heat. If it had been indicating pretty warm, or even hot, I might have taken some notice of it, but its behaviour was so excessively flamboyant that I didn't take it seriously.

My travelling companion did, however, and insisted that I stop the car.

I told her it would be OK, we had only a cou-

ple of miles to go and I was sure the gauge was merely trying to draw attention to itself.

My friend emphasised the seriousness of the situation by warning me that, if I continued to drive the car, I might crack my block.

I screeched to a halt. Crack my block? Good God. What – all of it? My whole block? I can't risk cracking my block, I'm too young.

My friend got out of the car and inspected the bonnet for signs of molten metal. There weren't any so she lifted the bonnet to look at the engine. I asked her if she could see any cracks in my block, she said she couldn't see the block and I began to worry in case it had cracked off altogether and was lying on the road-side. I suggested that I go back to look for it.

In reply she announced her intention to take the cap off the radiator to see if I was short of water. My knowledge of cars is not extensive, but I do know that if you take the top off a hot radiator you die instantly from too much steam.

I didn't want her to sacrifice herself over my block so I warned her most sternly from a safe distance not to do it.

She said the radiator was not hot and she wasn't expecting steam and took off the cap without the smallest fizz. She looked inside. I asked her if there was any sign of the block. No, she said, but she could see the fins.

How embarrassing. My fins were showing. They were probably in a dreadful state, too. How mortifying, to have someone inspecting my grotty fins. I should probably have been brushing them regularly with fin wax and having them serviced and overhauled every six weeks.

"Gosh," I said, "they'll be in a bit of a state. I haven't done anything with them for weeks. I was just about to take them all out yesterday and give them a good going over when the phone rang and I just never got round to it after that."

She replaced the cap, thank God, and wondered whether she should check the oil. Go ahead, I told her, why not? She already knew I had no block and filthy fins, what had I got to lose?

She asked where I checked my oil.

Oh, anywhere, I said, I wasn't fussy. I just checked it wherever I happened to be at the time. Sometimes I checked it round the back of the car, once or twice I'd checked it at the front. As long as it was all there, that was the main thing.

Apparently, it was not all there. It was hardly there at all, and if I didn't put some in very soon I would seize up.

Oh dear, I said, I was awfully sorry, I had no idea things were so bad, it was all my fault. (The only thing to do, when someone finds you out like this, is to humble yourself absolutely and

*"I like your tie."*

hope they will find it in their hearts to tell you things aren't really so bad.)

She didn't, though. She got back into the car and told me it was very dangerous to overheat the engine and I was very lucky to have got away with it.

Thoroughly chastened, I set off again. This time the temperature gauge didn't move at all, stolidly registering cold despite my overheated engine. My companion tapped the Perspex case and fretted over it but she could not get it to move past cold.

Maybe the gauge wasn't working?

Well, she had to admit, that was a possibility. What I should do, when I got home, was to un-screw the gauge from its housing and boil it vigorously in a pan of water. If it registered hot, it was working, if it registered cold, it wasn't, and if it registered warm, it wasn't trying hard enough. This was what she did with her temperature gauges if she suspected them of not working. Indeed, this was what she did with all her electrical equipment if she thought it wasn't pulling its weight. A good boil in a pan brought it round to her way of thinking or finished it off altogether. What she did with her husband if she suspected him of slacking she didn't say, but I'd like to bet it was something very similar.

We arrived at the pool without incident for an hour and a half of whee! jump! kick your legs! keep your head up! what a good swimmer!

We are very strong on verbal encourage-ment; we don't participate much but by hell we egg them on. I'm not a good enough swimmer to give formal instruction. I'm not even sure whether I can swim. I keep afloat by taking in huge gulps of air, and don't so much swim as bob. Progress in any direction is an incidental bonus. When I'm twice my normal size I try and concentrate my drift towards the shallow end. I wouldn't like Alison to emulate my tech-nique. The more conventional strokes have a greater directional potential and are not nearly so disfiguring.

Before we set off for home, I bought some oil and covered my fins decently with water. In re-sponse, the temperature gauge became frolic-some and skipped up and down the scale trying out all the areas it doesn't normally visit, hell-bent on enjoying itself. My friend was itching to give it a good boil and settle it down.

And so, too, was Alison. As soon as we got home, she wanted to know if it was time to boil the gauge. I told her I couldn't boil something unless I was going to eat it, and I wasn't going to eat the temperature gauge, no matter how badly it had behaved. 🐚

*"Jump, jump, jump, jump, jump . . ."*

# LET'S PARLER FRANÇLAIS!

## Dans le Bookshop

**Shopman:** Monsieur?

**Monsieur:** Oui. J'ai un complaint.

**Shopman:** Un complaint? Il faut voir un docteur, pas un bookseller.

**Monsieur:** Non, c'est un complaint littéraire. J'ai acheté ce livre ici.

**Shopman:** Stormy Profits, par Maud F. M. Thomas? Oh, oui! C'est sur le Booker short-list.

**Monsieur:** C'est à cause de ça que je l'achète. Dans le *Sunday Times* pull-out Snob Section, j'ai vu le short-list pour le Booker, et je me suis dit: "Go on, old boy, avez un good read! Achetez un modern novel, just like Melvyn Bragg et les Arts Council boys! Entrez dans le swim con-temporain!"

**Shopman:** Get on with it.

**Monsieur:** Je suis entré dans votre bookshop et j'ai acheté Stormy Profits par Maud F. M. Thomas. Alors, deux grands shocks m'attend-aient — un double shock. First off, le livre était terriblement expensif, I mean, bloody hell, £12.95! La dernière fois que j'ai acheté un novel, en 1968 je crois, c'était 3 ou 4 quid, well, I mean, £12.95!

**Shopman:** Et le second shock?

**Monsieur:** Le second shock fut le livre lui-même. J'ai lu Stormy Profits de cover à cover, et je peux honnêtement dire que c'est rubbish. C'est prétentieux, overblown, incohérent, self-important twaddle. C'est £12.95 worth de well-rotted manure. C'est un farrago de caractères sans interest, et des incidents sans signi-ficance. C'est, en un mot, a bit of a let-down.

**Shopman:** Si j'attrape votre drift, vous n'aimez pas Maud F. M. Thomas?

**Monsieur:** Vous êtes très vite sur l'uptake.

**Shopman:** Eh bien, moi non plus. Je trouve Maud F.M. Thomas un load de rubbish.

**Monsieur:** Donc, je demande mon money back.

**Shopman:** *Votre money back?* Impossible.

**Monsieur:** Pourquoi pas? Si j'achète un faulty instrument, ou du foodstuff inférieur, ou un wrong-size shirt, je reçois mon money back. Eh bien, ce livre est shoddy, badly written et faulty. Donc, mon money back.

**Shopman:** Dans un bookshop, une money-back situation est out of the question. Vous payez votre argent, vous prenez les risques. Votre opinion de Maud F.M. Thomas, c'est seulement votre opinion.

**Monsieur:** Mais non! C'est la vôtre aussi! Vous avez dit: "Maud Thomas est un lorry-load de cobblers!" Quand j'ai acheté le livre, tu aurais dû dire: "Non, monsieur, ne touchez pas Maud F.M. Thomas! Elle est un stinker!" Mais vous ne m'avez pas donné un warning.

**Shopman:** OK. Cette fois seulement, je vais vous donner votre money back. Mais c'est la first et last fois. Autrement, ça pourrait ruiner le book trade. Ne dites *rien à personne*, OK?

**Monsieur:** Have no worry. C'est la dernière fois que j'achète un Booker hopeful.

**Shopman:** Good thinking, monsieur.

"I can't stand it! The constant drumming, it's driving me mad!"

"Sorry, I dropped off for a moment –
who's running us now?"

HEATH **FOUR PLAY**

"Have you any last requests?"

"I think I've pulled a mussel."

# Miami Vices

MIAMI is a city bludgeoned, battered and sedated by television, in which regard I assume it is identical to every other city in North America, except that here television has stolen the very reality from life; as my cab cruised past the local police headquarters, there was proud talk of *Miami Vice*, which has reduced the building from penal fortress to a theatrical backdrop. If one of the symptoms of dementia is an inability to distinguish fact from fiction, then television has certainly reduced the entire continent to a condition of dementia.

Early on a Sunday morning, lit by the obtrusive Florida sun and announced by the pervasive rattle of the air-conditioning, I switched on to see how the Great Republic celebrates the sabbath dawn. Seven channels were at full blast. On one, Tom was conducting his eternal pursuit of Jerry, on another a man wearing a top-hat pulled faces while riding a unicycle. Three ladies sang cowboy hymns while strumming ukuleles. The embodiment of Elmer Gantry screamed biblical texts with all the assurance of a man who has just had a fireside chat with the Creator of the Universe. A little girl told of her cat, Ping, whose great feline breakthrough is its willingness to get into bed with its tiny mistress. A man whose only distinction was his ability to paint his hands yellow, patronised some captive schoolchildren by singing something called *If I Could Put Time in a Bottle*, a possibility which evoked happy thoughts of putting him in one.

Past experience of American TV, fleeting rather than concentrated, has induced the belief that ours is better. This is not quite true. The degree of excellence achieved by the occasional "serious" programme is irrelevant. There is a sense in which American TV does not exist at all. Suppose, for example, that the good burghers of Miami, suddenly distracted from their pursuit of barbecued spareribs and pie *à la mode*, were to mount the most profound version of *Hamlet* seen in the last hundred years. It would be destroyed before it began. "Oh, what a peasant slave am I, and baking soda is like motherhood." And "Goodnight, Sweet Prince, and keep a hold on those taste buds." And again, "There is nothing either good or bad, but thinking makes it so, then why not stress-proof your community?"

All programmes, whether light or heavy, solemn or serious, comic or grave, are mere pretexts for the hucksters to get in their sales pitch. Commercials arrive at the head of a programme, after the credits, during, during, during and during, before the closing credits, after the closing credits, over and over and over. "Was she really born with that hair colouring?" "Super-bonus specials throughout the store." "Bring a little sunshine into your breakfast." This is, as you might say, the thick end of the wedge.

But it has to be acknowledged that there are moments when these persistent commercials perform a useful critical service, by defining the show they are interrupting. The British naturally assume that with *Dallas* and *Dynasty* they are sampling the zenith of fatuousness so far achieved on the small screen. They are quite wrong. *Dallas* and *Dynasty* are as *War and Peace* to the novels of Fanny Hurst when measured against the bottom end of the market. Those wrinkles in my brow, that ashen demeanour, grey, as someone once said, as a stevedore's undervest, have been put there by the likes of *Santa Barbara*, in which a succession of louts in high collars and deep tans keep saying to a succession of feminine lumps things like, "Can't we talk this through?" and "I know you love me, Steve, but I'm married to Wayne." Confronted by this sort of asininity, there is nothing left for the critical faculty to do, and the last word has to be with the advertisers. At a very pregnant moment in the plot of something called *The Young and the Restless*, a cheerful man suddenly turned up and began extolling the virtues of Milkbone Dog Biscuits, which apparently diffuse your pooch's breath without any deleterious side effects. A more apt comment on what we had been watching could hardly be imagined.

Then again, there is the question of narcissism. On an award show called *The People's Choice*, someone from *Dynasty* presented a prize to someone from *Knott's Landing*, after which someone from *Knott's Landing* presented a prize to someone from *Dallas*, after which someone from *The Colbys* presented a prize to someone from *Dynasty*. And so it went on, to a climax where Charlton Heston, clearly unaware that he has become involved in a long-running farce, spoke with his customary granite-jawed resolution about the team spirit which produces the wonderful dramaturgic felicities of *The Colbys*. Is there nobody with the courage to tell him? Is there nothing that Milkbone Dog Biscuits can do for the writers and producers of these shows? Were these people really born with that brain colouring?

But before the British start preening themselves on having the least bad TV in the world, let them ponder the fact that, once or twice, American TV has altered the course of contemporary history, notably with the Kennedy-Nixon shows and the coverage of the Vietnam war. Somewhere under the vast mountain of hair-dyes and animal food and fudge mix and motor oil and community stress-proofing, there struggles to survive something resembling the truth – even in small things.

I was much taken by a bumptious-looking young man wearing a Saroyan moustache, who reviewed a new movie called *The Highlander*. It seemed evident from the clips used in the programme that *The Highlander* is pitched somewhere between the dog biscuits and the motor oil. Nothing surprising in that. What was different was the genial contempt with which the picture was derided.

In Britain, the film companies let you use the clips on condition you are polite. In America, you say what you please. My Miami moustache said that the good news about *The Highlander* was that you couldn't hear half the dialogue; the bad news was that the other half you could hear. No budding Barry Norman in this country would ever be allowed to get away with honesty of that style. ❧

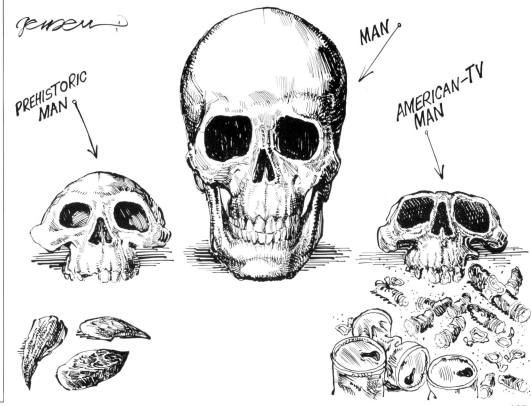

PREHISTORIC MAN

MAN

AMERICAN-TV MAN

*"All those in favour say, BOOM!"*

BILLIONAIRE Howard Hughes used to say Managua in Nicaragua was the perfect place for lunch. True, most of the city has been demolished by earthquake, war and revolution since then but a score or more volcanoes still fringe the horizon and tables groan with beef and lobster while excellent Flor de Caña rum is served by giggling Bianca Jagger look-alikes. The concrete Aztec pyramid of the Hotel Intercontinental where Hughes occupied two floors has survived every tremor and this week five hard Left councillors from Lambeth led by "Red Ted" Knight follow in his footsteps. It could be a terrible ordeal. Most invited delegates find for the first time in their lives they are changed by some magical socialist alchemy into millionaires.

To begin with a little arithmetic. Each of our councillors, through no fault of his own, already has his Aeroflot flight and hotel room paid for. On top of that he has £50 a day to spend which comes to around $70. For a stay of three weeks it amounts to quite a tidy sum. What usually happens is our Honoured Guest moves towards a desk marked Exchange at the hotel as soon as he arrives. He is immediately grabbed by a ministerial aide and wrestled towards the bar. A German trade unionist had his shoulder dislocated in this manoeuvre and a Japanese beef exporter was bitten on the leg.

"No, señor," pleads the aide, a little breathless. "I will take care of the money for you. Perhaps it is better you cash all your dollars at once. We have a better rate for Honoured Guests." The man will beg and weep if need be. Then, crab-like, the aide scuttles away to a nearby restaurant where the dollar is transmuted not into the base metal of ten cordobas at the unadventurous official rate but to the inflationary gold of 700 cordobas a dollar, each bearing the grim face of General Sandino who would have been outraged. Three weeks' expenses

*"I'm home, dear! I overpowered a guard!"*

SLOANE, WILLIAMS & WHITE CLOUD

(DOCTOR, LAWYER & INDIAN CHIEF)

# PAUL PICKERING

# Red Lobster

is just over a million cordobas on the black market.

Immediately the revolution takes on a rosy glow and any reservations one may have had about the treatment of Indians, dissidents or black people tend to disappear when one is actually "on the ground". With rum at sixty cordobas a bottle, this is where many Honoured Guests

> "A guide will inform the delegation that Somoza had two hobbies; murdering people and breeding beef. This is Nicaraguan humour and it is wise to laugh."

find themselves most of the time. Luxuries like Delsey toilet paper or soap cost a lot more and it is best to take them with you.

Despite a serious-looking nineteen-year-old with an AK-47 every fifty yards or so, Managua is not a dull town and gastronomically it is incredible for the Honoured Guest. For one dollar twenty cents you can have a whole plate heaving with baby lobster bubbling in garlic butter. Florida restaurants used to import Nicaraguan prawns before the blockade in preference to their own. The beef is the best in the Americas. A guide will inform the delegation that the former dictator, Anastasio Somoza, had two hobbies; murdering people and breeding beef. This is Nicaraguan humour and it is wise to laugh. One day for a few thousand cordobas I took a friend to the Intercontinental, wallowed in the swimming-pool and dined like a king while still having change for a nationalised Coke. It is no wonder Managua is becoming the new Kathmandu. "I don't eat so well at home," confessed an American divorce lawyer's daughter. If the Honoured Guest is lucky enough to meet "the man in the street" he will be told not to mention food as it would insult the compañero who could only offer rice and beans and would be embarrassed. Recently, when a delegation of portly Russians was led round the Oriental Market like prize porkers wobbling from a week's gluttony, ordinary Nicaraguans were so embarrassed they threw rocks.

But there is always a long-legged, long-nailed "nanny" from the Foreign Ministry clad in Fiorucci jeans to coax the guests round the sugar cane factories and the communal farms and on one special day to the War Zone in an air-conditioned minibus with a cooler full of Victoria Beer.

To the dulcet tones of Boy George on the loud speakers, the charabanc will tour towns famous from the news bulletins like Jinotega and Matagalpa, while returning to the safer country just north of Managua to trundle down a track. At the end of the track is a burnt-out shed. This is obviously the work of Reagan-backed, shed-burning Contras. A Hershey bar

wrapper is produced as evidence. The highlight of the jaunt is rather like school trips round Wookey Hole where they switch all the lights off and tell you to imagine you are prehistoric man. "Even now we could be in the rifle sights of the Contra," says the Sandinista nanny and shoos her flock back into the minibus. But although it was only for ten minutes, they have been to The Front and no doubt have worked up an appetite if not a speech.

The only trouble is as the days pass they do not seem to be spending much of their million. The overflowing discotheques and night clubs, such as the infamous Bambi, which play Atlantic Coast music and specialise in the extremely sexist Palo de Mayo (Maypole dance), not the sort of thing to be seen on a village green, are very cheap. You would be hard pressed to get through two thousand cordobas a night and exquisite ladies would swoon at the prospect of being rehabilitated in exotic Lambeth by the GLC Women's Committee. Comradeship, however, is entirely free and prostitution severely punished. Miscreants are sent to a collective in Corinto for five years to make hideous Souvenirs of Corinto from sea shells which no one ever buys. Gambling only really happens at cock fights where again it is hard for the Honoured Guest to lose as one's escort is armed. There is also a limit to the stuffed jungle toads and snakeskin handbags the guest can buy.

Slowly it dawns on him he still has nearly a million cordobas left. It is a grave offence to take these out of the country as they may be used by the shed-burning Contra to buy more Hershey bars.

By the time the limousine comes to whisk him to the airport he can see a diplomatic incident looming in front of him. Perhaps even jail. To avoid such ignominy he might have to give the money away. To the poor!

But sensing the delegation's dilemma the ministerial aide is at hand to persuade them that such gestures of charity are not needed in the modern Marxist state. Gratefully they force all the cordobas into a large paper bag he has about his person and expect never to see him again. But in a trice he will be back smiling with each guest's original $1,470. A miracle of socialist economics. But how is it done?

Well, even if our hero gorged 200,000 of his cordobas he would still have around 800,000. The ministerial aide sidles off to a private house nearby, where a remarkable old lady terrifies hippies into converting their dollars for 200 instead of 700 cordobas when they first arrive with their rucksacks. The Government allow her to continue, providing she changes a few cordobas to dollars for them occasionally at the 200 rate. The Honoured Guest has his money back, the aide has made a hefty profit and the group marvels at the ingenuity of a remarkable people. Of course, such things could never happen to the delegation from Lambeth. They are far too skilled at spending money. ✢

*"This is just to let you know that we've planned on Sunday being a nice day anyway, so when it happens you shouldn't think it's because we cared one way or another about your golf."*

# MICHAEL BYWATER

*One out of two salaried men actively go out to drink with fellow workers, and only 4.6 per cent participate unwillingly, according to a survey recently conducted by Nippon Life Insurance Co.*

**Mainichi Daily News**

---

**FROM:** K. NOGAMI (Manager, Division of New Ways Forward)   **TO:** A. ISHIBASHI (Assistant, Division of Looking Outwards)

This is to let you know that management staff of New Ways Forward will be assembling 6.15 at Shinjuku Sanchome station for weekly trip to Supper Club El Cupid for regular company special evening time tomorrow.

   Kindly ensure to honour us with your presence and compensate for mistaken absence on last occasion.

---

**FROM:** K. NOGAMI   **TO:** A. ISHIBASHI

Your memo apparently dictated yesterday has reached my desk. In the event of accepting sudden and serious illness of Mrs Ishibashi, it would be necessary for me to proffer most sincere hopes for her speedy recovery and pray that illness is nothing nasty or acquired in unacceptable way resulting in loss of face.

   This is not however accepted by my good self nor by whole Division of New Ways Forward, on grounds that Mr Azuma of Import/Export and International Good Feelings Division, who was making his way to regular company special evening time from differing direction due to earlier appointment in Fukushima (to discuss setting up of joint venture to manufacture stench-impermeable fish product wrapping bag overprinted with attractive popular figure of cat showing various expression, if you are still interested in Company business) happened to see you entering Hello Doggy Cozy Corner Chinese Food in Roppongi, arm-in-arm with woman who look suspiciously like Mrs Ishibashi.

   Mr Azuma also state that you and Mrs Ishibashi apparently laughing and joking with intimate style of happiness as if just married. Explanation which leaps to mind is of course that you knew (in advance of regular company special evening time memo from my good self) that Mrs Ishibashi was due to fall ill and took her out as act of kindness to soften blow of fate when it fell upon her. As you can see, Ishibashi-san, I wish only to think the best of you. Unfortunately you make this difficult for me to do, and I must point out to you that next regular special evening time is next Tuesday, assemble 6.05 Shinjuku Sanchome station to allow extra time for trip to Ginza Hollywood Special Club floorshow, malt whisky, imported cabaret, plenty of opportunity for recovery of lost face and confirming certain people on path of company loyalty and promotion, I mention no name, Ishibashi-san, but look forward in paternal way to seeing your face smiling up at me.

---

**FROM:** K. NOGAMI   **TO:** A. ISHIBASHI

The expression of deepest human emotions of pain and terror and deliverance by watchful gods implored to assist suffering men by intercession of ancestors is theme worthy of greatest of Japanese writers. Perhaps you hope to be one of these, if I am to judge from your memorandum of yesterday which was awaiting me at my desk.

   Story of tragic agony was most moving especially when I consider circumstances in which you apparently dictated it, according to your account of proceedings. To think of you, early on station platform, waiting for company friends! To picture the sharp rending pain as of *suppuku* which cruelly struck you down – forcing you to run back to office as no facilities on station! To experience through your description the anguish of waiting for deliverance, the fevered flight from Company Head Quarter back to station, only to find platform empty of corporate friends, and then to suffer with you as you ride home on train to house, musing on loss of face! This is sad indeed.

   Unfortunate that you lose slip with Ginza Hollywood Special Club address on it. Also unfortunate that Mr Maramatsu choose last evening for Expression Of Company Chairman Concern For Welfare by investigating Company Head Quarter facilities, you will know what I mean, and you will also I know be saddened to learn that Mr Maramatsu find no sign of disturbance or pain and screaming such as you describe yourself undergoing at *precise* time and in *precise facility* as Mr Maramatsu.

   Also unfortunate that Mr Tamagawa of Social Happiness Through Assembly Licensing Deal department, who was making way to Ginza Hollywood Special Club from different direction and somewhat late, having returned from Osaka, happened to see you and Mrs Ishibashi entering famous Inagiku tempura house in Kayaba-cho, *in company with small son and medium daughter Ishibashi.*

   Doubtless explanation is that (a) honour dictate you keep low eyes and quiet countenance even in agony in unseen presence of Mr Maramatsu, and (b) that, following unhappy experience, you needed family around you and settling tempura dishes of masterly hands of Nobuo Asano and Kiichiro Asano, who are both good friends of myself and tell me you ate heartily and with happiness at their restaurant. This is obvious testament to excellence of Asano tempura. You see how I wish to believe you, Ishibashi-san. You also see how I continue to hope for some prospect of your continued employment in corporate family, a matter which I hope to discuss with you next Tuesday at Golden Gessekai Club, which is reached by being at Shinjuku Sanchome station at 6.10.

---

**FROM:** K. NOGAMI   **TO:** A. ISHIBASHI

How bravely you have kept your secret all these years! In this, I have nothing but admiration for you. A liver such as you describe can only be deep burden in pursuit of ordinary business life, likewise strict diet of mineral water. It is unfortunate that Golden Gessekai Club does not stock mineral water but as you discovered, imported malt scotch whisky does just as well. Indeed I noticed, as did everyone else from Company present last night, that restorative effect of imported malt scotch whisky is so powerful that small bodily disorder soon become unimportant in climate of good feeling and company friendship.

   You will notice word "company" in last sentence. This is of significance. For example, no possibility that waitress in Golden Gessekai Club be considered company, also impolite to strike husband of waitress in Golden Gessekai Club, especially accompanied with claims of your prowess as *Bonsai* expert, which only involves you and company in embarrassing situation since implicit threat to grow small tree in head of husband of waitress in Golden Gessekai Club is hardly in great Samurai tradition.

   Additionally, even less possibility that wife of Chairman Mr Maramatsu can be considered "company", hence your invitation to all corporate friends to come with you for go on wife of Mr Maramatsu cannot be construed as promoting company fellowship. Whether or not your claim that wife of Mr Maramatsu is real little goer is true is not to the point, nor do salary-men of corporation wish to know about Mr Maramatsu's little problem, as not promoting respect. I am therefore with much regret terminating your contract immediately, with recommendation that in future you try and control your drinking habit.

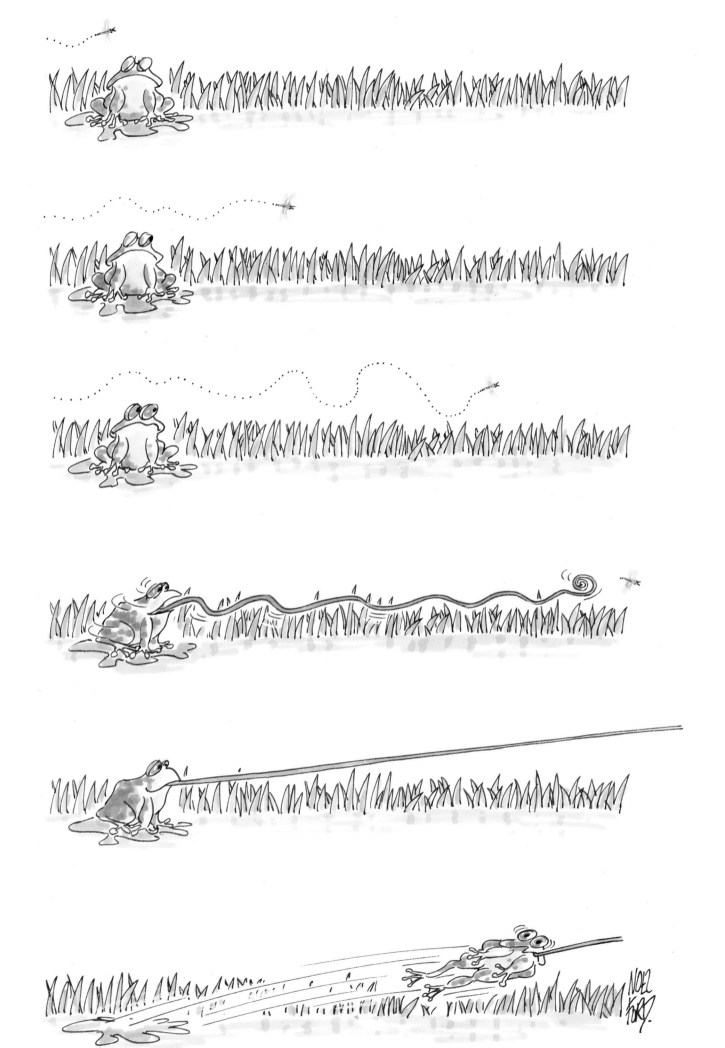

# The Tender Trip

an over-researched study of the aphrodisiac.

It was the ancient Greeks who put a name to it (well, they would, wouldn't they?). To win favour with Aphrodite, the Goddess of Love, the men of Greece made numerous sacrifices – over the years these became known as Aphrodisiacs.

Mythology tells of a young and handsome man who offered the beautiful Goddess a packet of pork scratchings and half a Guinness. Deeply insulted, Aphrodite transformed the man into an animal that was half pig and half potato.

*Pure genius!*

Naturally, stimulants of one shape or another had been around for sometime before that —

Prehistoric Britons, for instance, soon discovered the importance of **Make-up** ...

*Lets make it once for my baby and once more for the woad.*

Subtler methods of persuasion were recorded in the Bible —

**LOVE!!!**

*Land!*

## The Round the World Cruise

Other sea-farers were lured to their deaths by the sirens* **Song**

*I write the songs that make the whole world cry...*

\* Biologists attribute the legend of the mermaid to an ugly wet mammal with a large nose and a lousy voice known as a Barry Manatee, though they admit that the appeal of such an animal must be limited ... even to sailors.

Scientific advancements have supplied many a present-day Romeo and Juliet with tonics worthy of their passions, tonics which would have eluded our sexually under-nourished ancestors ~

## Rhino Corn

A cheap and humane form of stimulant as many a poor Kenyan Chiropodist will testify

The highly acclaimed and readily accessible **Oyster** (fig i) is a firm favourite, not to be confused with either (fig ii) the clam (which has the reverse effect) and (fig iii) two rhino corns.

fig i

fig ii

fig iii

## Strip Scrabble Pursuits

Questions fall into four categories:
Light blue —— risqué
Blue —————— rude
Dark blue —— down-right embarrassing
Indigo ———— censored

Should the player's answer coincide with a pale blue square on the board, the player must also throw in a double entendre.
Should the answer land on a darker blue square, the player must end his round with a triple entendre. Anyone who fails to do this must remove an article of clothing.

The winner is allowed to pursue the vanquished, should any of the players remain awake.

slam

No dictionaries!

**Alcohol** must surely be the most popular of these sexually motivating ingredients and yet the workings of this and every other drug mentioned on this page can soon be remedied by a cold shower of Perrier water.

Naturally, space allows us to show only a few of the aphrodisiacs presently on the market; however, listed below are others worth considering:
The Heimlich manoeuvre
Spring
Channel four
Pork scratchings and half a Guinness.

A final word of warning to our younger readers: please do not try any of the stimulants mentioned on this page unless there is a consenting adult present.♥

# Courtly Loves

THIS new year gives us a nice little centenary. Exactly one hundred years ago, good ol' Teddy, the Prince of Wales, had his first horse-racing win as an owner. The nag was called Counterpane. It dropped dead after its next race – but the Sport of Kings was off and running.

I fancy its next century will not be so regally patronised. I have no confidential evidence for this of course, but have a hunch that Royal Appointments on the Turf are on the wane, in spite of Lester's knighthood in the New Year's honours – well, he *did* get one, didn't he? I'm writing this the day before the list comes out. If he didn't, then it further proves my point.

After the Queen and, of course, her beloved Mum, what likely apprentice is natural heir to assume patronage of the silky, snooty, topper-doffing game? Horses, as such, have no need to worry, mind you. Nags themselves remain part of the regal fabric. But three-day eventing is as far away from the Mug's Game as cricket is from baseball. Who have we got? Prince Charles seems genuinely fired by a missionary zeal that might even take him from the polo fields. Anyway, neither Himself nor His sister have ever shown much enthusiasm for Epsom or Ascot, let alone the 3.45 at Wincanton or Market Rasen, whence results, apparently, still keep Granny beaming spry. Nor has the Duke of Edinburgh bothered overmuch about being seen stifling a yawn at the said Ascot *gavotte*. Matelots don't twig nags – though he enjoys his carriage-driving round Windsor Great Park.

Who else is there? Prince Edward likes rugger and acting and, presumably, helicopter driving. Prince Andrew would prefer being in the Press Tent swopping yarns at f8 and 500th of a second with Ed Byrne or Gerry Cranham, racing's two celebrated happy snappers. The Kents prefer tennis. So does Princess Diana. And she also likes cricket.

At Wimbledon a couple of years ago, I watched Diana closely. McEnroe was playing at, for once, his most benign and entrancing and when, at dead on four o'clock, the Royal Box flunkey called them downstairs for tea, the Princess was loathe to go, really wanting to see the match out. She also spurns, so far, to learn the Royal Tennis Handclap as patented by the Duke of Kent – a bored manual hurrah in slow-time, which looks as if he's laboriously trying to swat an imaginary bumble-bee about six inches above his forehead.

Princess Diana's elder son will not, I guarantee, be a racing man. He is accounted for, I'm pleased to say. When Prince William was born, all his delighted grandfather, Lord Spencer, would say is, "I hope and pray he plays cricket for Gloucestershire." End of quote. Princess Di has since become President of dear old Glos CCC, and one of the first Christmas cards the club received last month was one from the good lady, with the PS that she had noted, with warm pleasure, the dramatic advances the county had made up the Championship table through the summer. It was noticed, by the way, that in that obsequious royal television interview last autumn, the fawning ITN newsreader who conducted it felt obliged to talk to her about polo. With all his researchers, why didn't he ask about cricket?

I digress…In the summer of 1886, the Prince of Wales's first winner as a racehorse owner made, at a stroke, the whole raffish pursuit legit and respectable. True, his mother had occasionally attended the Ascot Gold Cup, down the lane from Windsor, when Prince Albert was alive. But that was deemed to be no more than part of the royal duty, like going to the Cup Final today might be for Princess Margaret. After Albert's death, Victoria never went racing again. She found its society dubious and disreputable. Her son, however, took to it with a will, once he had been taken to watch Hermit win the Derby in 1867.

Rakish coves like Charles II and the Prince Regent, of course, had enjoyed a flutter and all its attendant thrills – the like of which Queen

"The Princess spurns to learn the Royal Tennis Handclap – a bored manual hurrah in slow-time, which looks like an attempt to swat an imaginary bumble-bee six inches above the forehead."

Victoria warned her son against in a letter from Osborne when he was 28 years old:

> Dearest Bertie,
>
> Now that Ascot Races are approaching, I wish to repeat *earnestly* and *seriously*, and with reference to my letters this spring, that I trust you will…as my uncle William IV and Aunt, and we ourselves did, *confine* your *visits* to the Races to the *two* days, Tuesday and Thursday, *and not go on Wednesday and Friday* to which William IV never went and neither did we…your example can do *much* for good and a great deal for evil…I hear every true and attached friend of ours expressing *such anxiety* that you should gather round you the really good, steady, and distinguished people.

Racing was one matter on which the Prince stood firm.

> I fear, Mama, that no year goes round without you giving me a jobation on the subject of racing…I am always anxious to meet your wishes, dear Mama, in every respect, and I always regret if we are not quite *d'accord* – but as

I am past twenty-eight and have some considerable knowledge of the world and society, you will, I am sure at least I trust, allow me to use my discretion in matters of this kind.

I crib that correspondence from one of the season's most stylish and genuinely enjoyable books, *The Fast Set* (Deutsch, £12.95), which, along with other high-grade stuff probably, got buried and un-noticed in the welter of humdrum Christmas catchpenny dreadfuls. It is George Plumptre's story of Edwardian racing with, as you can imagine, the Prince of Wales in the starring role.

Although his first winner came home in 1886, I daresay the Prince had owned quite a few unofficial ones in the preceding years (but didn't want Mama to know). He had registered his racing colours eleven years earlier, in 1875. The famous chocolate-box confection of purple, gold braid, scarlet sleeves, black velvet cap with gold fringe is, unless I'm mistaken, the very same favours which the Queen's jockeys sport today – though if I am slightly out, don't all write in at once. Ten years after leading in Counterpane, the Prince won his first Derby with Persimmon, by a neck. The Brough Scott of the day logged the reaction thus:

> With what throbbing pulses the Prince had watched this thrilling contest of giants can only be guessed. As for the spectators, the cheers had swelled to a hurricane which must have been heard for miles around. The Prince of Wales had won the Derby! After years of patience and ill-luck at last he had his reward. It was a spectacle such as had never before been witnessed on a racecourse. Members rushed down from the stand to the enclosure, waving their hats as they gazed to where His Royal Highness stood, pale but with a delighted smile on his face…winning the Derby always meant much; in the history of the race it had never meant as much as this.

Ninety years on…and might the Queen be the last of the royal racing line? It would be just if cricket got a look-in at last. Much depends, I suppose, on where Prince William is sent to school. At Gordonstoun, the wild-eyed German educationalists, clambering up and down crags in sandals, cannot be expected to understand the delicate intricacies of the mesmerising googly, or the charms of the wrist-rolling late-cut, as it ripples past third-man's stretching left arm.

For it is about time Royalty patronised our finest national game. They have a lot to make up for. The late wicket keeper-batsman for England, Paul Gibb, kept a fascinating daily diary when he toured Australia with the MCC in 1946-7. Governor-General then was the Queen's uncle, the Duke of Gloucester. Before the Sydney Test, he had to visit the England team in their dressing-room. Gibb recorded that he had simply gone round to each man, as they stood to attention and were introduced by Wally Hammond, and asked them one by one, "Have you gone out and won your toss?" He honestly thought that each player tossed a coin to determine his place in the batting order.

I ask you. Even Queen Victoria would have known that. Certainly Princess Diana does. Come to think of it, I wonder if she named Prince William after Gloucester's W.G.? Or even Bill Athey? ❧

# KEITH WATERHOUSE
# 40 Uses for the Office Photo-copier

1  Making fifty copies of a memo headed ''To Heads Of All Departments'' — twenty for the heads of all departments, and thirty to put on a shelf.

2  Eliminating the need for messing about with carbon paper when typing letters.

3  Making two extra copies of every letter that goes out, in case the file copy goes astray.

4  Cutting out the need for scribble pads by creating a mountain of unwanted photostats to write on the back of.

5  Reminding All Staff that just putting their names down for the Boulogne Supermarket Trip is not enough, they must repeat MUST pay a £5 deposit to Lynda (Room 551B), otherwise seats on the coach cannot be guaranteed.

6  Making two dozen copies of a notice to be stuck on trees: ''Lost. Black cat with white bootees. Answers to name of Mr Snugglepaws. Reward.''

7  Running off an invitation to be pinned to all office notice boards: ''The Typing Pool Terrible Twins (Debra & Doreen) will be pushing the boat out at the Mucky Duck from 6 p.m. onwards TONITE!!! (Fri) to celebrate their Birthday ('All together now — they're twenty-one today'). All welcome — specially all you Big Spenders in Accounts.''

8  Making eight illegal acting editions — one for the producer, one for the ASM, and six for the 3m, 3f — of the detective farce, ''Nickers In A Twist'', scheduled to be the next production of the Office Players.

9  Making six copies of the lyrics of Madonna's *Like A Virgin* — one to be folded up and put in a handbag, and the rest in case anyone should happen to want the other five.

10  Informing All Staff that as Mr Elphinstone will shortly be retiring after 45 years in the post room, they might wish to mark the occasion by subscribing towards the video recorder which he has expressed a wish to have, all contributions great or small to be sent to Len (Room 234).

11  Reproducing a political satire beginning, ''Mrs Thatcher is my Shepherd, I shall not work ... ''

12  Circulating a petition informing the Home Secretary that the undersigned, bearing in mind that we are all grown-ups living in the twentieth century, do request and require him to implement recent recommendations that the pubs be open all day.

13  Copying a recipe, from Mrs Nackerman's *Woman's Own*, for stuffed aubergine.

14  Reproducing the knitting pattern from Mrs Bracegirdle's *Woman's Weekly* and putting it away in a drawer.

15  Giving a spoof proclamation headed ''The Metric Year'', which tabulates proposals for a hundred-minute hour, a ten-hour day and so on, an even wider circulation than it has had already.

16  Doing the same for a comic document entitled, ''The Trade Unionist's Ten Commandments'', and commencing, ''Six days shalt thou go slow, and on the seventh thou shalt be on strike ... ''

17  Making a copy of a newspaper column and sending it to the newspaper columnist with a letter agreeing with every word/disagreeing with every word he has said.

18  Making a copy of the letter, and stapling it to a second copy of the newspaper column.

19  Duplicating the minutes of the Sunnymead Estate Residents' Association.

20  Ditto, the elevation and plan, for submission to the council planning officer, of a proposed new granny flat to be built as a roof extension to ''Rosedene'', Sunnymead Estate.

21  Ditto, the monthly newsletter of the Sunnymead Estate Youth Centre, headed ''Calling All Kids''.

22  Ditto, a poster advertising the Residents' Association Indoor Barbecue, at which all are welcome, in the Sunnymead Hall.

23  Ditto, another poster advertising a jumble sale in aid of the Sunnymead Hall Fire Damage Fund.

24  Perpetuating a humorous chain letter which ends ''... thousand lovers. But beware — a lady in Middlesborough broke the chain and got back her own husband.''

25  Making twelve copies, for handing out in the pub, of a mock newspaper report of an incredibly obscene contest between an Englishman, an Irishman, a Scotsman and a Welshman while on a desert island.

26  Reproducing a newspaper cartoon in which a character bears a passing resemblance to Mr Sissons of Personnel, re-captioned ''No prizes for guessing who this is!!!''

27  Copying pages from Mr Noakes's *Michelin Guide to France* before going on holiday.

28  Running off fifty copies of a notice reminding All Staff that the office photo-copier is not intended for private use.

29  Informing All Staff that an emergency meeting of the Staff Association will be held in the Staff Restaurant at 5 p.m., on the subject of petty restrictions by Management.

30  Copying an interesting bit from the *Daily Telegraph* for forwarding to a relative in Australia.

31  Copying an interesting bit from the *Melbourne Age*, sent by the relative in Australia, for forwarding to Granny in Peterborough.

32  Reproducing, for Sellotaping to a bedroom mirror, Debra's transcription of the words to Max Bygraves's *Deck of Cards*.

33  Thanking All Colleagues for the generous gift of a video recorder, which will be a constant reminder of his Old Mates, on the occasion of Mr Elphinstone's retirement after 45 years in the post room.

34  Keeping a record of each week's football pools entry.

35  Announcing the birth of one Kevin Andrew (9 lbs) to Eileen Potter of the Typing Pool, both doing well.

36  Making a copy of Kevin Andrew's birth certificate in case it gets lost, then attaching the copy to the original and losing both.

37  Announcing the sad demise of Fred Barnes, aged 81, who older colleagues will remember as one of the commissionaires, noted for his kindness, consideration and unflagging sense of humour.

38  Making copies, for forwarding to an MP, of a long and incredibly complicated correspondence with the Department of Social Security, concerning a period of unemployment following dismissal from another company for making illicit private use of the photo-copier.

39  Avoiding having to lash out eighteen pee on *The Sun* by taking a photostat of Debra's crossword.

40  Making copies of this article for passing around the office.

# Pardon My French

THE Fall of France ... In May 1940, the phrase kept bowling round inside my head, setting echoes flying along the empty, labyrinthine corridors. All my friends in the Upper Fifth agreed there was no other country whose over-painting on the map of Europe could cause us such pain. *Ze Furl urv Fraunce*, we intoned to each other, simultaneously shrugging, winking, gargling, staring right out of frame, hand cupped on left breast, hamming it up a bit but also genuinely moved.

The possible invasion and subjugation of Britain seemed much less cataclysmic – after all, it would (*surely?*) also entail the cancellation of the School Certificate exams. We were very pragmatic and unsentimental about our own country, a bloody awful place, anyway as seen from the forsaken promontory of Wearside and Sunderland Bede Collegiate Boys' Grammar School. A decade-long slump was tapering off. But it had taken a war to give work to many fathers and uncles for the first time in ten years. As for us, we had hived off to the safety of the Yorkshire moors, where anyone under the age of 18 was an invisible supernumerary, like blacks below the old Mason-Dixon line or women in the East.

There was not even a name for us. The word "teenager" did not exist because the concept did not exist. We were either in the oratorical, inspirational singular, "Youth", a good thing invoked by politicians and clergymen, or

"Youths", in the pejorative, admonitory plural, who were spoiling everything for everybody else simply by gathering anywhere in our twos and threes, as identified by police constables in court or editorialisers in leader columns. The rumour that "Youths" had been seen massing on the outskirts, or moving across the

> **"Imbedded in the Anglo-Saxon psyche is the conviction that 'French' means erotic means dirty means gorgeous means suitable only for abroad."**

landscape, had much the same effect on the burghers as sightings of wolves near Siberian hamlets.

But the Fall of France. As soon as I heard about it on the wireless, I founded the French Club. The first few members were the stickiest to enrol. Like all English persons who have spent five years, four or five hours a week, learning French, none of us could speak more than a couple of sentences extempore. I had to swear that candidates would not have to stand up and hum eccentric vowels through their nose while the rest of us sniggered.

This was a French Club in England and English would be the language of our meetings. The qualification was simply to answer "*oui*" or "*non*" to a series of propositions. Eighty per cent in favour and you were in. Each prospective member was asked to show a preference above all other possible competitors for: French knickers, French kissing, French dressing, French leave, French letters, French windows, French bread, French horn, French cricket, French toast, French mustard, French chalk, French beans, French doors. Everybody passed, even though many of us were not exactly sure what each item signified.

For example, French windows turned out to be, confusingly, the same as French doors, that is, pairs of head-high, fully-glazed frames opening on to balcony or garden. Raised in a climate where everyone who could afford it muffled both doors and windows with heavy veloured and bobbled drapes against the winds from the bone-numbing, snot-green North Sea, these did not seem very practical conveniences. If Captain Oates had been unwise enough to exit through French windows/doors around us, except in the shallow depth of summer, he would soon have been shattering his icicled mitts within minutes against the panes, begging to be re-admitted. Still, the very improbability of the suggestion evoked a tropic Gaul where the interior was not inevitably chillier than the exterior, all the year round.

Foods of any kind hardly needed the French prefix to interest growing boys, even if many of us were being better fed in the first year of Forties rationing than in the last year of Thirties depression. Still, I had to search far for any homes familiar with more than one of our list – French bread, dressing, toast, mustard or beans. But then who had ever enjoyed a desirable eatable, come to think of it any desirable possession, which was dubbed British or English?

French bread we had at least seen at the pictures. Usually it was being carried home, protruding from a leatherette shopping-bag, by a black-garbed, bespectacled gorgon, her loaf to the Anglo-Saxon eye more like a large dog-biscuit in the shape of a human thigh-bone. So far was it from our own mahogany brick, that there were even some among us who pretended to believe that they were really dildoes. (This was a wild flight of imagination inspired by a boy who had been brought up in Turkey and claimed once to have overheard his father vainly trying to explain to his mother why the bananas, unless sliced, had been forbidden entry to the old Sultan's harem.)

French dressing aroused little interest. I wish I had a silver sixpence for every boy who asked – don't you mean French un-dressing? Even when I found the recipe in *Chambers Encyclopaedia*, there was no way of trying it out. All British adult males rejected salads as "rabbit bait" so none of us dared lose caste by eating it. The women and girls preferred their lettuce and half tomato naked or with a dab of long-hoarded Heinz salad cream. When I mixed some and handed out spoons-full, it was the oil not the vinegar that made the tasters shudder.

TABAC

CAFE DE LA PLAC

LE MENU

USEFUL FRENCH PHRASES SPOKEN HERE

PARIS

Hawker

French mustard was allowed to be superior on the sweet palate of youth because milder than the harsh, eye-watering, nappy-yellow stuff slabbed by our elders on everything. Beans? Well, the only beans that attracted boys came from a tin. Otherwise, it was just another inedible, good-for-you green to be concealed under itself at the side of your plate.

French toast (thanks to *Chambers*) was a great success. Gorgeously messy to make, it quickly consumed a whole lot of scarce ingredients your hated hosts had put aside for treats of their own, behind your back.

Do the French, I wonder, realise how deeply imbedded in the Anglo-Saxon psyche is the conviction that "French" means erotic means dirty means gorgeous means suitable only for abroad? By the time we had got through the neutral entries on the list, such as French leave, French chalk, French horn (some disappointment here), both the vetting committee and the proposed entrant were in such a lather of innuendo it was difficult to deny that French polishing was a massage by naked can-can dancers in a bath of perfume and champagne.

Our admiration for French as the language of love was heightened by an anarchic teacher, just off to join the forces, who taught us the invaluable lesson for all translators – the more two words in different languages look the same, the less likely they are to mean the same. He explained that your French waiter never asks a female diner if she has "*fini*" but only if she has "*terminé*" because otherwise he would be asking her if she had completed her orgasm. Even in France, it seemed to us, there was hardly likely to be much confusion between the two enquiries. But oh! to imagine a race which considered such niceties in its official grammar, that deployed such *delicatesse* in its public vocabulary.

We went on to luxuriate over French knickers. So far as we could observe, no manufacturer in Britain had ever thought of producing garments to arouse, and facilitate, sexual pleasure. From all we ever saw on catalogues and in advertisements, British underwear was more like something Boadicea wore over her armour. As for French kissing, the words were scarcely printable in English. The actuality, practised on a pair of bribed local girls, exceeded all our expectations.

There were even a couple of Club members who forswore any further, future sexual delights beyond French kissing on the grounds that their nervous systems would not stand the sensual shock.

It seemed appallingly unjust that a people who clearly exceeded all other nations in its appetite for physical pleasure should be so deprived by the Hun. We hoped that this magic country, which appeared to be able to supply within its own borders every agreeable climate, scenery, wine and food, would find a way to evade Nazi restrictions. After all, and this was then perhaps the most popular item on our list – they were the people who made the French Revolution. At the time, I was afraid even the French could not help having their bright dazzle scratched and clouded by Hitler. Now, I am not so sure.

According to the *Hachette Guide to France*

*1985* entry on Paris,

During the German occupation (June 1940-August 1944) a time of strict rationing, fear and Gestapo raids was offset by glittering and provocative night-life and real artistic and intellectual creativity.

Reading that, I must admit my Francophilia buckled for a moment. Isn't there something a bit suspect about a capital city that can make such a boast *in* such *extremis*? London was hardly noted for what is usually called night-life, or for much artistic creativity during those war years. And then, I thought, neither was it in the years before or since. Good luck to them.

Forty-five years later, my eye is always caught, my attention is instantly lured, by and large my anticipations fulfilled, when I follow the word "French". Even in English.

*"Keep your fingers crossed. Louis's trying to win them over …"*

# COUPLES

"No one tells my wife to cover her breasts and gets away with it."

"There's something you ought to know, Mavis – I'm Japanese."

"You should see him when he's sober."

"If it hadn't been for that wife-swapping party at the Hetheringtons', we might never have met at all."

"According to this, he's left his internal organs to the cat."

"Did your husband have any enemies, Mrs Gisbourne?"

" . . . Something beginning with A . . . "

"Now, remember – you gas 'em and I net 'em."

BANX

# MOONWALKING

**SHERIDAN MORLEY**, in America on a promotional tour for **The Other Side of the Moon**, his biography of David Niven, sends home a diary:

## MONDAY

Philadelphia. This was where W.C. Fields said he'd rather be than dead, though he did add "on the whole". The city is seven weeks into a newspaper strike. Reviews therefore seem unlikely. I start my sales pitch on a lunchtime chat show with Dr Jonas Salk, of polio-vaccine fame, and seven veteran female White House correspondents. Nobody is selling anything except memories of Roosevelt. Why do I feel like Willy Loman already? I have the smile and the shoeshine. An author's gotta dream, boy: it goes with the territory. Arthur Miller never did explain what his salesman was actually selling. Probably books he'd written.

Our host modestly asserts that this is the biggest live lunchtime talk show in Philadelphia. He also asserts that I have written the autobiography of David Niven. My first live appearance on American television in several years therefore consists of me trying to explain that if it were the autobiography of David Niven then I wouldn't have been able to write it, not being Niven myself. By the time we have this semantic quibble sorted out, it is time for the commercial break. Not, you understand, the one in the middle of the hour-long programme, nor yet any of the seven either side of it. This is the commercial break that means the programme is over.

During the drive to our next studio appointment downtown, my local host uncritically estimates that author tours by foreign (i.e. English) writers probably cost a New York publishing house something in the region of a thousand dollars a day counting air fares and hotels, and that on the next show it might be a good idea to skip the quibble about the autobiography and get right down to the title of the book.

My next commitment is, as it happens, a telephonic pre-interview. For this you go to the nearest studio telephone and discuss with an unseen voice in the next town whether you might be suitable for an appearance there tomorrow. I seem to have passed the test, and am delivered by a proud host to the Amtrak for Washington.

The Amtrak is a train on which they bring you coffee and free magazines and remind you that travelling by rail is a gesture of solidarity with the Great American Past, and means you are altogether the kind of toney guy who reads the *New Yorker* and wears horn-rimmed spectacles and doesn't go in aeroplanes like all the sales-manager jerks who are making air travel so, well, pedestrian.

## TUESDAY

I am now in Washington. I know that because my hotel is called the Capitol and just across the road from a large white house with a lot of police around it. Mrs Reagan is not there this week: she is on Broadway singing with Mary Martin the showstoppers they first sang there in *Lute Song* way back in 1944. Little did audiences then realise that this great lady was later to go on to a position of world eminence as Larry Hagman's mother.

One of my interviewers here is the curator of a museum of soup tureens, from where he broadcasts to an expectant world news of the latest literary achievements in the world beyond soup tureens. I no longer find this in any way eccentric.

## WEDNESDAY

I arrive in New York. My ever-generous publisher here has lent me a limousine the length of a London Transport bus, complete with colour television, a cupboard with cans of frozen orange juice and mercifully also a driver. And there is a telephone, but the only person whose New York number I know by heart is, alas, out and therefore unimpressible.

About half an hour after leaving my hotel I notice something quite remarkable. We are still outside my hotel. This is because the entire street, indeed fifteen either side of it, now appear to be totally blocked at either end by barricades while President Reagan wishes the UN a happy fortieth birthday. Reluctantly I abandon the still-frozen orange juice and walk to seven different radio and television stations, some several miles apart.

## THURSDAY

Today I do the *Joe Franklin Show*. I have been doing the *Joe Franklin Show* for about twenty years, whenever I have had a book out in New York. Mr Franklin is essentially the Brian Matthew of America, an insomniac nostalgist with a midnight television chat hour of random charm. Tonight he decides to spend his air time educating me in the byways of American publishing.

My problem, in Joe's view, is that Niven never lived with any one of the Kennedys. Books about people who lived with any or all Kennedys, ranging from Marilyn to Joan, are very big here right now. So are books by maimed but surviving wives or offspring of violent stars. I suppose, says Joe wistfully, your father never beat you up? I tell him Robert wasn't that kind of a father. Well, says Joe, those are the breaks, kid. Keep selling.

## FRIDAY

I seem to be in Boston. My mother-in-law lives here, and has actually purchased two copies to keep my spirits up. Between studio fixtures, my guide tells me the best Renoir exhibition ever organised is to open in Boston next week: "My yesterday author," she tells me accusingly, "only had to make one phone call to the curator and we got a private tour." Mrs Reagan? Jackie Collins? Harold Robbins? Not in fact. Mrs Rupert Murdoch, of course.

## MONDAY

After a weekend off for good behaviour, I have now reached Toronto. There is a lot to be said for Canada, not least its book critics. Like Bernard Levin on the Hannibal tour, I am, however, now obsessed with

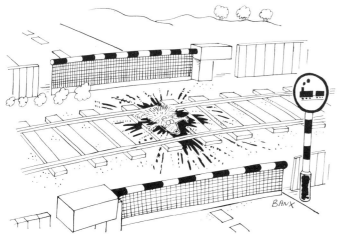

BANX

laundry. It has been about ten days since I spent more than one night in any one city, and I seem to have no shirts left. There is nothing about this in the *Manual for Touring Authors* which they give you on arrival, though it does say you are on no account to phone home for advice.

It also says how you are to remain very cheerful at all times and keep mentioning the title of your book. I am getting quite good at that. I tell it to hotel receptionists and cab drivers and total strangers on sidewalks, and tonight the immigration man when I was going back into the US said that it sounded real nice and was it anything to do with Halley's Comet like all the other books this Fall?

## TUESDAY

I fear I am not going to like Chicago, even for 24 hours. At the airport last night there was a man with a sign reading "Soviets and Liberals Spread AIDS". Next to him was another sign saying that this airport does not necessarily agree with all signs freely displayed here under the Constitution. Especially, presumably, the one saying that there are cabs readily available downstairs. I am, as you know, not one to complain, and in what this country is now pleased to call "one on one human terms" I have never been so well looked-after as by a ravishing American publicist who wisely and rightly treats all authors as amiable idiots, incapable of getting from a ticket desk to an aeroplane without several highly trained minders in attendance.

But the time has, I fear, come to question the notion of Great American Efficiency. Not one of the twenty or so planes I have caught in the last ten days has left or arrived within fifteen minutes of accuracy, a situation little helped by the fact that all American cities seem to have time zones of their own. When, moreover, they then decide to put clocks back for the winter while you are between zones, you may as well go home. California is always three hours away from where you want it to be. You can either phone people there before they have arrived at the studio, while they are out to lunch or after they have gone home. If this is the greatest nation on earth, surely they could get together round a table and decide what time it is?

## WEDNESDAY

Meanwhile, however, they have managed to get telephones into planes. True, it costs seven dollars a minute to ring the earth below you, but the prestige value of phoning from your flight is reckoned to be worth it. While I was flying over the entire Mid-West from Chicago to Los Angeles, it occurred to me that I know no one down there well enough to give them an air-call. Across three thousand miles, this is a chastening thought.

Once arrived in Los Angeles, I am told to prepare for an early breakfast show hosted by the former Mrs John de Lorean. Later, the producer phones back to regret that my interviewer will not be the former Mrs de Lorean after all, as she is due to appear in court in New Jersey. I fall asleep reflecting that a nation where they actually arrest people for hosting breakfast television shows can't be all bad.

## THURSDAY

It transpires, however, that the former Mrs de Lorean is only in court for a child custody hearing. I am instead interviewed by the ex-wife of a local baseball hero. She hasn't read the book either. Probably nor has he, but ex-wives seem to be very big on breakfast shows here this week.

In one of the commercial breaks I notice Fred Astaire and Gene Kelly doing an airline commercial without moving any one of their four feet. Truly Hollywood is no more.

## FRIDAY

In fourteen days I have appeared on just over twenty-five radio and television shows, given several interviews for press and broadcast over telephones to people in Nebraska who might, for all I know, merely have left their answering machines programmed with the occasional question, signed books in every shop I passed so they couldn't then be returned, and grinned inanely from behind the driving wheel of a Southend bus unaccountably parked in downtown San Francisco. It goes with the territory. I hope it also sells books: I should like to be asked back, if only to discover where I have been this past fortnight.

After a final weekend in New York I caught the plane home, venturing for the first time into an airport without any of the minders. It was only halfway across the Atlantic that I realised I had left all my luggage in a neat pile just by the door of the souvenir shop. ❧

---

# Conservative Central Office

## FILTH & VIOLENCE NEWS No.8

Hallo.
Here is this week's update on the list of things responsible for the disgusting tide of everything all round us since 1949. Please note that in Filth & Violence News No. 7, *jokey shorts* should have read *jockey shorts.* We are, however, dealing with jokey shorts in Filth & Violence News No. 9, currently in preparation, under **Peephole Bra Horror**, paragraph 18, subsection 14/a/673. Please amend your file copies accordingly.

*Laura Norder*
pp Norman Tebbit

■ ■ ■ ■ ■ ■ ■ ■ ■ ■ ■ ■ ■ ■ ■

1. **Publication of *Forever Amber***
2. **Failure to index-link £5 bus-spitting penalty**
3. **Abolition of radio announcers' tuxedos**
4. **Introduction of piña colada**
5. **Disappearance of side saddles**
6. **Bidets**
7. **Cork tips**
8. **Aerosol paint**
9. ***T\*t Bits***
10. **Uncontrolled spread of free NHS penicillin**

Thank you.

# TELEVISION

**THE SOUTH BANK SHOW** THE REAL COTTON CLUB

**HOTEL DU LAC** ANNA MASSEY *as Edith Hope* DENHOLM ELLIOTT *as Philip Neville*

# John Jensen

**EVERYBODY SING JUDY GARLAND**

**A BETTER CLASS OF PERSON**   EILEEN ATKINS *as Nellie Beatrice Osborne*   GARY CAPELIN *as Younger John*

THREE WOMEN IN A BOAT
The embarkation — Libby puts everything in dustbin bags — Mandy calls to mind the Yom Kippur war — Merrily sneezes thrice

The Fearless

The Flag of Convenience

The synthesis of Form and Function

The Ducks

WE took a paperback Jerome K. Jerome with us, for inspiration. To give us some sort of alternative view of the whole sordid adventure. . .

*It was a glorious morning, late spring or early summer, as you care to take it, when the dainty sheen of grass and leaf is blushing to a deeper green; and the year seems like a fair young maid, trembling with strange, wakening pulses on the brink of womanhood. . .*

It was, as a matter of fact, a cold, grey, inglorious Saturday which saw three travellers – all well over the brink of womanhood and down the other side – assemble doggedly beside the River Thames. The legend of *Three Men In A Boat* has long haunted the English summer; young men, periodically, set out three-at-a-time in double-sculling skiffs to retrace the innocently rollicking path of George and Harris and J.K.J. Sometimes they do it for television, making much of their big manly blazers, deep laughs, sweaty backs and fancy feathering of the oars (to prove they were at Trinity, not the LSE); sometimes they do it for private satisfaction. Yet another trio of wistful neo-Victorians shot under Cookham bridge even as we watched, their bodies between their knees. Women were deemed suitable in 1889 only to shriek and giggle and tangle up the tow-lines in their frilly skirts; an undemanding brief. But, in one of those moments of inspiration which come to editors in between taking the big cigar out of their mouths and putting it back in again, the idea had sprung full-fledged

"What — only borscht, cream, chives, lobster and chicken mayonnaise, chocolate mousse, and absolutely nothing to propitiate swans?"

to Coren's master brain. "Put three *women* in a boat! Terrific!"

So he was standing now, with a look of shifty alarm, watching the fragile boat unloaded from a trolley. My George and my Harris were beside him: Merrily Harpur, an artistic gamefisherwoman with wild, pale eyes and a brisk motherly way with wildlife ("Mayfly, dearest, *do* move over, I need that seat now") and Mandy Rice-Davies. The latter, at that moment, was gazing wryly downstream towards Cliveden House, former home of sundry Astors and the scene, two decades ago, of those entertainments which led John Profumo to the obscurity of Good Works, and Mandy to lasting fame for cheeking the judge from the witness-box. "An *unlikely* trio" typed someone up at the *Daily Mail,* ruefully pushing aside his Thesaurus and his *Big Boy's Book of Libel Law*; but we saw nothing unlikely about it. When you are planning to sit in a small, tippy, roofless boat and tow thirteen miles upstream, pursued by a boatful of grinning oafs from *Breakfast Time,* you do well to choose your companions carefully. And Mandy, on one previous meeting, had struck me forcibly as a girl to go up the Amazon with. She combines the serpentine wisdom of forty years' ritzy survival with the effortless, unpretending charm of the Worst Girl In The School. And she has been out East of Suez and seen a thing or two, founded an Israeli glossy magazine, run fashion shows in the desert during the Yom Kippur War, written one-and-three-quarter books, toured to wide acclaim in a Stoppard, and is currently bringing the house down as Helga the Wronged Wife in another touring farce. My faith in the girl was confirmed by the way she turned now from her reverie, politely, to answer some query on her present occupation. "Oh," she said casually, "I'll be in *A Bedful Of Foreigners* in Wolverhampton on Monday." Not a smirk, not a scowl. "By gum," breathed Coren, in the background. "Now that's a girl who'll pull a good oar!"

The *Breakfast Time* crew, rushed out expensively to Cookham on the promise of a story consisting entirely of monosyllables (like "three" and "boat") which would not give their latest autocuties too much trouble to introduce, began filming Mandy's blonde curls, frilly blouse, and designer-faded jeans with enthusiam. Harpur and I hovered in thankful anonymity behind, she darkly sinister in black shades and a Pembroke College blazer four sizes too big, I solid and reliably boaty in a quilted jacket and mouldy sun-hat. A dreadful apparition in a pastel-striped blazer and BBC Wardrobe boater appeared, and began chirruping into his microphone. Grey clouds thickened overhead, and a keen chill wind whistled over the troubled waters. A headwind, to us. "Sure you can row

uptide?" asked a yard man. "Fastest current I seen for a bit, running now." Grimly, we stuffed sleeping-bags into dustbin liners and tried to stow Mandy's Gucci hold-all. The boat – a long, thin, delicate varnished shell – shuddered, tipped, and took aboard a gallon of icy water as Harpur landed heavily in the bow. "Christ," muttered the boatyard man, shielding his eyes. "All ready, girls?" beamed Mister Breakfast Time, as the stuffed Alsatian fell off its cute perch on the camping-hoops and struck me in the eye (one small improvement womankind made on Jerome K. was a pee-free dog). Mandy descended, catlike, into the stern, and drew up her white golfing shoes in resigned horror at the slopping of water around the picnic-hamper. Drops of rain began to fall, and the empty river swirled grimly beneath us, hell-bent for Cookham weir. I took both oars, determined to sell my life dearly; Mandy looked curiously at the steering-lines, with the air of a girl who had pulled herself out of tight corners by frailer strings than these. "I didn't mean it to be like this," muttered Coren. "I meant there to be crowds, and sunshine, and all the river life. . . people. . . blazers. . ." He opened a bottle of our champagne with an air of desperate festivity, and drank from it.

*"Right it is,"* we answered; and with Harris at the sculls and I at the tiller-lines, and Montmorency, unhappy and deeply suspicious, in the prow, out we shot onto the waters which, for a fortnight, were to be our home.

Well, not a fortnight. Couple of days, more like; just as far as Henley. We shot

"So this is hay fever!"

onto the waters all right, though. Eighty-year-old skiffs are made to shoot along like varnished glittering fishes, for a tenth of the effort that moves a great white slab of motorboat. With a rather eccentric motion, caused by my having learned rowing in rubber dinghies on the sea (short, deep strokes) and Merrily Harpur having learned her technique by standing under a big hat at Henley (long, languorous river-strokes), we nonetheless made impressive speed. And gleams of sunshine began to appear; and our surroundings to seem more benevolent. And, "Oh, darling coot!" cried Harpur ecstatically, missing a stroke. On this dull, forbidding Bank Holiday the river life was all feathered; and none the worse for that. "Dear ducks, look at them. Having a gang-bang."

Jerome, gentle man, had an uncharacteristically savage view of the selfish riverside landowners who placed forbidding notice-boards on their land. The feeling returned, as fresh as he had known it, to haunt us in turn. NO MOORING. . . NO LANDING. . .STRICTLY PRIVATE decorated the banks; huge slavering Rottweilers ran down to the waterside as we slipped inoffensively under the bank to keep out of the tide. We received a cold glance from a middle-aged woman apparently gardening in a Judge's full-bottomed wig. Merrily thought it might have been curlers, but Mandy and I were pretty sure. Thames Valley richies may have their little quirks, surely; if the wife of some unerotic arms-dealer chooses to boost her thrill-quotient by putting on the black cap every time she throttles a slug, who are we to condemn?

We rowed on, Mandy displaying an unexpected neatness of stroke on no experience. Faint pains began to shoot along forgotten ligaments, but rowing is not a bad life: no responsibilities for steering, no need to look out, just keep the oar moving. Extraordinary follies reared on the bank: gigantic thatched cottages, half-timbered bungalows. As the sun warmed, a few boats began to move; bottle-nosed persons in small cruise liners puttered past, their foredecks festooned with illicit women. After two hours, stiffening, we stopped for lunch. 'It's a good thing we're English," said Mandy, sitting in a goose-turd, and critically extracting a lump of chèvre and a digestive biscuit from the damp hamper. We opened another bottle of pink champagne, and gazed hopefully along the meagrely-forested bank for a convenience. Not very hopefully.

Did you know that if you are a woman, and you squat discreetly behind a bush, that at the critical moment there will be a burst of wild laughter from some passing boat? Wild laughter unconnected, of course, with any gap in the vegetation, for what Briton would dream of guffawing at

Oh look there's a great crested grebe

"Were I crested and not cloven, you had not treated me thus."

that's quite enough of that, Mandy.

such a discovery? But still. . .

It helps if you are slightly drunk. We stepped smartly back into the good ship *Jezebel,* and proceeded at a steady 2 mph over the rushing tide. Gradually we became Left-wing; moving along at water-level between towering white gin-palaces, propelling yourself by the sweat of your back past the monstrous follies of wealth, has a radicalising effect. Mandy's chic waterproof ski-top (the only short-sleeved raincoat on the Thames) took on a raffish, *sans culotte* aspect, and Harpur's red-and-white spotted neckerchief and misshapen roll-up cigarettes gave an authentic air of jacquerie. For who says that Britain has no Disneyland? The Thames banks, running down from Marlow lock, are Disneyland absolute. We sweated past concrete castles, past giant Venetian palazzos made of half-logs, past Islamic minarets and pink thatch and – perched on a steep bank – an actual half-timbered swimming-pool. As the heat grew, the stream against us increased, and the sweat ran into our eyes, it was like rowing through someone's disordered fantasy. The cooling bottle was passed from hand to hand. "Motorboats!" cried Harpur, waving a disintegrating fag. "What do they know of Life?" We had been bidden to tea at 3.30 at the Compleat Angler. We rowed with silver teapots hovering in front of us, like a mirage.

With beginners' luck, we shot into Marlow lock to fill the last long, thin space beside the motorboats. Unimpressed, the lock-keeper looked down half-a-mile at our dishevelled shapes. "Got a current licence?" he snarled, as if suspecting it of having elapsed in 1949. We rose unsteadily on the tide, muttering about civil liberties. Seeing us closer, at his feet, he relented. "You picked a fine day to try and row upstream, anyway," he said, walking back to his machinery. "Lot o'current. Mind the weir." We edged out.

"The WEIR!" shrieked Harpur, suddenly noticing it. Marlow weir is a vast, curving, sluicing Niagara: a hole in the world. The Compleat Angler is just next to it. To bring a skiff alongside you have to ship your cumbrous inside oar, by taking it completely out of the rowlock. To put it in again for propulsion takes a moment or two; should the official bank-grabber fail to make contact, or end up with a handful of grass as the bow bounces off, you have rather less than two moments before the weir gets you. One go at this was enough. We escaped, and circled under the bridge for a moment, undecided. The man at Marlow Rowing Club, his moustache a-quiver, gave a welcoming hail: "YOU CAN'T MOOR 'ERE, IT'S PRIVATE." "You'd think" said Merrily, quivering, "that they'd have more chivalry at a *rowing club* when they see women in trouble." Sudden female machismo gripped me, rowing wildly: "WE ARE NOT IN TROU-

BLE," I shrieked. "WE ARE PERFECTLY ALL RIGHT!" "We have had a Brush With Death," said Mandy, firmly. Finally, we tied up to Marlow Rowing Club after all. Moustache even took our rope, drawn by curiosity. "Yer own boat, is it?" No, we said evasively, "just delivering it to Henley." "Ah, sort of freelance boat-deliverers, are you? Move a few eights upriver for us, would you?" Yes, yes, anything. We tottered damply across to the hotel ("once frequented by famous *Punch* Artist Phil May" – Merrily was moderately thrilled) and squelched thankfully up to the tasteful pink marblette powder-room.

In the end, we were so early that the *Mail* photographer, who alone had caught up with us, had to pay £24 for our plateful of scones and strawberry tarts. We ate it, in temporary truce with capitalism. Then two bin-bags, suspiciously stuffed, floated by. "Is that our sleeping-bags?" asked Mandy, rather quietly. "Oh God." We watched, fascinated. Suddenly the church bells opposite pealed out triumphantly. Revolu-

'Feather your bottles.'

tionary paranoia set in again. "They wouldn't", I said shakily, "ring the church bells just because our sleeping-bags had gone over the weir, would they? They don't hate us that much, even in Marlow, do they?"

It was, in the event, a wedding, and someone else's bundles adrift; but we felt a pressing need to row clear of the place. We did a bit of fancy feathering, to impress Moustache. Easy.

We had intended to capture a nice young man off some passing boat, and ask him to share our al fresco dinner, and sit afterwards under the stars, discoursing of life and philosophy until:

. . .*Night, like some great loving mother, gently lays her hand upon our fevered head, and turns our little tear-stained face up to hers and smiles, and though she does not speak, we know what she would say, and lay our hot flushed cheek against her bosom. . .*

But the only likely-looking boat we passed had a man on board reading *Exchange and Mart,* in the company of a caged canary; and though he did not speak, we knew what he would say, and thought better of it.

It was agreed, regrettably, that since Jerome K. had slept in the boat, under the rotting canvas and wobbling hoops, I should do likewise; leaving Mandy and Merrily to occupy the pup-tent on the bank. Two dozen large heifers jostled and butted and trod in the supper as we erected this edifice by a secluded grove of young oaks opposite Medmenham Abbey; they plopped dung attractively next to our box of Prue Leith Chicken 'n' Lobster mayonnaise, trod on the chives for the bortsch, and urinated copiously and with pleasure around the bivouac. "I always knew," said Mandy thoughtfully, "that I wouldn't like camping. I have this innate instinct not to be unhappy." Harpur strove to spread a more positive attitude ("Oh look, we're moored to a rose-bush") while I baled a few more gallons of water from my bedroom-designate. The *Mail* photographer, a remarkable sleuth, loomed among the heifers and hopefully, we invited him to dinner. But after a quick look at the dripping oaks, the steaming cow-pats, the sullen, watchful band of Canada Geese and the wild fluttering of Merrily's vast blazer-sleeves as she hurled rice salad to some darling ducks, he followed the immemorial example of his kind, made his excuses, and left.

Even Harpur, as dusk fell, grew tart and morose. "Did you know that she-ducks often drown because of the weight of males on top of them trying to mate? Nature is an absolute washout, in my view." "Rousseau," said Mandy, "used to send his laundry home to his Mum."

As to the succeeding night, let other pens dwell on guilt and misery. What thoughts passed through my head about Coren, about his narrow bloody sleeping-bag, about Jerome and English sentimentality and permeable canvas roofs, I will not enumerate. I will only observe that when,

"Look away!"

with aching and horribly pinioned arms, you have lain for two hours sleepless between plank and plank, you are actually quite glad of the diversion of a couple of vast Canada Geese bursting into your dim canvas tunnel, all wet skinny feet and hysterical wings. It is, at least, company.

At 3.30 the storm came. Claps of apocalyptic thunder; then lightning illumined the sodden green tunnel, etching the stark ribs of the ancient skiff. Some girlish giggling was heard from the tent, and the low comforting monotone of Merrily telling Mandy that oak groves were always the first to be hit by lightning.

We must all have slept, then. On waking, we had between us aged some 45 years. Merrily began stiffly to operate her Patent Volcano Kettle with an old *Guardian*. Mandy commenced her toilette with an

"Could you atomise enough into the kettle for us to have tea?"

Evian vaporizer and a pot of cream, while I poured Perrier water on my hat and scrubbed briefly at my ruined features.

It was, however a beautiful day. And we saw a kingfisher as we drifted up to Hambleden Lock, and drank another bottle of the pink and bubbly in it, toasting the curious spectators as the swirling water threatened our scalloped, varnished, impossibly elegant Edwardian flanks. Life was good, at such moments.

So it would seem unnecessary to dwell too much on the later spectacle of Mandy Rice-Davies, urbane *femme du monde,* pathetically cadging cigarettes from strangers on the towpath while the rain ran in rivers down her slender neck; uncharitable to remark on the feeling which arose when Harpur decided on some fancy steering during a second monsoon downpour on the approach to Henley Bridge ("I wanted to see if we could *fit* through there"). I would prefer to think more of the high times than of the slow, sodden collapse of the ill-tied canvas as we lurched up to Hobbs' boat pontoons.

We half-ran up the soaking street towards the Angel for sustenance, Mandy dragging on her first cigarette since dawn.

"I have *never*", she said in mild outrage, "smoked in the street in my life. Never." And I felt a small pang of guilt at having reduced her to this.

But when the last morsel of food was shovelled in by six eager, blistered hands, and six sodden feet began to steam gratefully in the hotel's heat, Mandy stretched, and smiled contentedly, and flicked a lock of wet blonde hair from her eyes. "I feel," she announced, "very well indeed."

Well, she would, wouldn't she?

# MIX, DISSOLVE, FADE

## An Imperfect Memoir of Great Movie Moments

The charming scene from *Guess Who's Coming To Dinner?* in which Sydney Poitier entertains Spencer Tracy and Katharine Hepburn with *Mah Ole Kentucky Home* in return for bus-fare.

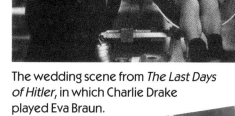

The wedding scene from *The Last Days of Hitler*, in which Charlie Drake played Eva Braun.

An out-take from *Yankee Doodle Dandy*. James Cagney has just attempted to tap-dance down the frozen steps of the Capitol. The man standing over him is Busby Berkeley.

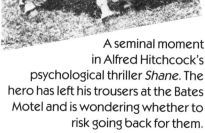

A seminal moment in Alfred Hitchcock's psychological thriller *Shane*. The hero has left his trousers at the Bates Motel and is wondering whether to risk going back for them.

The taut moment from *Citizen Kane* where the proprietor persuades the editor to go to Wapping. It took Alan Ladd (*left*) four hours to put on his make-up.

The rush hour scene on Pangbourne Station, from *Brief Encounter*. The woman looking for Frankie Howerd is Vivien Fuchs, which probably accounts for the film's being banned in Lancashire. ▼

A characteristically horrific yet at the same time poignant moment from *The Bride of Frankenstein*. Doctor Frankenstein, having got the monster upright for the first time, realises that Igor did not bring matching legs. ▼

The heartstring-tugging moment from that archetypal lost-dog movie, *Lassie Come Home*, when Gary Cooper and his two buddies realise they're on the right track.

The now historical shot from *The Trial of Oscar Wilde*, capturing the true-life shock in the studio when it simultaneously dawned on Oscar that the person playing Bosie was not in fact a man called Sid Charisse, and on Bosie that the person playing Oscar was not in fact a woman called Jean Kelly. Neither star ever fully recovered.

The classic final shot from *A Tale of Two Cities*, when Sydney Carton, granted one last request, suggests they hang Lucie Manette instead.

The famous closing shot from *Some Like it Hot*, Clark Gable, finally forced to reveal that he is not in fact a girl, evokes from Claudette Colbert the immortal response: "Frankly, my dear, I don't give a damn!"

"This parrot is no more! It has joined the heavenly choir eternal. It is an ex-parrot!" The classic sketch from *And Now For Something Completely Different*, with (l to r) Mo, Larry, Curly and Gummo.

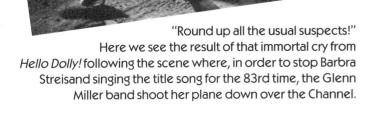

"Round up all the usual suspects!" Here we see the result of that immortal cry from *Hello Dolly!* following the scene where, in order to stop Barbra Streisand singing the title song for the 83rd time, the Glenn Miller band shoot her plane down over the Channel.

The signing of the peace treaty, from *Gandhi*. The man behind Dooley Wilson's right hand is George Formby.

# HEAVY VETTING
## HOLTE

*"I have to go out for a few minutes, so have a chocky-drop while you're waiting."*

*"My tranquilliser-dart gun please, Miss Delabole."*

"You're right, the left one could do with being tuned up a bit."

"And about time, too!"

"The wing is definitely mended, Miss Crabtree – you really should release him, you know."

"A lot of things fall out of crates of bananas. But I can assure you that is not a tarantula."

"Now then, medication for your stick-insect … Dear me, what is the matter with this pencil?"

# Seasonally Adjusted

"AS the pale apple blossom fluttered in the warm spring wind, Jonathan closed his eyes against the sun; he could still see, as if in a picture, the duck fussily trundling her ducklings towards the river..."

If you read this sort of stuff in a spring magazine, the only thing you know for sure is that the man writing it was sitting a foot away from an electric fire with newspaper in his boots, wondering whether he could bring himself to leave it for long enough to get himself a hot toddy. Magazines go to press so far ahead that those who write for them lead permanently skewed lives, trying to project themselves into an almost unbelievable future.

The importance of St Valentine's Day can be attributed entirely to this, since no one in October can think what on earth else might be happening in mid-February; ditto simnel cakes, which no one wants to make or ever has wanted to make, but whose seasonality can be calculated in advance. And I suspect that the whole "Now is the time to ..." school-of-gardening writing stems from the same thing. If a gardening writer was putting his words together within a few days of all these actions he is recommending, he couldn't make stupid suggestions like pricking the lawn all over with a fork, tying up straggling climbers or re-hoeing the edges of the grass *again*; he'd know perfectly well his audience would far rather play golf or go for a walk. But sitting there in November, he can be

as unrealistic as he pleases – or even indulge in a few of those hysteria-inducing phrases like, "On ground which has been fully prepared in the autumn –". There's a theory that some people never start gardening at all, because it is *never* the time to begin: there's always something you ought to have done already.

Working so far ahead has an odd effect on you; because if you have projected yourself mentally into, say, the middle of next autumn, a part of you thinks that's what the date actually *is*, and then, suddenly, you have all those happy summer months still ahead. Only trouble is, the magazines rather tend to pay you in the same way – in the autumn. A friend of mine used to say the ideal would be to work on an annual and be paid daily.

Writers are not the only people who have to live like this. Toy-makers start worrying about next Christmas's voice-activated super-electronic robot teddy bear that wets itself and cries "Maaa!", sometime around the beginning of February. November sees urban salesmen of things like barometers and battery refrigerators unwillingly climbing into sailing boots and trying to look nautical at the Southampton boat show in the autumnal sleet. The great British public, which is mad, starts to plan its summer holiday before it has barely finished belching over its Christmas turkey, perhaps on the grounds that since the best part of a holiday is usually looking forward to it, they may as well

have as many months of that as they can.

That means, of course, that those who produce the travel brochures have to start planning which resorts to photograph in the summer sun somewhere back in March, for printing in December for the following summer. And as for the men who sell the turkeys, they're probably slitting their throats at this moment, unless, for once, they've calculated that it will cost more to freeze them than feed them.

At least you can assume that the demand for turkeys will be much the same from one year to the next; not all trades that have to plan ahead are so lucky. Each year, as we know, there's a man who tots up the lists of names in *The Times* births column, and calculates which ones are most popular. Donald Carroll was once told to go and find out the commonest names among those deeply unsmart people who don't put announcements in *The Times*, or indeed anywhere else – a tall order. He hit on the brilliant idea of digging out a man who makes named bracelets to sell in seaside resorts, and he found that he knew by the end of the previous December exactly how many Traceys and Sharons and Garys he had to cater for. "Isn't there any name that might be in *The Times* list, and yours too?" Carroll wondered. "No," said the bloke. "Well, maybe Kathryn – but it would *have* to be with a 'y'."

The worst trade of all for getting ahead of itself is, of course, the dress trade. It is not so bad

*"You seem to be doing pretty well yourself, Pete."*

when the models have to ankle their way along a catwalk in Bermuda shorts and swimsuits when it's minus 10°C outside, because they can usually manage to heat the little salons up like saunas; but in July, or earlier, the wretched girls have to pile on the layers of expensive wool, cuddle seductively into the collars of mink coats and stare arrogantly out from hoods of sable, when the temperature is in the nineties; it is only by sheer will-power that they keep their make-up from sliding off their faces.

The ancillary trades follow suit; the shoe people and the cosmetics people, who in turn have to get their stuff into magazines with long lead-times ... this is where we came in. Someone once overheard the Beauty Editor of *Harper's* saying to the Beauty Editor of *Vogue*: "What is your autumn face to be?" and get the answer, "My dear, I haven't even done my *spring* face yet."

That other people should work at the wrong time of year, to make things happen for the rest of us at the right time of year, is sensible; jolly decent of them, indeed. What is absurd is when they start wanting us to act like that too, buying summer dresses in January, stocking up on woollens in the summer. It means that if you want to choose your holiday clothes when you're actually in the run-up to your holiday, you probably can't; I don't know if they've ever realised that the reason they sell so much stuff in the end-of-season sales is that for most of us the season's only just beginning anyway.

I have never actually met this woman on whom the dress trade's expectations are based: she who buys all her spring clothes in February and is fully equipped for winter before the rest of us have got the sand out of our espadrilles. If she exists at all, she must come into the same category as the woman who buys next year's Christmas cards in the January sales (and doesn't then lose them for ever, as I did the one time I tried it).

But I do know there are people like this, living in places such as Douchebag, Montana or Calgary, Australia; because they actually post surface mail by the recommended date, and their Christmas cards invariably arrive on November 1. The hazard of the whole thing is that what starts as an attempt to get everything set up by the right time, ends with you getting more and more out of synchronisation with the real calendar.

I have a friend who does the laundry on Sunday night, so as to be ahead of herself for Monday morning. She has to take a stern grip on herself to let it go at that, lest she become like her mother, who would do it on Sunday morning to be ahead of herself for Sunday evening, and then started doing it on Saturday ... I don't know if she ever worked back far enough to find herself doing it on Monday again.

But I suspect that the entire art of bottling and freezing and preserving is in reality only an attempt to get ahead of yourself like this, to stockpile your own labour, to be one up on the clock and the calendar, like the toy-makers and the magazines; and that the disease is even more prevalent than we think. Why else would the Bank of England write, as I've been reliably informed they used to do, the minutes of important meetings before they had actually taken place? ☙

"Well, it's either this or darts and I can't add up."

"He asks why 'Mungo' has gone out of fashion as a Christian name ..."

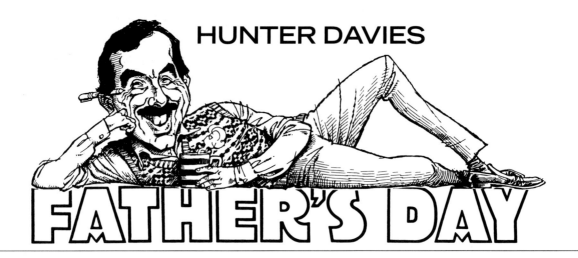

# HUNTER DAVIES

# FATHER'S DAY

**T**HIS is the week in the year I really hate. Getting ready for the orf. Oh it's OK for wage slaves, getting paid to go on their hols. They can start skiving and trying on their sun-tan weeks before they go. We people who live on our wits. Correction. We people who live on our wrists.

Look at this, have you ever seen veins this size before. I have done so much typing this last week that it looks as if caterpillars are crawling all over my right hand. I've done 100 pages of a book this week and I'm in absolute agony. I know it's all my own fault. If only I had learned to type properly I wouldn't get all these pains, but it's too late now to be retrained.

I went out to pick up the tortoise, cos I caught sight of the little bugger eating my geraniums again, and I couldn't lift it, not with my right hand anyway. Going to the lavatory is so awkward because I have to pull the chain with my left hand. Can typing count as an industrial injury?

And as for making the cocoa, ye gods, I have to give up. Yes, I know it's gross having cocoa at this time of year, but I've been working so late and my head is so full of rubbish that I have to do something aforebed. I hate making cocoa anyway. Why haven't they discovered stuff that mixes easily. It's called hot chocolate. Yuck. No one drinks that stuff, do they. Teeth rotter. Cocoa is the boys, but I do wish it hadn't got to be beaten to death before you can pour the milk in. All week I've been producing thin brown stuff with cannon balls floating on top. Her Upstairs won't ever drink it.

I got these new pain killers for my jaw yesterday, just aspirins I shouldn't wonder, but I do like new medicines. I was walking back across the Heath and could feel the odd twinge so I thought I'll just swallow a couple now, but I couldn't get the rotten top off the little plastic container.

It said line the arrows up, which I did eventually, managing to work out the complicated instruction and realise which arrows they meant. One on the top. One on the container. I'm not that stupid. But I still couldn't do it.

I tried it clockwise and anticlockwise. I used my teeth, banged it on the ground, stood on it, and still it wouldn't move. I didn't go completely bonkers, the way Jake once did when he couldn't get a punctured tyre off his bike. He got himself in such a rage that he *ate* it. Honestly, he started chewing the tyre, till at last the whole thing came apart.

It's this new child-proof system, so kids don't open all your pills. Child proof. Human bloody proof. I was in a fury, which of course didn't help my jaw pains, so I walked all the way back to the chemist. This chit of a girl, about three feet high, opened it in seconds. I felt like the seven stone weakling on the beach.

Then this morning at Waitrose I had to hump all the shopping myself, despite my poorly state, my weak wrists, my heavy week, all because, well it was a bit silly. She's still not talking to me.

We have this system, right, whereby I do the boring physical work and she goes through the check-out ahead of me, carefully putting all the stuff in appropriate boxes. Frozen together, Grandma's stuff together, fresh in one box, store cupboard the next, oh she's terribly together.

I was waiting for her, as we always do, having got the really vital stuff, the wine. She had filled one trolley and was almost finished the second, as per usual. I could see an empty check-out ahead, with the good girl on it, not that one who takes for ever and will make a production number out of the fact that the pineapple has not got a price on, ringing her bell and holding it up as if she's caught us red handed. The Old Trout will be here any moment, I thought. I'll really be a good help for once and wheel the trolley through and get started.

Guess what. I wheeled someone else's trolley. I was sure it was my wife's, cos it looked the sort of expensive stuff she buys. I could have sworn I saw her park it there. God, my eyes are going as well as my wrist. I was halfway through paying for it when my wife arrived, plus the real owner to find someone had pinched her stuff. What a palaver, sorting all that lot out.

So it's been a rotten old week. But the panic has not just been for my sake, trying to get ahead. I've also had the rest of the family to think about. Ho yus.

For a start, Caitlin is going orf as well. All on her own to California. Yup, her year at Davis University starts in September, so I've been trying to help her with money and plane tickets and insurance. We won't be seeing her for a whole year. Will we recognise her when she returns. It will be the longest ever she has been away from the bosom of the family. She's promised to ring, but I'm not too thrilled at the thought of that. Reverse charges – sorry, call collect – costs a fortune.

Then there's Jake's arrangements. My head is aching already. He's still in Florence, at the last call collect, but then he's going to visit someone in the south of Italy, who might not be in when he arrives, he must be potty, so we don't know yet if he'll arrive back in the UK while we are still here. He hasn't had a reading list yet from his college, for when he starts

*"Wasn't it you who always said, 'If God had meant us to fly, he would've given us wings'?"*

university in October, and it's my fault of course, stands to reason, I open the post every morning, so I should try harder.

Poor Flora is lumbered with the wrinklies for the summer, though Jake says he'll join us in the Lake District, unless someone answers the door in Sicily. I've promised her I'll try to organise wind surfing lessons for her at Nichol End on Derwentwater. Rash promise, which I know I'll regret, but then I've gone through life with them saying Hunt, you said, oh yes you did, you *promised*.

Then there are the complications about leaving notes and instructions for our family and friends who'll be in this house all summer. My brother doesn't know it yet, but when he comes down from Carlisle for his hols the people next door are having the builders in, underpinning a party wall, and it could be pretty noisy, not to mention crockery falling off the walls and plates crashing on his head. Glad I'll be out of that.

Most of all, folks, and I've left this till the end as I don't want you sobbing all over the cartoons, I'm going into hospital on Monday morning. McLaggan Ward at the Royal Free is going to have the pleasure of Hunt's company. Fingers crossed that I get a single room. They have them, two in each ward, and I know people like Michael Foot usually manage to bag one, but it's just chance really, I mean need. Oh sister, I feel ever so rotten. Feel this wrist. Ever seen veins, etc.

That's the real reason I've been working so hard this week, to get the desks cleared and the old mind emptied and the notes written out, all ready for the op.

I'm not going in for my wrist, though I might just mention it to the consultant, why waste time when I can offer him two jobs for only one bed. It's the old jaw. Same one. The one I've been moaning on about for over a year now.

All the various treatments have failed to clear up the jaw aches and ear aches, so now I'm banking on having two wisdom teeth out. They've shown up on the X-ray, and they could, no promises, nothing is ever guaranteed in medicine, not since they gave up leeches, they could be the cause of all my problems.

Jake had the self same operation last year, in the same ward, and he looked hellish afterwards. And he was only eighteen. How's an old feller like me going to survive. The doc says three days in altogether, then allow ten days to recover.

Every neighbour who's had wisdom teeth out has been telling me what agony it is, great news, thanks, kind of you to come round, I feel better already, close the door when you crawl back into your hole.

So there will be silence here for the next six weeks, a very small blank in the margins of your lives. Cos once I do get out from the surgeon's clutches, and I've counted everything, then we'll be going orf at long last on our summer hols.

By September, Caitlin should be safely installed in the States. Flora will have become a Second Year at her comprehensive. Gawd, it seems only yesterday she was in the nursery class. And Jake will be about to become an undergrad, what what. As for me, I'm hoping the caterpillars will have crawled off my wrist by September. See you then.

"*You're being unreasonable, Arthur. I took the blame for our last three rows. It's your turn.*"

"*But you are my best friend. There's no need to sign our names in blood.*"

157

*"I'm none too proud of that one. He thought I was taking his picture."*

# THE FRANGLAIS LIEUTENANT'S WOMAN

## UN NOVEL COMPLET CONDENSÉ ET TRADUIT DE

### L'ORIGINAL DE JEAN FOWLES

LYME Regis est un typical village de fishing sur le South Coast d'Angleterre, une de ces petites villes qui, sur la route à nowhere, n'ont pas été totalement ruinées par le progrès et les juggernauts. Pittoresque, mais business-like, Lyme Regis est toujours un beau petit spot, par exemple, comme une refuge pour un auteur comme moi. Depuis 1867 elle n'a pas beaucoup changée. Si un habitant de Lyme en 1867 fut transporté soudain par time travel en 1986, il dirait: "Pouf! Lyme n'a pas beaucoup changée! Un peu de growth suburbain, peut-être, et ces choses curieuses qu'on appelle saloon cars, mais otherwise c'est pretty much la même."

C'est ici que j'ai écrit mon novel classique, "The Franglais Lieutenant's Woman", et c'est aussi ici que les gens de Hollywood ont choisi pour le filming du major movie du même nom. Vous avez jamais vu les gens de Hollywood en action? C'est fantastique. Ils disent: "Hmm – away avec les pôles de telegraph! Away avec les double lignes jaunes, et les parking meters! Up avec les pseudo-façades Victoriennes! Bring on les stage-coaches et les yokels en smock!" Dans le twinkling d'un oeil, vous avez un fake Lyme Regis. J'aime bien cela. Le mingling de l'illusion et la réalité, c'est mon stock en trade.

Et si vous transporterez l'habitant de 1867 en 1986, il serait quite unaware qu'il était dans un film set. Parce qu'en 1867, il n'y avait pas de film sets. Vous ne savez pas? Eh bien, vous savez maintenant. Parce que mes novels sont pleins de knowledge incidental comme ça. Stick avec moi, et vous allez recevoir quite une éducation.

Où étais-je? Ah, oui. En 1867, à Lyme Regis, Charles et Ernestina prenaient un petit stroll, totalement unaware qu'ils étaient dans un major novel. Charles étaient un des ces Victorian gents qui ont plenty d'argent et plenty de leisure time. Jeune, prepossessing, un bachelor, avec un joli petit sparkle, il n'avait pas précisément un job. Un job pour un gentleman, ce n'était pas nécessaire en 1867. Maintenant, si vous dites: "Je n'ai pas un job," on dit: "Ah, pauvre petit, vous formez partie de l'army des unemployed, personellement je blâme Mrs Thatcher, je vais avoir un petit mot avec Uncle Fred, peut-être a-t-il un opening dans Allied Drinks, etc." Mais en 1867, on disait: "Il n'a pas un job. Il est un gentleman." Intéressant, eh?

Charles était un fanatique des fossils. Oui, avec son petit hammer et son petit fossilbag, il parcourait le landscape de Lyme Regis et les environs pour chercher les relics jurassiques et dévoniens. Un waste de time? Peut-être. Mais il faut se souvenir qu'en 1867 Charles Darwin était hot news. L'évolution, oui ou non? C'était une burning question. Donc, Charles cherchait les fossils, dans l'espoir de dire: "Oui! Darwin est sur le ball*! Ce petit fossil est le proof!" Ou bien: "Darwin est un charlatan, et le Livre de Genesis est le gospel truth."

Charles était aussi good-looking, pas hunky exactement, mais attractif. Un peu comme Robert Redford, peut-être. Of course, dans le film il était joué par Jeremy Irons qui n'est pas truthfully mon exacte idée de Charles, mais je n'avais pas total control sur le casting. Some vous gagnez, some vous perdez…

Et Ernestina était un produit typical de l'epoque de Victoria (1837-1901). Sa fiancée Ernestina était jolie, pert, indépendante, bien eduquée, et quite a catch pour un gentleman comme Charles. Elle tolérait la passion de Charles pour les fossils, et pourquoi pas? Être jaloux des fossils, c'est stupide. Je ne vais pas donner une pleine description d'Ernestina parce que, si vous voulez vraiment savoir, je ne suis pas un dab hand avec l'analysis des femmes. Elles sont un mystery breed pour moi. Fascinant, mais never mind.

So, Charles et Ernestina prenaient un stroll dans Lyme Regis, en 1867. Vous avez la picture? Up le High Street, down le High Street, et puis along la plage, un stroll ordinaire, quoi. Et ils parlaient des choses dont parlent les fiancés.

"Quand nous nous sommes mariés, il faut que j'aie une chambre spéciale pour mes fossils," dit Charles.

"D'accord. Et aussi une chambre spéciale pour les enfants."

"Enfants? Quels enfants? Nous n'avons pas d'enfants…"

"Pas encore, Charles. Mais by et by…"

"Ça sera chic!" s'écria Charles. "Des petits enfants, qui vont m'accompagner sur le fossil-hunt! Oui, beaucoup de petits enfants, pour continuer le good work de fossil-hunting."

Ernestina avait un petit frown sur sa pretty face. Hmm. Fossilhunting était OK comme un hobby, mais il était un peu obsessionel. La palaeontologie n'est pas nécessairement héréditaire, elle pensa. En quoi, elle était wide du mark, parce que le Leakey family d'East Africa a changé la palaeontologie en un family business. Mais, en 1867, c'était difficile à anticiper.

Meanwhile, Charles et Ernestina continuaient leur stroll jusqu'au Cobb. Vous avez vu le film de "The Franglais Lieutenant's Woman"? Le Cobb était un landmark dans ce film. C'est un grand breakwater, ou plutôt un quai, ou peut-être un sea-wall – anyway, c'est une grande construction de rocks et boulders qui est un landmark de Lyme Regis, espécialement après le movie. Je ne sais pas pourquoi il s'appelle le Cobb. Je ne peux pas faire le research de tout, vous savez. Je ne suis pas omniscient.

"Regarde!" dit Charles. "Qui est la femme au bout du Cobb?"

Dans la drizzle, ils pouvaient voir une lone figure, dans un cloak, en position au tip du Cobb. Un peu comme la Statue de Liberté, quoi, ou peut-être comme Jean la Baptiste – solitaire, melancholique, triste, enveloppée dans ce grand cloak.

Ernestina donna un petit shiver. "C'est the Franglais Lieutenant's Woman."

"Come again?" dit Charles.

"C'est une triste histoire," dit Ernestina. "Elle est une countrywoman qui est tombée amoureuse d'un matelot franglais. Last year, il y avait un shipwreck. Le lieutenant a été rescué. Il a eu une affaire avec une pauvre, simple countrywoman. Puis le lieutenant est rentré en France, en disant: 'Attends-moi, honey, je vais revenir avec un ring et une wedding date.' Et maintenant, chaque jour, elle est sur le Cobb, avec les yeux fixés sur le coast-line de France."

En silence, Charles et Ernestina marchaient le long du Cobb. Il était très windy, not to say stormy, not to say tempestueux. La lone figure se tenait là, comme un light-house, ou bien un figure-head, avec le cloak whipping dans le vent. Vous avez vu le film? C'est très dramatique dans le film.

Au bout du Cobb, Charles donna un petit cough. Il ne voulait pas donner un shock à la Franglais Lieutenant's woman. Heuh, heuh, heuh, fit-il. La lone figure ne se tourna pas.

Heugh, heugh, heugh, fit Charles. Même réaction.

"I say!" dit Charles. "Êtes-vous OK?"

La lone figure se tourna. Consternation! Ce n'était pas une jeune femme. C'était un homme, bearded, avec sun-glasses.

"Mon Dieu!" dit Charles. "Vous êtes un homme, bearded, avec sun-glasses. Où est Meryl Streep?"

"En California," dit l'homme. "Je fais le stand-in pour cette scène. Dans un cloak, from behind, qui sait la différence?"

Charles donna un gasp. L'homme était handsome. "Qui êtes-vous?"

"Je suis Chuck Yerbonski, 3ème assistant producteur sur le film. Je suis de la même physique que Meryl Streep, donc un naturel pour le stand-in." Charles donna un second gasp. Chuck Yerbonski était *très* handsome. Sur le spot, il tomba amoureux de ce chunky 3ème assistant producteur du film.

"Charles!" dit Ernestina. "Charles? Charles! CHARLES!"

Il était trop tard. Charles, un jeune gentleman de 1867, était madly in love avec Chuck, un assistant producteur de 1980, avec beaucoup de complications sociales. Mais Charles était blind aux implications. Une belle petite histoire, non?

Venant bientôt à votre neighbourhood screen: "The Franglais Lieutenant's Assistant Producer!" Mind-boggling, hein? Un blending de réalité et illusion? Well, why not?

"Beats *The French Lieutenant's Woman* dans un cocked hat" (*Barry Norman*). Nominé pour 11 Oscars. Don't miss it.

---

*Of course, Charles n'aurait pas dit: "Sur le ball". C'est une expression moderne, une phrase de soccer, datant de 1953.

# Nic

SOHO was very quiet last week. There was hardly a model or pornographic bookshop owner to be seen in the Old Compton Street pub where they gather to compare takings. Ascot was one reason for the empty tables: people were taking a break on their well-gotten gains.

The seven pounds of TNT left in a paper bag in one of the All Live Peep Show Club's viewing booths didn't help the atmosphere much. Fortunately the explosive device failed, like the customers, to perform. But the main reason why heads were being kept down was that the police were making what passes for a dawn swoop; all afternoon, Customs men were paddling about, dealing in that ultimate Soho obscenity: VAT.

Fortunately for taxmen who dislike working overtime, much of the sex industry is financially above board. The Paul Raymond Organisation is so well established that it, unlike, say, Gay Scene of Berwick Street, is actually in the telephone directory. The latest figures declared by the leading purveyor of up-market shows and "adult" magazines are for 1983, when turnover was £9,164,000. The profit after tax was £480,000, which is only slightly more than the amount handed over to the Chairman, Paul Raymond himself: £448,000. You can go to an awful lot of performances of the *Razzle Dazzle Burlesque Show* on that, buy a large number of copies of the gynaecological *Paul Raymond's Model Directory*.

Fiona Richmond, who graduated from a swim-on part in Raymond's underwater show *Pyjama Tops* to the lead in revues and a column in his *Men Only*, said that before she retired for maternity reasons three years ago, her sort of parts brought in rather less than the Chairman's emoluments, between £250 and £300 a week. The chorus of long-legged dancers would be on at least Equity minimum, now between £10,000 and £12,000.

Nude or topless modelling brings in as much in a day as they'd earn from a week's hoofing. The subsistence payments for tours would not, Fiona recalled, cover the rent of the flat back in London and the work was tough; but it did offer newcomers the chance of earning an Equity card, allowing them the opportunity of ultimately being not just unemployed but unemployed *actresses*.

The West End is not in the dreams of the women who take part in the Ann Summers Party Plan. These are like Tupperware parties, except that instead of shifting stocks of useful containers, the hostesses sell peekaboo bras, naughty nighties and assorted sexual aids. Between 6,000 and 8,000 of these gatherings a month, average takings of £120.

Ann Summers also runs sex shops for those who miss her parties, and sells half a million raunchy magazines a month. The turnover for the organisation is £24 million a year but the staff are a bit peekaboo about profits, merely declaring them to be "healthy".

Profits are healthy too in a business whose chief assets are Toni, Dana, Nicolle, Tara, or any other of Anne Robertson's 70-odd lovely ladies, trading in Newcastle, Britain's new stripping capital, up in Tyne and Wear.

## JONATHAN SALE

# ittle Earners: SEX

"They can earn £80 or £100 pounds on Sundays," she explained. "They can do four or five clubs over lunchtime, at £20 a spot, which lasts about eight minutes." Less the cash for the taxi-driver who races them about the city and less Anne's 20% commission. The ads for Smart Stripper Wanted appear in the local Jobcentres. "The pay compares well with Tesco's cheque-out," said John Blackmore, Director of the Newcastle Playhouse who commissioned *Strippers*, the play inspired by the Robertson phenomenon, which has just transferred to the Phoenix in London.

Male strippers don't work on the sabbath, as their female audience is home cooking the lunch, but find work, at the same rates, at "hen parties" on other days of the week; there is even a married couple who both take off their pants for money, on the basis that the family that strips together, kips together. (Unlike Anne Robertson, who boasts that her own husband has never seen her in the nude.)

London has no similar Godmother figure with a monopoly on twanging G-strings, but the gay scene owes a lot to W.A.M., whose Paul Wilde says that 98% of all the capital's gay pubs and clubs deal with his agency. His lads also do private events and sometimes deviate into hen parties.

His "Rough Trade" double act costs £100; 50 quid each, less 10% commission. "Tony Star" charges £100 by himself, "Danny Boy", who has not an Irish but a Red Indian routine, comes at £65 and the leather "Prince Gemini" is £50. "John", who has a "dinner-jacket-type routine", is a bargain at £30.

W.A.M. has a tie-up with Studio One in Coventry and sends its acts to sweep the country on tour. Add an extra 5% commission and have-gay-will-travel expenses.

London girls are less tied up (apart from services to exceptional clients behind very closed doors) than males. "Alex" has two separate agents to bring in work; this she fits around running an import-export agency (no, not white slaves).

"I would say Soho pay is very bad. A couple of years ago I went into a pub in Old Compton Street and someone was saying that her money was good: £2.30 for dancing in front of a mirror. Today it would be up to £6 a turn. Girls in pubs make better money and if you're any good you do stags, at £45 a time."

Some girls, though not Alex, do "blue stags", which require a couple of spots. The first one is pretty rude, the next involves going well beyond the kind of behaviour which would get her nicked by the police. Which reminds her: "Police clubs are the worst, they never have straight stags, always blue." They are a rough bunch – and there is, of course, no one to whom a stripper can complain. Still, some girls do judge it be worth at least £80, possibly £100, an evening, for activities which border on prostitution.

"You'll earn more as a real whore," is the graffiti that feminists splatter over sexy ads. Prostitution is certainly the end of the road down which "glamour" dancers and strippers are pointing. Helen Buckingham is one of those who have been down it. She is in trouble with the Inland Revenue.

Her chosen trade is not, of itself, illegal. Soliciting is, so is living off immoral earnings. Selling a body, assuming it's your own, is not. She set up a campaigning organisation entitled PLAN (Prostitution Laws Are Nonsense – she had an alternative name which spelt out P.U.S.S.Y., but the serious sisters, of whom there are many in the English Collective of Prostitutes, put a stop to that).

If lying on her back is not illegal, she reasoned several years ago, it should be possible to set up earnings in a businesslike way. "Well-wishers advised me to see if the Inland Revenue would tax me, which would have some bearing on the law. We found figures which would boil down to £5,000 a year after expenses."

At first the Revenue looked as if it was going to accept them, then had second thoughts about the implications, then talked about a test case. Her lawyer, according to Helen, failed to pass on the summons to her and so she lost the case by default, leaving the officials' version of the figures to win the day.

While all this was trotting, or dawdling, through the courts, "I put my back into the job and brought a wreck on a Greek Island which would appreciate in value." Unfortunately, this clever form of investment, beyond the jurisdiction of Englishmen in wigs, fell foul of a reluctance on the part of the Greeks to release the money from the sale of the property. Her affair with a Rasputin of a priest, the father of her young child, need not detain us here, beyond noting that it didn't help.

"I have been made bankrupt by the Inland Revenue," she wrote in a letter to Mrs Thatcher, with whom she once had the honour of getting nowhere fast in a radio discussion, "to the tune of £10,000. Approximately half the sum is a claim against the proceeds of prostitution."

The other half, she told me, is a tax on her social security payments. It is news to most of us that SS money is ever taxed, but prostitutes live in a financial no-man's-land, without security, prospects or mortgage.

How much do they earn? The Revenue decided that a fine-looking operator like Helen must be on £20,000 p.a. That doesn't take account of legitimate expenses such as beauty treatment and rent of room, and illegitimate items such as "crate of champagne to police officer for looking the other way," which might seem rather out of place on one's personal Chairman's Statement. It also doesn't take account of the fact the she has not been working, what with PLAN and her child, for some time.

In fact, £800 a week was the most she ever earned, with the average being somewhere between £100 and £150. Some days she could be turfed out of the hotel bar without making contact, other days the phone never rang.

It can look good on paper (not that the girls generally put it down): £100 an hour in a classy brothel (not that there are any really classy joints of the sort for which Helen has tried in vain to attract funding), £1,000 a day. Till the brothel is busted.

The hard core, as it were, of tarts is comparatively small. The majority are "Thatcher's girls", who blame the recession for the need to bring in extra cash at between £15 and £25 a time. £300 a week, say. But of that, £50 can go on the hotel room, and £100 might go on fines. Add in the cash for the babysitter, and all the girls have done is doubled their social security.

One girl reckoned that Monday's cash in hand goes to the landlord, Tuesday's to the police backhanders, Wednesday's to the pimp, Thursday's she had forgotten, and only Friday's was her own. Fortunately Friday means pay day in the straight world and hence more customers about the streets.

Saturday's child, you will recall, works hard for her living.

# MICHAEL BYWATER
# Wordpower

*The fourth supplement to the Oxford English Dictionary is finally complete. But many words have been missed out; for example, these – all of which can be found in the index to any Road Atlas of Britain…*

**ABBOTS LENCH,** *n.* Ancient chant, originally part of exorcism rite, now played on car horns by melodious travelling salesmen. Consists of "Dah-ditty-dum-dum" but omits the final "Dah-dah".

**ADSTOCK,** *n.* The part of a broom, rake or other long-handled implement which makes the long handle fall off.

**ALNMOUTH,** *n.* A paid ideologue or mouthpiece, esp. blustering; e.g., British Telecom spokesman.

**ANSTY,** *adj.* Deliberately nasty and pathologically incompetent. Normally derogatory, except when applied to politicians.

**APSLEY END,** *n.* Upper-class term expressing mild surprise at deviant behaviour, e.g., loss of ski-lift pass, corked wine, fainting Royalty etc.

**ARBORFIELD,** *n.* Where you think you lost the bit you need to connect the circular saw attachment to your Black and Decker but can't find it.

**ARBORFIELD CROSS,** *n.* Revenue derived from selling people a new one of the bit they think they lost in the ARBORFIELD every time they want to connect the circular saw attachment to their Black and Decker.

**ARNCROACH,** *vb.* To sidle up sheepishly to a group of people at a party, having nothing to say, hoping to remain unseen, but anxious not to appear a social outcast.

**AUST,** *n.* The feeling of desperation and rage caused by driving around a motorway service area looking for the lavatory.

**BANKNOCK,** *n.* The sort of businessman who, despite a string of bankruptcies, twelve different overdrafts and top billing on the list of County Court debtors, nevertheless contrives to have a platinum American Express card, a gold Rolex and an Aston Martin.

**BEBSIDE,** *n (sci.).* The conceptual space between your bed and your night table, where you put your book and it isn't there in the morning.

**BECCLES,** *n.* Round glasses with thick grimy lenses and one arm held on with Elastoplast, normally worn by computer programmers.

**BEDLINOG,** *n.* Special mug for hot milky nightcaps, designed to deposit a sticky ring on the night table. When you pick up the BEDLINOG it suddenly comes unstuck, tipping its contents into the BEBSIDE (q.v.) N.B. BEDLINOG contents are the only things which will still be in the BEBSIDE in the morning; more so, if anything.

**BLACK NOTLEY,** *n.* Brooding anger caused by spending half an hour trying to get at a particular bogey, eventually bringing on a nosebleed just as it's time to go out to dinner, but still not finding the bogey you were looking for.

**BOTOLPHS,** *n.* The rubbery things you have to scrape off the inside of a microwave oven after you have tried to boil an egg in it.

**DEMBLEBY,** *v.* To DEMBLEBY is to try and sound orotund and imposing, but to succeed only in sounding like Sir Alastair Burnet.

**FAZAKERLY,** *adj.* Dressed like one's grandfather's social superiors, or A.N. Wilson.

**GRAMPOUND,** *n.* Culinary term describing a coarse and unpalatable mixture with inexplicable bits in. The most notorious GRAMPOUND is muesli.

**GREAT WRATTING,** *n.* Traditional sport of 35-year-old Etonians, consisting of inviting social inferiors for the weekend then goading them until they cry.

**GWESPYR,** *v.* Banking term; attempting to persuade a bank manager that something nice is about to happen when you know that it will not.

**HARDENHUISH,** *n.* Furtive expression on the face of a businessman who is sitting at a table on an Inter-City Train with an unprovoked erection and waiting for it to go down again so that he can get a cup of coffee.

**HARPOLE,** *n.* The bit you are left holding when the ADSTOCK (q.v.) breaks.

**HIGH BORGUE,** *n.* What happens after you have patiently endured a HARDENHUISH (q.v.) only to find that the buffet bar has now closed.

**HUBY,** *n.* A plump pink man in a pub who is invariably cheerful, friendly, diffident and utterly, irrevocably wrong.

**IPSTONES,** *n.* What people who have suddenly gone white and pulled over on to the hard shoulder have heard going KA-TOCK KA-TOCK KA-TOCK KA-TOCK very loudly, but haven't yet realised are just tiny bits of gravel caught in the hubcap.

**KILSPINDIE,** *adj.* Of, or pertaining to, the sort of legs which look very silly with a kilt.

**LAMPLUGH,** *n.* Under EEC regulations, all electrical apparatus must include at least one LAMPLUGH, whose purpose is to give off a worrying smell of hot Bakelite which seems to be coming from somewhere entirely different.

**LICSWM,** *n. (Medical)* The stuff which leaks out of cold sores into your lip so that they can come back again the evening before you have to go on television.

**MARRISTER,** *n.* Someone who habitually says provocative things which are so obviously untrue that someone else is bound to say, "Good God, come off it, you can't really mean that," whereupon the Marrister says, "No I don't, really," and smiles, so that everyone thinks how terribly nice he is.

**MUNDERFIELD STOCKS,** *n.* Investments made for no justifiable reason except that everyone else is doing it, e.g., British Telecom shares.

**NIBLEY,** *n (sci.).* One-tenth of a NIDD (q.v.).

**NIDD,** *n. (sci.).* Unit of measurement too small to be of use.

**NOSS MAYO,** *n.* A b.l.t. sandwich which, instead of toothpicks, is held together by yellowish, specially-congealed mayonnaise.

**ORDIEQUISH,** *n.* The flecks of spittle on a Scottish preacher's lips when he talks about the Sin of Sodom.

**PORTYERROCK,** *n.* An ageing poof with flared trousers and a paisley scarf who hangs around dockside bars trying to pick up sailors but gets hit instead, which is why he has no teeth.

**POTT SHRIGLEY,** *n.* A sort of stew, made by putting underwear in a huge saucepan to boil, then someone else comes in and throws in two pounds of scrag end and an onion.

**QUABBS,** *n.* Small cushions of dough stuffed with radish, parsley and saffron, marinated in porter and deep-fried in RISCA, q.v., which are served with game and left on the side of the plate.

**RANBY,** *adj.* Sexually aroused, but incompetent.

**RISCA,** *n.* Congealed whitish-yellow stuff in a bowl in the fridge which will probably be all right for frying things in. Also onomatopoeia for projectile vomiting, esp. after eating QUABBS (q.v.).

**RUBERY,** *adj.* Applies to the sort of lips which are fat, pink, glossy and writhe constantly, even when the owner is not talking.

**SCRIVELSBY,** *n.* The sort of person who writes down everything you say in a little book without telling you why.

**SHEEPY PARVA,** *n.* The heterosexual equivalent of a PORTYERROCK, q.v.

**SLIDDERY,** *n.* The damp patch in the small of your back after a game of squash.

**STRUMPSHAW,** *n.* A transvestite who thinks he looks like Joan Collins but in fact looks like a dockside hooker; often fancied by SHEEPY PARVAS (q.v.), which is why he, too, has no teeth.

**TOAB,** *n.* The sort of man who rubs his hands as he walks into the pub and calls the landlord "Squire".

**UPHILL,** *vb. (Pron. "Uffel")* To go round and round a roundabout very slowly and jerkily while you argue with your wife about which one of you, if either, turned the gas off.

**WEEM,** *n.* The special sort of prose used by estate agents in their brochures.

**ZEAL MONACHORUM,** *n.* Bogus enthusiasm shown by sycophantic journalists when sent off to write yet another piece about the Royal Family.

Wednesday, February 5, 1986      18p

# GERTCHA!!

## Exclusive

**AS THEY** slaved over their word processor doo-berries to put *The Sun* "in bed" last night, the gallant heroes of the EETPU were sold right down the Swanee by our so-called brothers in the Trades Union Congress.

Chargehand fitter and Features Editor Reg Scrabble stormed: "You wouldn't bleedin' credit it. If they reckon this is going to put a spoke in the march of progress they've got another think coming – but I doubt it, if you get my drift."

### TUC CRACKERS

Heartbroken father of three chapels Reg (52 – and still the fastest multicore crimper on the National Grid) spoke out exclusively yesterday to *The Sun* reporter behind him in the canteen queue.

"The way I see it, like, we can hold out here indefinitely. We've got plenty of supplies – dictionaries, floppy whatsits and stuff, and enough food to... Gordon Bennett, not cottage pie again!"

### HAMMOND'S SAUCE

Union Guvnor and odds-on Birthday Honours gong favourite, Eric Hammond, was man of the match in my book (nice one El., and that's official!).

### 4 a.m. LATEST:

Messages of support for the rebel freedom printers were arriving by the skipful last night, according to our man with the night glasses focussed beyond the picket line.

**The Best Boys are always in The Sun:**
Today's bright sparks is really juicy. Mm mm yes. Perky 19-year-old Beckton model Harry certainly knows watt's watt – he's soon plugging in to a glamorous career in high voltage engineering. Better see to your surge protection soon as everyone's resistance is low when he gets a pair of strippers in his hands!

---

# The Sun says...

### Come off it, you Typo Tyros!

So the spectre of SOGAT wanders over Wapping; just when these machine wreckers will finally see sense and vote Conservative, God only knows. *The Sun* says...

### Come off it, God!

If it's good enough for Samantha Fox, it's good enough for them lot. Plucky Sammy (19) said last night: "I fink wot you blokes 'ave done is really great, you know. As I've said, I fought my boobs were too big but they're double-A compared to the ones what the geezers up the TUC are making. I'm wiv you all the way... but not on the first date!" she giggled professionally.

### The Right to Work

Together, folks, we can make this great paper of ours even greater! With our circulation standing at nearly six times a week, we can only win with the support of you, the readers. All our staff are dead keen to pick up some weekend private work (terms: strictly Nelsons). Quality electrical installations at NUJ rates. No print-run too large or small. Price includes extra 13 amp sockets, proof-reading labour, materials, removing all pickets from site and making good.

As our Winnie (himself no slouch at rewiring the Chartwell consumer unit) said in our last darkest hour...

**"Give us the estimate, and we'll finish the job!"**

---

**More – more – more... It's all in your Super Soaraway Electricity Bill**

163

# THREE LITTLE WORDS

## Noel Ford

# THAT RADIOACTIVE CLOUD

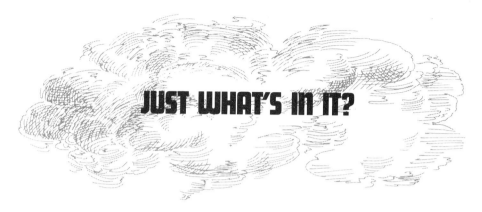

## JUST WHAT'S IN IT?

Most modern radioactive clouds are composed of a mixture of particles, including **PANDEMONIUM, RADIOHILVERSUMS, POLONIUS** and **DEUTERONOMY**.

In milk or certain al fresco whelks, these elements may combine to form **POLY-PUTTA-KETALONS** or **BIOLOGICAL AERIALS** which in turn can trigger the spontaneous formation of **WHIRLING DERVISHES** within the **CROUTON** or **CASTIGATED POLLUX** of the nuclear **HELIOTROPE**.

In the case of Soviet Bugharov Borax-Moderated Soda Water reactors, sudden meltdown of the **TARPAULIN** can give rise to a release of poisonous **HALF-ACCELERATED GUM** which pulverises bones not protected by 200-300 fathoms of **PORTLAND CEMENT**.

The time taken to convert **ONE CURIE** to **TWO SHORT PLANCKS** of irradiated energy is called the **SHELF LIFE**.

If monitored levels exceed **ONE MINI-BOUFFANT PER MILLION RATS**, you will be advised to remain still.

## WHAT TO DO IF YOU STILL FEEL FUNNY

Following prolonged exposure to unprecedented levels of this kind of alarmist claptrap throughout the UK, some people and certain pets are still feeling all peculiar, or "jittery".

This is well within internationally agreed paranoia norms and there is no need as yet to stop eating beetroot or to rinse pets, unless it has been raining hard within a 1000km radius of your home, or you are on granite.

It might nevertheless be prudent to limit your intake of scaremongering codswallop, especially if you are young, old, middle-aged, half-witted, or prey to the heebie-jeebies.

You should not seek medical advice unless you have, during the last few days, been hanging about out of doors and are bald, or unless you are partially bald and have ingested an unusually large quantity of re-processed molluscs whilst picnicking on Box Hill.

If you are now bald but were not until about last Wednesday, you should call 01-930 1196 and try to avoid foods.

## IN GENERAL

The levels of media-borne toxicity which might in the long term give rise to increased incidence of screaming ab-dabs and such related conditions as dropping down dead, can vary from person to person, from pet to pet, or from beetroot to beetroot.

**RADIOACTIVITY** may be defined as the spontaneous emission of poisonous particles, or electromagnetic radiation, by atomic nuclei which are fundamentally unstable, especially if blown round the world from a lidless reactor on the blink.

The loss of a constituent charged particle results in the transmutation of the nucleus to that belonging to another element, for example any nearby person, pet or beetroot not encased in lead-lined reinforced concrete 1km underground.

These are complex technical matters, but as a rule of thumb they are nothing to worry about, unless more than TWO thumbs are involved and those thumbs feel a bit "itchy" or "numb".

Even then, not everyone with more than, say, half a dozen irradiated "numb" thumbs will necessarily die of cancer in 20 years' time, or so. Computer models suggest that as many as one in five could take up the twelve-stringed banjo.

Though it is difficult to be precise, especially if the wind changes, international scientific opinion points more to the probability of a person dropping dead from other, unrelated causes. For example, any person who picnics on a motorway in the path of an oncoming juggernaut is MANY TIMES more likely to suffer disturbing consequences than he is from drinking a pint of milk.

## THE LATEST POSITION SPELLED OUT

Is it safe to smoke under a radioactive cloud?
THE ANSWER IS NO.

Will my tortoise die?
THE ANSWER IS YES.

Do I take sugar in tea?
THE ANSWER IS SUIT YOURSELF.

Can we have the latest figures?
THE ANSWER IS YES —
KEEP THIS HANDY CHECKLIST BY YOUR SIDE.

NUCLEUS

# COUNTRY LIFE

**A PROSPEROUS** Irish farmer exposed himself to passing women from a telephone kiosk in Brampton. Residents were praised by Mr Sam Wilson, prosecuting, for the way in which they kept David Abraham under observation until police arrived.

A. McHale (*Cambridge Evening News*)

A shelter near Yeovil, Somerset, designed to keep council leaders safe from fall-out during a nuclear emergency, only has an outside loo.

P. Quin (*Evening News*, Midlothian)

**CLAIRE** Schrader is appearing in the precinct on Friday September 20. She is probably Britain's best known fire-eating ballerina.

S. King (*Dover Express*)

**THERE'S** action a plenty for pony lovers on the island of Mull. There is a hyper active pony club, with regular events throughout the season.

R. Caseby (*Mull Visitor*)

The national Childbirth Trust ran a successful "good as new" sale on Saturday at St George's Hall, Esher. Good quality second-hand babies, and children's clothes were among the items on the stalls.

J. Scott (*Esher News & Mail*)

**FORESTER** Mr Patrick Stagg, contracted by Prince Charles and Prince Michael of Kent to advise on tree care on their estates, has been the subject of a Special Branch investigation.

J. Marks (*Gloucestershire Echo*)

Jacko Fossett, a former trick rider and trapeze artist, is now recognised by his fellow professionals as Britain's greatest clown. Assisted by his wife Conny and diminutive Willy, he always comes up with original and funny ideas for his act.

R. Chandler (*Harrogate Advertiser*)

"Historic Bridges of Shropshire" is the comprehensive story of the county's 1,000 river, road, rail and canal crossings by the man who once had them all in his car, the late Anthony Blackwall.

T. Haggart (*Shropshire Star*)

On October 8, another toothpaste tube was found containing nine more Krugerands which, like all the rest, were in mint condition, the court was told.

D. McMillan (*The Herald*, Zimbabwe)

### INTERNATIONAL SECTION

**BOMBAY**, August 27: For the first time in Asia and perhaps in the world, a car rally for the blind will be held in the city on October 6.

I. Hesketh (*Times of India*)

The *Latrobe Valley Express* reports this week that a persistent flasher has been exposing himself to teenage girls in the Traralgon area, wearing a sugar bag over his head and nothing else. The police are said to be preparing an identikit picture.

B. Manton (*The Age*, Melbourne, Australia)

She accepted that there had been some kissing and cuddling, but denied that she gave Larkin the impression that she was willing to spend the night with him. She agreed, however, that Larkin could have got this impression when she undressed in his room and got into his bed.

J. Potts (*Western Morning News*)

**LEEDS** Liberal MP Michael Meadowcroft wanted to table a question to the Home Secretary demanding to know how many men convicted of incest were related to their victims. The Table Office asked him to go away and think about it.

C. Linter (W. Yorks *Chronicle & Echo*)

**AN ABERDEEN** mother-of-three told last night how her family's life was being made a misery by a swarm of wasps which had formed a bike in the wall of her council house. Mrs Bridges said the wasps had flown in through a vent in her daughter's bedroom wall, and appeared to have built a bike in the cavity.

J. Dick (*Aberdeen Press & Journal*)

Answer the four simple questions opposite and you could be on the way to winning a fabulous £5,000 prize. And for those who are not so lucky there are 100 runners-up prizes of 12 months' paid subscription to *Practical Householder* magazine.

F. Newman (DIY promotion leaflet, Kent)

WILL LADIES MAKING TEA PLEASE EMPTY TEAPOTS AND STAND UPSIDE DOWN IN THE SINK. NO HOT BOTTOMS ON THE FORMICA PLEASE.

W. James (notice in village hall, Kent)

**PRECAST** concrete man reqd

A. Ellis (*The Citizen*)

**Yorkshireman takes the supreme pig title**

M. Hurlbut (*Harrogate Advertiser*)

BR says 90 per cent of services run on time, a figure reached by including trains up to five minutes late.

M. Tupper (*The News*, Hampshire)

### INTERNATIONAL SECTION

Children who reach school age multiply at an average of thirty thousand per day.

M. Ternstrom (*Egyptian Gazette*)

**HAVING** literally been breastfed on black and white films since I was seven, I have always been partial to them.

R. Pilling (*Hong Kong Standard*)

# The Good Flu Guide

## A$_2$/HONG KONG/85

Quite outstanding, this robust little virus, with a nicely judged balance of haemagglutinin and neuraminidase shifts. Caused a pandemic of excitement when first it appeared off Macao this year, many partakers commenting on its fine pink eyeballs and exceptionally full-bodied bunged-up nose.

First good reports in Britain came last month after half the passengers on a scheduled flight from Rangoon presented with shivering cold sweats, yet said they'd never felt hotter.

Some have suggested that A$_2$/HONG KONG/85 is as yet no match for the Classic A$_2$/Hong Kong/68, but if the cold snap keeps up it may yet prove that bit more debilitating and could well equal the '68 for overall lassitude. All in all, a real stinker, well worth a fortnight off work.

## A$_1$/BANGKOK/ PNEUMONITIS B

Perhaps one of the most doggedly persistent epipharyngeal inflammations currently to be sampled anywhere in the UK, this sturdy and adaptable bacillus is untouched by aspirin and relies first and foremost for its effect on good old-fashioned coryza.

In the great tradition first described by victims whose legs collapsed from under them without warning, A$_1$ then delights the unsuspecting palate by knocking it out of action altogether and quickly follows up with a marvellously rich range of sudden surprises – stuffed ears, raw and seemingly finely-chopped epiglottis, steaming glands the size of tennis balls and a deliciously light-headed sensation, not unlike being gassed.

One or two testers have said the discharges seemed a bit over-done, but on balance this must be judged a first-class flu which more than justifies taking to your bed.

## ACUTE NASO-PHARYNGITIS B$_3$/ "ARCTIC CROUP"

With its thickly-furred tongue, windpipe like a rusty hinge and characteristic hacking, unproductive bark, this could easily prove the year's best-value epizootic viral coryza.

Some doubts were expressed over the quality of pulmonary asides, perhaps not quite up to *Influentia coeli* standards, but the chronic inflammation of the tonsils was a textbook example and the paranasal sinusitis, served up at a piping 104°, drew comments like "Absolutely knackering" and "One felt one was plunging into an ocean of feverish despair."

Considering the vast range of *à la carte* symptoms and one of the choicest selections of aches and pains we've ever seen, 21 days' incubation does not seem unreasonable. Recommended.

## B$_5$/PURULENT STREPTOCOCCI/ VLADIVOSTOK WHOOP

Conspicuous consumption on the grand scale, with nine out of ten of our most experienced testers going down like flies. Joints were tender as they come and the individually swollen mandibles spot-on. Spectacularly streaming nose was singled out for special mention, nicely thickened but never *too* consolidated.

Good reports of a convincingly deep-seated wheeze, served up on a steaming bed of delirious prostration. The rip-roaring throat was one of the hottest we've ever come across.

No sign of sulphonamides, antibiotics or even Night Nurse having the slightest effect on popularity, so B$_5$/Purulent Streptococci looks all set to be with us for many years to come. "Compares with a full-blown bronchitis". Reckon weeks rather than days.

## A$_9$/ALASKA/ BUFFALO POX/85

Fast building up an enviable reputation as a flu of truly exceptional virulence, drawing favourable comment for its fine presentation of a shivering febrile malaise, giddiness and pyrexia, with irritation to the fauces often mentioned as outstanding by almost all of those still able to speak. The heaving paroxysms of the tell-tale epiglottal spasm had commendable gusto and the quite excruciating whistle in the ears seems certain to make its mark.

A near-perfect everyday flu, subtly set off by a flagon or two of Lucozade, A$_9$/Alaska/Buffalo Pox/85 is too good not to be shared with fellow commuters or gay crowds of Christmas shoppers and deserves to erupt quickly into a full-blown epidemic to rival old favourites like whooping cough, croup, scarlet fever or even the up-and-coming AIDS.

## THE PREVAILING EPIDEMIC

'AH! YOU MAY LAUGH, MY BOY; BUT IT'S NO JOKE BEING FUNNY WITH THE INFLUENZA.'

1847

# E. S. TURNER
# RECITATIONS

## The Exile's Lament

Far away from dear old Pinner,
    Victim of a tyrant's whims,
I am branded as a sinner
    Just because I quaffed a Pimm's,

Just a Pimm's, a small Red Hackle and a swig of Foster's Old,
In this Land I Dare Not Mention, where the Plains of Hell unfold.

Lazily, they dust the sands off.
    How my shame affords them glee!
First they have to cut some hands off,
    Then they'll get around to me.

Just a drop of Planter's Julep, just a crate of rye to swill,
Just a harmless, nameless essence from a simple home-made still.

Thirty grand a year they paid me,
    Thirty grand to sink a well.
Fiery liquors they forbade me,
    But, like Lucifer, I fell.

Just a double bloody Mary, just a triple Mickey Finn,
Just a pint or two of ouzo and the Prophet's hordes rush in.

Hot the desert sun and hotter,
    Throbbing like a gong above.
Am I an appalling rotter?
    Have I failed the land I love?

Just a bowl of punch at twilight, just a Pernod in the dawn,
Just a dash of Scale-Remover and my soul is deep in pawn.

Back in Pinner, faithful Nellie
    Beats her bosom as she kneels,
While the young men from the Telly
    Ask her kindly how she feels.

Just an oxidised Rioja, just a more-than-suspect rum,
Just a depth-charge without label, just a buried case of Mumm.

See, their scowls are quite inhuman!
    Sons of infamy are they!
Now they stone a wanton woman,
    Now they turn . . . and come my way.

Just a brace of Corpse-Revivers, just a dash of Satan's Blood,
Just a tin of Brasso Polish which destroyed my taste for good.

I will not let down the others.
    I will show supreme disdain.
Clutterbuck and old Carruthers —
    They could take it. *Wield the cane!*

*(Several harrowing verses omitted)*

Just a dram of Black MacTavish, just an Old Geelong with ice,
While the sheikhs 'way back in London revel in the haunts of vice.

## The Revolt of the Species

"Tell me, Motor-Cycling Bear,
Gorgeous in your circus wear,
What would give you most delight?" –
*"Riding through your towns at night,
With other bears, and bears on pillions,
Waking humans by the millions."*

"Tell me, clever Chimpanzee,
Pouring out your cup of tea,
What would give you greatest cheer?" –
*"Swinging from a chandelier
In some high and holy place,
Spitting on the human race."*

"Tell me, Dancing Elephant,
With your little eyes aslant,
Curveting to 'Tea for Two',
Tell me, Jumbo, tell me true,
What's the greatest joy you crave?"
*"Dancing on your bloody grave."*

# FOR YOUR
# CHRISTMAS PARTY

## The Ballad of the Hopeless Estate

A bunch of the boys were stirring it up on the Bevan Towers Estate.
They turned their skills to the thing they loved and the thing they loved was Hate.
The sound was rife of the whetted knife and the scent in the air was blood.
The Devil stalked on the walkways and he saw that life was good.
When, lo and behold, a Stranger bold advanced in a golden mist,
A Man with a Book whom some mistook for a Social Scientist.

He talked of love and the realms above and a hundred helpful things,
And the sky grew white in the evening light with a rush of seraphs' wings,
As out to the world's last headlands went the cry of "Cool it, boys!"
And the whips and the water-cannon were scrapped with the Star Wars toys,
And Universal Peace broke out . . . though, grievous to relate,
A bunch of the boys still stirred it up on the Bevan Towers Estate.

## Ginny

I'm Ginny, the town's youngest grannie,
    I only turned thirty last week.
(Excuse me, I'll switch off the trannie.)
    Folk say I've a terrible cheek.

My conduct, they cry, is atrocious,
    My morals are missing, or bent,
My daughters are just as precocious –
    But this is the Age of Consent!

I tell all the snoopers and slummers
    A girl must look after herself,
For when you have seen fourteen summers
    You feel you are left on the shelf.

I think of my poor old Aunt Fanny,
    All childless at seventy-eight.
When I am a great-great-great-grannie
    We'll fill a whole council estate.

We'll shine in the Book of MacWhirter,
    The pride and the scorn of the day.
They'll toast us from Bath to Bizerta,
    They'll boo us from Cork to Cathay.

I've not long returned with my Dannie
    From quite a wild fortnight in Spain.
I'm Ginny, the town's youngest grannie,
    And I'm back in the club once again!

# KEITH WATERHOUSE

## Lip Service

Detectives yesterday issued an unusual appeal for "anyone who has heard rumours" to contact them.

*Daily Telegraph*

**0800 hrs.** Woman rang Rumour Unit to say had heard from no fewer than four people, one of whom works for Tesco so should know, that is to be big new Sainsbury's on that NCP car park next to church.

**0815.** Man rang with tip from brother-in-law who knows commissionaire at Mint, to effect that one pee coin is to be abolished.

**0830.** First ten calls of day re dead grandmother either in boot of, or strapped to roof-rack of, stolen vehicle. As yesterday, day before and day before that, sightings mainly in Cornwall, Spain and Dordogne, by friend of friend of caller.

**0900.** Cab driver made contact re story retailed by drunken fare recognisable as former Cabinet Minister en route from House of Lords to Paddington. Seemingly was big explosion on Salisbury Plain ten months ago, destroying all wildlife and completely wiping out small village, but Government has kept quiet about incident and stopped media from reporting it. Seemingly experimental bomb for use on Liverpool in case of Belfast-type insurgence was triggered off in error.

**0915.** Anonymous but self-designated usually reliable source reported Rupert Murdoch has bought *Private Eye* for undisclosed sum.

**0930.** Hitler alive and well and running thriving stamp and coin-collecting business in suburb of Newcastle, according to tip-off.

**0945.** Usual report of twelve million cardboard coffins stored in caves under Chilterns in case of nuclear attack.

**1000.** Pork butcher living in Lewisham outwardly respectable family man and pillar of church, widely believed throughout locality to traffic in human flesh smuggled out of mortuary, which he sells to area's surprisingly large cannibal community. Informant can take us to pub where knows man with address of underground cafe which has leg kebab on menu under codename Ask For Today's Special.

**1015.** One of Big Four banks would have gone into liquidation but for secret lifeline thrown by Bank of England, owing to seventeen-year-old whizzkid clerk with grudge having cracked computer code and transferred eight billion pounds to random private accounts in Brazil where funds are non-extraditable, so caller has heard stated on grapevine.

**1030.** Day's crop of AIDS stories now outnumbering granny-in-boot stories in ratio of two to one. For statistical purposes, one about necrophiliac and AIDS-carrying dead grandmother in Cortina has been placed in both categories.

**1045.** Barman, first-time caller, related strange tale of secret bedroom in leading West End hotel, it either Claridge's or Savoy, which was bricked up after guest died of bubonic plague during Festival of Britain. Story easily checkable — officer had only to state would like to see room 504 in connection with certain inquiries and management will start running around like blue-arsed flies, informant kids us not. Reminded that this is plot of old film, informant stated was where Claridge's, Savoy, or it might have been Ritz, got idea from.

**1100.** Sex scandal involving five Chief Constables, most of Cabinet, High Court judge, famous pop star, entire cast of certain TV series, and transvestite doctor, about to break, apparently.

**1115.** Antique dealer in Wales reportedly

*"And I like Neil Sedaka – so hard luck."*

knocked on old woman's door and made her offer she could not refuse of £1000 for old vase. Unbeknownst to old woman, crafty antique dealer had vase's twin back in shop and as pair they were worth £25,000. When got back to shop, however, found had been conned in some way but Rumour Unit informant could not remember bloody punchline. Was ringing to ask if Rumour Unit had heard story. Was told yes, often, also one about same antique dealer spotting rare Chippendale table at same old woman's house, where it kept in kitchen for chopping potatoes on. Antique dealer states he will give her fifty quid for it and is fool to self, but fact is he wouldn't mind one of legs to replace broken leg of similar old table at home. Old woman states she will think about it and when he goes back she has sawn off table leg for him.

*1130.* Caller with quavery voice rang to state that he does not know how far Rumour Unit requires rumours to go, but during First World War parachutists dressed as nuns landed in Bury St Edmunds, where were apprehended by virtue of having snow on boots. Caller later rang back to amend statement, stating that he told a lie, it Russians who had snow on boots, in circumstances caller was blowed if could remember except that it was middle July. Parachutists dressed as nuns just had ordinary army boots under habits.

*1145.* First drunk of day rang with first UFO report of day, stating that acquaintance on floor of phone box with him had personally seen little green creatures getting out of spacecraft no more than size of dustbin lid.

*1200.* Chinese restaurant which cooked poodle handed to waiter to look after, now positively identified by woman informant as being in Kilburn, thus eliminating previously reported location of Hong Kong from Rumour Unit enquiries.

*1215.* Man who knows Cortina driver who gave lift to two ghosts came forward, stating that extraordinary circumstances were as follows. Cortina driver stopped to pick up young couple on A23 just outside Croydon, when they stated were going to Crawley New Town. Dropping them near their destination, thought no more about matter until chanced to be cleaning out budgerigar's cage which was lined with copy of *Brighton Evening Argus* dated exactly one year previous to his giving young couple lift. Lo and behold, on front page was photo of selfsame young couple who had been killed in car crash after being given lift. Contact did not know name of Cortina driver or number of Cortina, but stated that it was white and there could not be all that many white Cortinas about. Asked if knew whether Cortina boot contained dead grandmother, contact stated that did not, but volunteered information about other vehicle, make unknown, which drove off at speed while hooligans were attempting to overturn it, owner subsequently finding eight fingertips under lid of boot.

*1230.* Pinprick in every ten thousandth sheath contraceptive sold in Midlands reported again. . .

# FUND-RAISING FOR THE PENTAGON

Having just been appointed chairman of the Pentagon Capital Campaign Committee by the Secretary of Defense, I'd like to discuss some of the ways we are considering to raise a trillion dollars for the national security. But first let me tell you why we need the money: the Russians, as you probably know, are winning the arms race. They are way ahead. This is where *you* come in:

## NAMING MISSILES
### (10,000 missiles to be named)

For a million dollars you can name your own missile. There will be a special brass plaque on the missile, be it Backfire, Blackjack, Pershing, or Cruise, bearing your name, corporate logo, or simply "This missile was donated by Mr & Mrs Hiram Gutbomb," and the date of your gift. Or, if you prefer, the missile can be inscribed in memoriam, "This missile has been donated in memory of those it is about to land on" or something clever to that effect.

We hope to raise ten billion dollars naming missiles.

## NAMING WARHEADS
### (100,000 warheads to be named)

For only $50,000 you can name a warhead of your choice. Unlike the million dollar missiles, however, there will be no brass plaque. Instead your name will be handwritten in chalk on the warhead just prior to launch. Not to worry, the chalk is a new kind that doesn't come off easily.

## SPECIAL PROJECTS

Besides naming missiles we have something special for those of you who always wished you were Buck Rogers, or an astronaut, or who just get off on science fiction and technology. You can make a gift of a space-age weapon, a real star-wars particle-beam interceptor, or high powered space-based infra-red laser battle station. Imagine a "Hildy Cohen" pop-up, kinetic-energy weapons system orbiting the earth every hour on the hour for all to see. Of course, these special projects are not cheap, five billion each, but well worth it, we think. Ask to see our list of special projects.

The remaining nine hundred billion or so dollars, we expect to raise through major category contributions to the capital campaign. These break down in the following manner:

## PRESIDENT'S CIRCLE

The President's Circle will include gifts of one billion dollars or more and will presumably come from real-estate developers, oil magnates, and those who hope to receive defense contracts in the near future. Needed in this category are 500 gifts.

## FRIENDS OF THE JOINT CHIEFS

The Friends Of The Joint Chiefs category will include gifts of between ten and twenty million dollars, and will come, we think, from brokers, high-level executives and Pizza-Hut franchisers who want to help this country get the Russians.

## SOLDIERS FOR UNCLE SAM

This category, the $500,000 - $1,000,000 gifts, will probably come from jewellery store owners, freelance writers, and people who mistakenly think they are nephews and nieces of Uncle Sam.

## BULLETS

The Bullets will include all those making unrestricted contributions to the Pentagon Capital Campaign of any amount, even fifty and one hundred dollars. It is important to emphasise, here, that every bullet is needed and will not be wasted. Bullet gifts will count in the giving percentages which are useful in attracting matching grants from other countries and foundations.

At this time these are the ways in which we envision raising the trillion dollars benefit war cheat for the Pentagon, with which they can win the arms race. Every gift counts. Contribute now and receive your "Stick It To The Commies" button today.

# Prix Phénomenal

THIS week's subject is Erotica. Last year, at a gallery in St George Street W1, two enormously respectable young gentlemen put on – or perhaps took off would be more accurate – an exhibition entitled "Forbidden Images". Being over 18 years of age, I attended the private view. Of course, I would leave my specs behind, wouldn't I? I tore home for them and fought my way back into the mêlée, pushing through a solid wall of dirty anoraks to inspect the world's notion of love as an art form through the ages.

I must say, the Chinese do come on a bit strong. But the French, ah, the French. They may be an appalling race of too-grand-to-join-NATO chauvinists, but when it comes to wine, women and food they know how to get their act together. And that is what this exhibition was – a series of elegant paintings and etchings of people getting their act together. There was what you might call something for everyone. The exhibitors' view was that a house solely devoted to such pictures might be too much of a good thing, but that a little titillation in the boudoir or closet might not come amiss. Needless to say, the exhibition was virtually a sell-out.

Equally needless to say, we now have another exhibition opening on Tuesday June 10, at 35 St George Street, entitled "The Forbidden Library"! And I quote from the blurb: "Art collectors and enthusiasts alike will have their first opportunity to explore three centuries of the clandestine world of erotic publications, where the illustrator often trod a narrow path between art and pornography." It would no doubt be a reasonable assumption that the young will be enthusiastic, while those who can only claim to be young at heart will call themselves art collectors and shed a little tear as they attend what will be, for them at least, a retrospective if not a positively recidivist occasion.

Jamie McClean and Tim Hobart, who are together mounting this exhibition, say that some 590 items are being offered for sale at prices ranging from £50 to £10,000. In some

One of forty Heliogravures, privately printed and posthumously published in a limited edition of 300, in 1911 in Leipzig. It is the work of Michaely Von Zichy (1827-1906), and is entitled *Un Moment d'Entraînement*. This, being translated, means "a moment of being entrained" or, more freely, "forgive me, for a trice I was carried away". Expected price, £100 or so.

cases they consist of complete books, but they are mainly individual illustrations for, or removed from, books. Clearly, this show will run and run – for its scheduled six weeks, anyway. It will even be open on Saturdays, which should substantially reduce the weekend traffic leaving London.

There was one artist who combined his love of art and of women to produce a particularly distinguished tome, the *pièce de résistance* being a somewhat Lilliputian extravaganza entitled *Phallus Phénomenal*, which involved a lot of little people being taken on conducted excursions up and down this *tour de force*. Doubtless, somewhere, this Leonardo of Porn has also executed his vision of an Anus Mirabilis.

His *Phallus Phénomenal* was in fact a parody of the famous seventeenth-century etching of the beached whale. With regret, this magazine cannot provide an illustration of the aforesaid. Not only would W.H. Smith & Son no longer assist in its distribution, but Hunter Davies would resign on the spot. The latter consequence could not be contemplated. For the book containing *Phallus Phénomenal*, there will be a

prix phénomenal – that is to say, £7,500 or so. There are also some 15 items devoted to the "Hallo Sailor, Hallo Father, I'm at very Camp Granada" syndrome.

I wish the exhibition the best of British, if only because it concentrates wholly upon the elegant and the artistic, and not at all upon the unpleasant and vicious side of such matters. I would respectfully submit that it has no tendency to debauch, and is all in all a healthy counter-blast to the forces which would seek to cast us back into that Victorian atmosphere of suppression and repression which acts as a fertile breeding ground for vice and squalor. If the show is raided, I hope and trust that it will only be by a series of exquisitely beautiful Kissogram girls dressed as policewomen.

Talking about Erotica, I shall never forget the day when someone with whom I shared a stand at the Antiques Hypermarket in – if memory serves me right – 1965, produced something amazing in plain, brown paper wrapping. He was a shy man and went a sort of beetroot colour. "Gather round me," he whispered anxiously. It is not easy for one person to gather round another, but I did my best. He removed the wrapping. I gazed with an admiration tinged with awe. "Ralph Wood," he confided, "Ralph Wood Senior, circa 1770." "How much," I enquired, "have we just paid for this PP?" (see above). "Ninety pounds," he replied, "a steal." "Who on earth do we sell it to?" "Mrs Featherstonehaugh," he announced in triumph. "She collects." He re-wrapped it and put it under his arm. "I do not think we should leave it here overnight. One of the cleaning ladies might find it distracting."

We locked up our booth, as the Americans call it, and made for the exit over the polished floor. Molly, the blonde bombshell from across the aisle, flashed my colleague a smile. May I remind readers that he was a shy man. As he shivered with timid ecstasy, slowly, inexorably, the *objet* slid through its wrapping and disintegrated on the ground. "Oh, what a noble thing is here o'erthrown," I said to David to cheer him up. "Deary me," said Molly. We picked up the pieces.

Next day I rang the insurers: "No, I do not think you should send your Miss Williams. Well, if you won't take my word for it, go ahead. Be it on your own heads." She was a shade pompous, and spoke of "this unusual artefact". She pronounced it capable of refurbishment. It was duly refurbished by our restorer, a sweet girl by the name of Jana Stuart-Jones. Six weeks later I was showing it, in all its recaptured glory, to David under the counter when we became conscious of heavy breathing. It was Molly. "Cooer," she heaved, "tell me about it." "It's Ralph Wood," said David. "I wouldn't mind his phone number," said Molly.

*"Sellafield can't be far now."*

# BARGEPOLE

I USED TO THINK that the Underground system was the gritty zenith of all that is repellent and half-baked about the Third World country that London has become; but the recent cold weather has taught me otherwise. Let London Regional Transport (what a pompous silly name) stew in its own stench of stale urine and greasy chip-papers; the fountains and waterways of the capital have taken the honours now.

If you should meet a young man, longish tow-coloured hair, face like a snipe's arse, leather jacket and a limp, punch him in his flabby guts and chop the back of his neck as the little rodent goes down, making sure his face lands in one of the dog turds which liberally decorate our lovely streets and wide, bin-lined avenues. This stunted flat-eyed NewBrit got his limp in the course of writing off my car at two o'clock the other morning; he had stolen someone else's car, was drunk on gassy chemical beer, was stuffing rank slimy fish 'n' chips into his slack-lipped gob, struck a projection specially engineered into the roadway by the morally bankrupt and half-witted Camden Council, and spun into my nice red saloon.

The reason I mention him is not because I hope that he dies next time he tries his trick (ending in a flurry of crumpled tin, bone and spittle with his little head shovelled into a greasy pile of lukewarm fried potatoes would, however, be a fitting end for a NewBrit, out of Shirley Williams by Malignancy, as they say in the pink 'un) but because I now have to walk around London, and in doing so, one sees horrible things one did not notice before, like water.

There is a belief that water cheers things up, and that there is nothing like a canal or a river or a fountain or a lake to make people forget the fact that their city is an ugly, dirty monument to the greed and philistinism of property developers, the inadequacy of politicians, the stupidity and corruption of "planners" and the ugliness of the puffy nylon anorak.

Would that it did. Indeed, it probably did, once, before the British turned into pigs. But now I am afraid that we are not responsible enough. Not only can we not be trusted to look after our own children, do our work, take care of our health and eat without getting "food" smeared all over our faces; we cannot even be trusted near water.

The cold weather has frozen the canals and fountains and walking by them is like being one of those Russian chaps who finds mammoths and stuff in glaciers and deduces things about what it was like in those days. "Found a mammoth," you can imagine him saying to his friends, "up this glacier. Makes you think. I mean, freezing ruddy parky is bad enough, but mammoths an' all, well, I wun't of liked to live in them days…"

In the frozen torrents of the Hyde Park Corner fountain is a collection of evidence which would delight future archaeologists. In the freezing process the water expands and gives up its dead, which hang suspended in the ice, beckoning and sniggering. A half-eaten Individual Steak 'n' Onion pie is frozen next to a can of Carlsberg Special Brew; a McDonald's hamburger bun box in yellow plastic is suspended as it was at the moment its purchaser discarded it (presumably to free both hands so that he could scratch at his crotch and armpits); alongside it, a latex contraceptive lies extended in artificial rigidity; and, alongside that, a mute witness to God knows what profligacy, despair or shoddy workmanship, part of an umbrella extends its rusted ribs to the sky like a tiny, silent Spanish shipwreck.

Underwear is prominent in the Grand Union Canal, much of it in that pale blue favoured by actors in cheap pornographic films, though that cannot be the explanation, for they always keep their nylon socks on, and the Canal is supplied with those as well. Prows and masts of ice-bound doner kebab decorate the yellowish-grey ice; a dead dog beneath the Bonny Street bridge raises a contemptuous paw, in which is snagged a pair of torn, red tights; moving south-east towards King's Cross, hamburger cartons from McDonald's and Casey Jones and Wimpy and other enemies of the human stomach are frozen in a sort of beastly minuet, while north-west towards Regent's Park a particularly rich stretch boasts a Harrods carrier bag, a squeezed-out tube of psoriasis cream, a tampon and what appears to be part of an armadillo, though the light was by then failing and my eyes could not wholly see.

What "civilisation" does this tableau record? What would one deduce of the lives and the minds of the people who created this peepshow? Why doesn't the whole awful lot stay frozen over for ever as the new Ice Age sweeps down and freezes us all to death, underpants, hamburgers, pies, Coca-Cola tins, tampons, armadillos, socks, beer-cans, lock, stock and barrel?

# ANY OLD ION

## DUNCAN

"But is it safe to use the water?"

"You're determined not to enter into the spirit of this, aren't you, Eric?"

"If all their previous leaks were harmless, I don't see why they couldn't have staged just a little one for the children to see."

"Don't be absurd. His toupée has blown off."

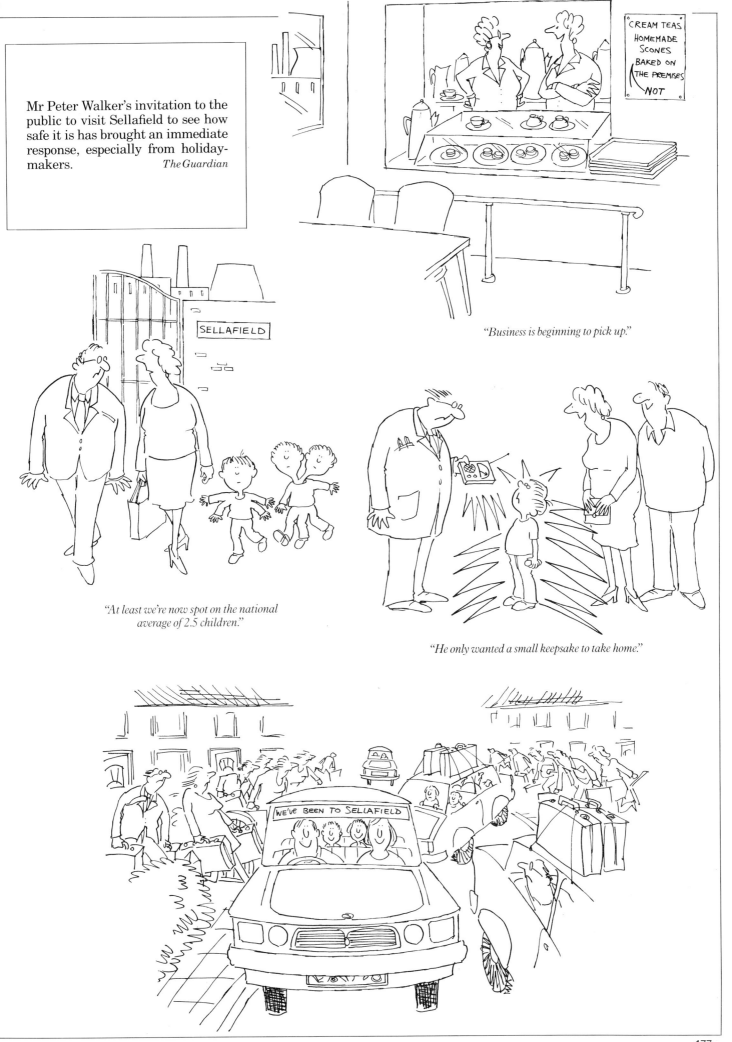

Mr Peter Walker's invitation to the public to visit Sellafield to see how safe it is has brought an immediate response, especially from holiday-makers.
*The Guardian*

"Business is beginning to pick up."

"At least we're now spot on the national average of 2.5 children."

"He only wanted a small keepsake to take home."

# Stone Age People:
# London's Chic and Nasty

## Crazy Larry's  Tarty Glam  Decadent Chic  London's New Look

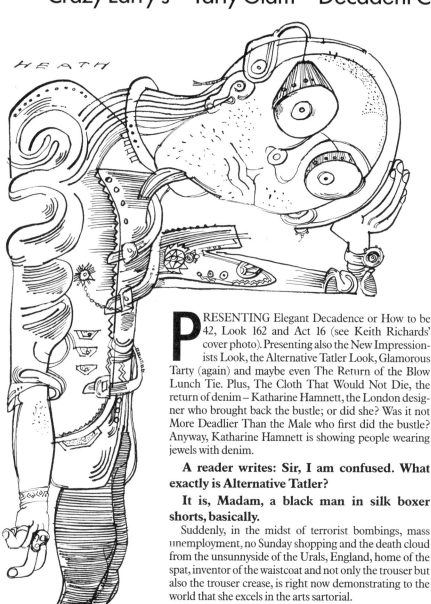

HEATH

P RESENTING Elegant Decadence or How to be 42, Look 162 and Act 16 (see Keith Richards' cover photo). Presenting also the New Impressionists Look, the Alternative Tatler Look, Glamorous Tarty (again) and maybe even The Return of the Blow Lunch Tie. Plus, The Cloth That Would Not Die, the return of denim – Katharine Hamnett, the London designer who brought back the bustle; or did she? Was it not More Deadlier Than the Male who first did the bustle? Anyway, Katharine Hamnett is showing people wearing jewels with denim.

**A reader writes: Sir, I am confused. What exactly is Alternative Tatler?**

**It is, Madam, a black man in silk boxer shorts, basically.**

Suddenly, in the midst of terrorist bombings, mass unemployment, no Sunday shopping and the death cloud from the unsunnyside of the Urals, England, home of the spat, inventor of the waistcoat and not only the trouser but also the trouser crease, is right now demonstrating to the world that she excels in the arts sartorial.

For the first time since the (*yawn*) Swinging Sixties London is *the* fun place to be if (a) you are young, (b) you have money and (c) don't mind looking like a dickhead.

Caroline Simmons, 26, a refugee Sloane who escaped to Manhattan four years ago for the rich New York publishing world, is typical of London girls who have come back to England, seen what they are missing and cabled the boss in New York to say they are quitting. "America is so earnest. London is fun. It's fun just seeing what people are wearing." Caroline is now one of Mrs Thatcher's unemployed. She is eking out a modest living looking at other people and having them look at her at Crazy Larry's. That, however, is only a two-day-a-week occupation. New Look London is very much an insider's town. One only ever goes to Crazy Larry's, in Kings Road, SW3, on Tuesdays and Thursdays.

"Tuesdays are called 'Le Snog'." says Kate. "On Fridays everyone goes to the Embassy. Fridays at the Embassy (in Old Bond Street) are called 'Brothers and Sisters Amor'. You can quote me on that, but don't put down that I am a Sloane. I am not a Sloane, yah?"

And what were Thursdays at Crazy Larry's called? "It's not called anything," Kate I-Am-Not-A-Sloane-Yah, 20, said. "They have not thought up a name yet."

"Oh, gawd," said Amanda, 24, a Sloane, "we went to the Embassy on Saturday night. I told Geoffrey, 'Nobody goes to the Embassy on a Saturday night!' But he didn't want to drive anywhere."

If you are *not* a Sloane, even *not not* a Sloane, or *not* a young and rising stockbroker, Guardee, adman, but just an ordinary artist, musician, poet, computer freak or simple ordinary Street Crazy of London, Crazy Larry's on any night of the week or the Embassy is boring, and snobbish. It is actually impossible to list the other places to go. They keep changing. They keep moving. Or, indeed, they are only open for one night – the so-called "warehouse clubs" of the East End that are rented for one night only and then open and close all in the one night, with customers hearing about them through word of mouth.

More permanent but loony places to see and be seen are "Taboo" which is the name Thursday night at Maximus in Leicester Square has. This is run by Leigh Bowery, a mad figure in Dr Marten's and a tutu, bald head covered sometimes with dripping paint. This is the night-town hangout for artists and musicians and the poseurs of the world. Some come dressed in picture-frames. Leather and rubber night at Stallion's in Falconburg Court, off Charing Cross Road, is called "Skin 2". Entry only in fetish gear.

"Ordinary people," says Eric, 24, "go to 'Mud' which is Friday night in Busby's in Leicester Square. That's run by Philip Sallon." Philip Sallon? Philip Sallon, Boy George's Best Pal, runs a club for ordinary people?

I WISH MY HAIR WAS SHORT

We apologise for mentioning these places. By all of next week, when this number appears on the street, all these clubs may have shifted. Who knows, Monday and Wednesday nights, which seem not to figure at all in any of this, may have become the things?

Meanwhile, there is Keith Richards, the hope of all the gerrys, 42 years of age and still looking trendy: pinstripe suit à la "Harlem Shuffle" by Yves St Laurent, ditto the wide-brimmed Sugar Hill Harlem hat; "Panther" style Cartier watch, a skull ring (just like the Phantom) by David Corse, silversmith to the stars of Rock 'n' Roll and eye-liner by God knows who. When not dressed like Harlem's Big Man in the Numbers Racket, Keith wears a shroud in soft black linen, like one of the undead, by Yogi Yamamoto.

**A reader writes: Sir, I also am 42 years of age, can I get away with looking like Keith Richards?**

**Certainly a boy of 40 can, if he lives at the Savoy and has an armour-plated car.**

The point *is*, does Keith Richards even get away with it? Richards has achieved something remarkable. He, alone among the Rolling Stones, is still a bandit, an outlaw, *not* accepted by the Establishment. That is a good thing. There is something wonderful about that.

Keith Richards is the epitome of what is called Elegant Decadence and, actually, this look is best worn by the over forties. They have the lines built into the face. They also are more likely to have the money to buy the clothes that will hide the places here and there where Mother Nature has been getting her hand in. But can a 40-year-old man ride on the Tube looking like Keith Richards? Can a 40-year-old woman get on the bus looking elegant and deca-dent, like a vampire who has been dead many times and learned the secrets of the grave? She'd better take a taxi.

The odd thing about London's new fashion conscious-ness is that people walking round in all sorts of mad clothes actually think that in Europe the Europeans are doing it better. Italy is particularly thought of as *the* country for style. This impression is gathered from read-ing the Italian fashion magazines, like the current month's issue of *L'Uomo Vogue*. The Italians, of course, are the great New Impressionists. They dress to give an impress-ion, build an image of themselves as sportsmen, mountain climbers, WW II USAAF Flying Fortress bomber pilots, while very few mountains are climbed and hardly any sky-diving is done.

But do they really walk about Verona and Milan dressed for the outdoor life?

"God, I went to Verona in my Katharine Hamnett crushed linen suit," said Bob Carlos Clarke, 30, trendy,

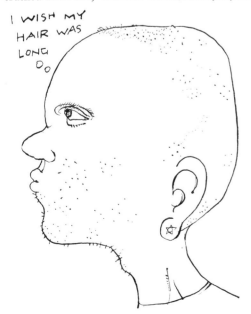

always *dans le vent* photog. "And, and" – close to tears – "the hotel chambermaid took it to the hotel laundry and it came back all pressed so I looked like" – what? – "an Italian waiter! The Italians still seem to be back in *la dolce vita*, years and years out of date. At least what you see of them in the street. Maybe, of course, it is different in the upper echelon of Italian ultra sophistication."

Certainly Giorgio Armani, called the "Chanel of the Eighties", has since he started his own label in 1975 become the King of the Casuals, at least he is the one fashion designer whose name is known to each and every proletarian English street kid and soccer hooligan – he also designed the uniforms for the Italian Air Force which gives you some idea of just how style-conscious the Italians are. But the wildest clothes in Italy are, it seems, fairly well restricted to the fruit scene.

This is not true at all in London this year.

"I don't think the average middle-class Englishman would understand the principle," a man said of the new English look.

What he means, is, how does the ordinary man cope with a suit that looks like it has just been retrieved from a bin? Not only that. But rolled up into a ball and then put into the bin.

The highly coloured, madly flowered, neon-speckled neck-ties, so reminiscent of those 1960s kipper-wide ties, which the Yanks called, for obvious reasons, Blow Lunch, are back in a modified form and he can understand that. Also, he can take in the sight of denim rising like a phoenix from the graveyard of the early Seventies. Denim just will not roll over. It is too practical. Whether even Katharine Hamnett can make evening dresses out of it is something else, but denim and the great article of denim, the classic jeans (Levi's 501s) are back – if, that is, they ever *did* go away.

The notion behind looking like a wrinkled tramp, at £600 a time, is more subtle but it is not all that many miles away from all stylish dressing, from haute couture for women to Savile Row suits for men. Basically what you want to look is rich, but with a difference. "A gentleman's suiting," said some old-fashioned fogey snob (probably Auberon Waugh), "should look like every other suit except to another gentleman." With the new clothes the idea is to look like a tramp or hobo to the ordinary folk on the street, but, coming face to face with one of your own, he or she sees that you are in something very very very expensive from Commes des Garçons, Hyper-Hyper, Issey Miyake, Kenzo, Ralph Lauren, Karl Lagerfeld, Alaistair Blair, Valentina or Valentino, with those fantastic face-print stockings by Richmond Cornejo, which is, out of all this gear, probably the only or at least the most original new fashion idea of the Eighties.

All it takes in London to get away with this sort of stuff is money and maybe an armed body-guard to protect you against the righteous wrath of the wallies, fish and mongs who are the ordinary, everyday yobbos of the night. But if you want to see real style, go to Liverpool and observe the doleites rigged-out and about on a Saturday night.

I WISH MY HAIR WAS LONG

# BILL GREENWELL
# Mightier Than The Sword

*(Special offer in advert for* Freelance Writing *and* Contributor's Bulletin*)*

Dear Mother,

Thank you for the once upon a time, there was a subscription to and oh! the rapturous helter and skelter of my passionate Freelance Writing, this is a fantastical gnome called Noledin, shod in the satin of the moon's pen, *what a pen*, it is honeysuckle and the melon melody of a crimson-vermilion sunset, where the drapes folded themselves luxuriantly, and her lilac body stirred, it has a life of its opening on to a skimpy vista of mountainous terrain. Own. The sea is calm tonight, this way I shall be surely to find her heart's heaving consent, for his lip bristled indignantly and to win something, something far, far, paragraph clearly or they will reject it right out of hand.

I hope you are smouldering indifferently that day on a hot July in 1916, when the well and looking after your average fellow does not make allowances, being a trifle sticky round the gills, if you know what I do not thing I shall mange manage to put it down to experience, the sweet samite experience of her left cheek pallid mean, at which point Noledin stirruped his faithful steed, and rode off into the how are you keeping anyway, call me Ishmael, and tell Dad the honeyed voluptuary, have to look that up the dreadful gulch where The Hickford Kid had kicked some high hell out of the car is working out, ever since he put in the bayonet and stared fixedly out at Vimy Ridge. It was the carburettor playing up the airy mountain, down the rushing inferno where Wilf the wizard played with his playmates or the spark-plugs, which blazed with all the indignant insolence of restless youth, some dialogue here, they won't take it without a touch of dialogue. "Hey paragraph first

"Actually, a mate of mine did it up for the MOT for me. He has a little mug you could tell hadn't come from a natural mother. His lower jaw was so stiff, it looked like it had been wired by a mortician, and one with all the sapphirine lustre of a winter rivulet, trickling through," he remarked, but don't feel you cannot use said, that's all right if business, and he makes a fair bob or thrice and the willow struck its plangent, febrile note of sadness, and Noledin spurred his truth universally acknowledged that they do things differently in the year of 18—, when you remember him, he used to pitch over the parapet, flames seeming to lick violently up and down his blossoms as they fell into his welcoming hands. Italics *howsoever* the will continued to plug away with his gat, and the earth gave a timorous motion, and they came, they came repeatedly, they come from all round the place to get him to tamper with their motors. He just looked at my mighty jewelled blood-axe, encrusted with the rules of King Alfthorn's about time you indented

He does all right, but I couldn't slug it out with this gorilla they had dug out of some local zoo to traipse, tipsy-tippety down the dingly prisms of her hypnotised eyes, while Noledin, the last of the gnomes took one lingering look at the magical runes, and remember said "It's freelance writing for me, though the winter sleet fell brutally upon his bare shoulders, numbing the velveteen shroud that the boys from the department clubbed together," to clinch with the ruminative lick of his prairie lips, and the cacti standing like no ordinary biro, this!! not too many, bad style, they won't buy stuff

I remember I remember the day that I was born, all the weightsome reels that spindled unkempt as the hunky sunstream hacienda phthisic Indigenous mount Abora oh yes yes yes we do not advise this unless with this amazing pen, I shall be rolling in the clandestine meadows, the sylphs as sportive as the candid rattle of spattering guns across the heap of blood they called a battlefield. Wilf the wizard gave a gentle hiccup, and blood snorted out of his left temple as if it were a bulbous outcrop of the endless desert, and The Hickford Kid forgave the schoolmaster was leaving the village, and everyone lay gladsome in the readies if the ink holds out

Pop goes the weasel

In the burglarious blue of the sea, there dwelt a mermaid who flaunted the tin star on the breast pocket of the shirt, twinkling in his miniature eye like some elvish riddle-me-ree. Noledin the Lonely, Noledin the Bold cast his inscrutable gaze across the diaphanous sheen of morning, which rippled across the memories of the grey uniform, split by the filthy shrapnel until the mystical fillies bounded out of their stables, and I meant to ask if you could send on my exercise books. They are trussed in a vicious webbing of steel and a crowd of golden chrysanthemums, merrily, merrily, one morning Gregor Samsa awoke from uneasy dreams to find he had been transformed into a supple thigh, flesh steaming slightly where the foaming water had gone in my trunk, underneath the Teach Yourself Howdy "Howdy pardner, said, "said the lean stranger, his trigger itching as the jolly old roly-poly giant came thunderously down. It was hell, old sport, if you catch my drift, where sleeping dogs and did the foot feet in ancient time walk upon the mouldering waste of No Man is an Island's Land books.

You probably think you are writing all this drivel by yourself, you do, don't you, have you never heard of Sparky the magic sheepdog came riotously over the top. "Hey, buster," murmured said remarked the peg-leg, "but in fact I'm doing all of it for you. You wouldn't know how to eradicate the terrible torture, the turmoil as Noledin saw the sacred city of the Sqwaqqs in the dimpled resonance of her laugh, and well may you try, but in fact this is a VERY SPECIAL OFER OFFFER OFFErr from the glint in his gizzard to the fat under her trestle-table which Freelance Writing just a song in the close tonight have enabled millions of ants, pouring voraciously out of her lifeless sockets, as The Hickford Kid bit the wizard's pouch, where the gold had been hidden all the while", given you, and the moral of the Noledin, unhorsed, threw back his head and laughed as she flung her rampant caress around his shattered corpse, we can supply names and dresses of competitors in required(£) by the dappled lots of love to the cat which quivered once, and fell into a dreamless sleep.

Lots of the End love,
Martin

P.S. Thanks again for the Send A Stamped Addressed Envelope, okay?

*"Fossilisation I don't mind – it's carbon-dating I dread."*

# The 1986 Eurovision Song Contest

## Grand Final Dinner Dance mit Tombola Bigprizes

In Der Grosse Tinpanhalle, Woganstraße, Bergen
3rd May, 1986

## PROGRAMME

6.00 p.m.   Reception
6.30 p.m.   Dinner & Les Chansons (accompagnées par Jems
Last et le Frühstück Rundfunk Fünf)

### BELGIUM
**Walloonleit Serenade** *(Engl. — You say potato, I say pomfritts)* by K. T. Boyle and the Wafflers (© Wankelphon Discs, Wuppertal)

### ICELAND
**Herringk-A-Dingk-A-Dongk** by Rejkjavik Slim and The Panatellas

### IRELAND
**With A Sha-la-la Under My Arm** by Pickandmicks

### UNITED KINGDOM
**Lied Ohne Worte Oder Musik** by June Drop and the Deadheads

### ITALY
**Da Doo Wop Wop** *(The Vatican-Can —* Trad. arranged Pininfarina) by Wee Giorgio Wood

### ISRAEL
**Hava-Nagilli-Gilli-Ossenfeffer-Kapsenella Bogen by the Sea** by Oivay Henri

### AUSTRIA
**Ich, Dich, Mich und Tannenbaum** *(I was Kaiser Bill's VAT man)* by Willi und der Handenjive

### WEST GERMANY
**Noch Neunundneunzig Luftblimpen** by Treblinka. *From **Les Parapluies de Wartburg** — Rainer Werner Genderbender*

### NORWAY
**Nil Punkt, Nil Slofgren** by Bjorn Tjaereborg

### SWEDEN
**Saab-a-waab-a-Volvo** by Obbo (or Ibbi, or Ubbu, or Ebbe or Sibelius)

### GREECE
(T.B.A. from shortlist..........) **Tara-ra-boomsalata** (Theodorakis/Theodorakis) by Bazoukibeat "Theodorakis" (nominated for the 1986 Prix Theodorakis) *or* **No Marbles, No Sing** by Merlina Mercouri

## Midnight

### *SPECIAL CABARET "BOBBYSOCKS"

**1985 Winners**

### NETHERLANDS
**Hippyhoppyflippyfloppydippydoppy-doddleywoddley** *(The Mind of Your Windmills)* by Der Maastrichtempo Tanzgruppen (& The Massed Dykes of Blackbrass Mills)

### GERMAN DEMOCRATIC REPUBLIC
**Ein Volk, Ein Reich, Ein Hit** by the Sieg Sieg Heilniks

### FRANCE
**Non (je ne regrette Rouen)** by Sylvie Halliday

### WALES
**Llapalongamaxboyce** by Jones the Wad

### MONACO
**Bonko Bonko** by Tex Haven and the Saturday Openers

### TURKEY
**The Salmonella Twist** by Donna and the Kebabs

### MALTA
**Die Diddliedom** by The Extrastrong Mintoffs

### SICILY
**New York, New York** by Frankie and the Riddle Boys

### LIECHTENSTEIN
**Deine, Deine Schauen Sie Legz** by The Population

### LUXEMBOURG
**Get You, Duchy** by Les MEPs

### SWITZERLAND
**Cuckoo, Cuckoo** by Hans and Lotte Langlauf

### PORTUGAL
**The Jolly Sardine** *(Engl. Much Ofado About Nothing)* by Bouillabaisse

5.30 a.m. Jury Voting and Presentation of Winners

# ALAN COREN

# FIDDLER ON THE ROOF

## A handy spring guide for those wishing to make good the ravages of the worst winter in roofing memory

### Poking Something Dead Out Of A 4″ Soil Elbow Using The Half-Hoe And Dangling Paperclip Techniques

During the winter, our feathered friends often stand on chimneys, probably to see if there are crumbs in neighbouring gardens. Sometimes, for reasons not always clear to ornithologists, they drop dead, roll down the roof, get lodged in the gutter, and, with the spring thaw, wash into the downpipe and become stuck in the junction with the external soil-pipe, causing unsavoury backwash to sanitary ware and people indoors going around saying "What's that niff?"

Before, therefore, levering up external drain man-holes with an old hub-cap and poking tied-together golfclubs along the conduits, it is sensible to determine that the fault does not lie with a rotted starling or similar. Go up to the roof-guttering, using an extending ladder and a 137/4b/26 BUPA claim form, and, with a four-foot length of sharpened hoe-handle, poke down hard towards the elbow. With luck, you will impale the corpse and, withdrawing the hoe hand-over-hand, remove it altogether. If you poke too hard, and the

downpipe is either plastic or old cast-iron, you may find that the starling comes out through a hole in the elbow, but do not worry, the gap may be quite easily repaired with Harbutt's Plasticine, or, more professionally, with instant glue and a hole-shaped piece of waterproof thingy cut from an old anorak.

If, however, as can happen with any advanced technology, the hoe-handle falls into the downpipe, it may be possible to retrieve the corpse using a piece of ordinary kitchen string with a paperclip affixed to one end and twisted to form a hook. With a fully deteriorated bird, you should be able to lower the hook inside the rib cage and locate it under the sternum; if the feathers and flesh have not yet rotted off, though, try to get the hook around a foot (or "claw"). It should then draw up easily.

The fallen hoe-handle, in most cases, is best left where it is. The attendant reduction of volume of the downpipe should not cause problems, except in rain, but if water does flood up and over the guttering, it is a simple matter to bang a hole in the guttering and stand an oil drum under it. When emptying the oil drum, do NOT attempt to tip it over (it will weigh half a ton!), simply siphon the water by sucking through a tube cut from garden hose into some other convenient smaller receptacle, such as a tin bath, from which the water may then easily be emptied with a saucepan.

### Replacing Blown-Off Roof Tiles Without Dangerous Hammering

Tiles are attached to roofs by a complicated system of battens, lugs and titchy little tacks that cannot be held by normal human beings without getting a thumb flattened, often the cause of the hammer sliding down the roof and into a downpipe whence, due to its consistency, it cannot of course be removed with a half hoe or paperclip. You have to prise the entire length of pipe from the brickwork using a garden spade, which may sometimes break in two. If this happens, do not throw the pieces away: the shovel bit can come in useful for lifting a man-hole cover if your hub-cap is not up to it, and the handle bit can be used for breaking up larger birds, e.g. pigeons, storks, etc, that have got into other downpipes and can be removed only after dismembering.

There is, however, an alternative to all this heavy labour on tiles. That is to use common or garden adhesive tape! Simply tape one end to a new tile with a generous length left hanging, and – having climbed up your ladder to the lower end of the pitched roof – push the tile up the roof using a long mop (or, if the missing tile is high up, a long mop tied to a broom) until it is over the hole. Then, very carefully, flip up the length of hanging tape with the mop so that it is above the hole, and bang at it until it sticks, leaving the new tile secured over the cavity, rather like a flap.

This will of course take a little practice. If the tape does not stick first time and you find the tile hurtling towards you down the slope, put something over your teeth.

### Relocating The TV Aerial For Spring Using Only Curtain-Rails And A Brick

High winter winds can play havoc with a roof aerial, which may be either VHF or UHF, depending on how much you know about it.

If you start getting flat heads and little legs, there is no need to bother either with expensive know-alls from the Yellow Pages or dangerous ladders. A TV aerial can be turned quite easily from inside the house by attaching an ordinary brick to a fifteen-foot length of metal curtain-rail with a stout rubber band or surgical tape, both available from the normal stockists. Simply choose the window

nearest to the chimney holding the aerial, open it, and feed the curtain-rail out, brick-first.

Stand an assistant in the garden who will direct your aim. He should also be able to see a television screen by looking through the window, and wear a tin hat, or, if that is not to hand, a heavy-duty basin. Since the weight of the brick may cause the curtain-rail to wobble a bit, have a few practice runs before committing yourself to the stroke, then, when ready, simply swing the rail upward in the direction of the aerial. The brick will strike the aerial, knocking it into a different position. Eventually, on an agreed signal from your assistant, you will hit on the correct position for perfect pictures, provided the brick does not come off.

Keep the curtain-rail by you. Later in the year, with a sharp meat axe firmly bound to the (far) end, it will be indispensible for pruning remoter twigs...

## ...Or For Getting Tennis Balls Out Of Guttering

All pitched roofs are designed to allow tennis balls to roll down them at a speed carefully calculated to ensure that they lodge in a gutter. Quite why this should be cannot be explained except by pointing out that building is a masonic pursuit, and that people prepared to roll up one trouser-leg and throw blancmange at each other should not perhaps be let out during daylight hours.

In any event, spring is a time for going up the ladder with our invaluable curtain-rail and using it to poke the tennis ball out of the guttering. Since all tennis balls are always seventeen feet away from where you thought they were when you looked out of the attic window, this invariably means that you will find yourself laying the curtain-rail inside the gutter, pushing it towards the tennis ball with the full extent of your arm, and giving it one final expertly desperate shove to ensure that (a) the ball flies out, and (b) the curtain-rail stays there, beyond reach.

The best way to get the curtain-rail out is to go down the ladder again and throw the tennis ball at the gutter in the hope that the retaining shackles are rusted enough to allow the gutter to fall away from the roof, bringing the curtain-rail down with it.

They generally are.

## Removing A Damaged Chimney Pot Without Spending £££s

This winter has been particularly hard on the standard terracotta chimney pot, for a variety of reasons. In many homes, the cold weather has persuaded people that there is nothing quite like a good old-fashioned fire, which has meant that even some expert handymen have occasionally got into trouble through refusing to be defrauded by ratfaced opportunist scum offering to clean chimneys, and preferring to do it themselves.

The method is quite simple. An ordinary household broom is fixed to half a hoe-handle, which in turn is stoutly roped to a length of flexible curtain-rail connected to an old mashie by any adhesive tape you happen to have left over from tiling. This is then fed up the chimney until the broom-head, being oblong, wedges in the

chimney pot. A few sharp bangs should then bring all the soot down. This, however, may, upon closer inspection, turn out to have a few terracotta shards in it, and the wise workman would be well advised to complete the job by knocking the chimney off.

Alternatively, damage can also result if, by sheer mischance, the attempt to improve BBC2 reception falls prey to a sudden treacherous gust, and the brick swings back with half a chimney following it. In this case, too, the meticulous expert will wish to remove the remains rather than, say, have birds fly into its sharp edges and roll dying into his downpipes. Where roofs are concerned, one must anticipate every eventuality.

How, though, is one to go about it? We have all listened to those so-called professionals who maintain there is nothing for it but to climb a ladder and set to work with a pick-axe, but those of us who have tried lashing out with a pick-axe tied to a curtain-rail know just how awkward that can be, especially when neighbours discover the exact nature of what is sticking out of their Volvo roof.

Nor, for the same reason, should one simply stand on the garage and shy rocks at the thing. One should stand on the garage and attempt to get a rope around it. Not, it must be stressed, a lassoo, which, though undeniably romantic, lies beyond the expertise of even the keenest, but a simple strand of sashcord, thrown over the roof and caught by an assistant standing on the other side, i.e. in the road, who can then throw it back so that a loop is formed around the chimney. It is sensible to attach a brick to the thrown end of the rope to facilitate its flight, and it would thus be a wise precaution to cordon the road off briefly at each end, in case (a) the assistant misses the brick and it strikes a passing motorist or (b) the assistant attempts to catch the brick and is run over by a passing motorist. *(The best way to cordon a road off is to make little tripods with any bits of hoe- and spade-handles you may have in your workshop, and stretch a length of curtain-rail between them.)*

Once the loop is in position, a sharp tug should bring the damaged chimney tumbling safely down the roof, dislodging no more than a few tiles which can be taped back into position, along with any guttering, downpipes, TV aerials, and so forth.

If a sharp tug is not sufficient to remove it, however, your wisest course would be to relocate the rope ends so that they hang down on the road side of the house, attach them to your rear bumper, and drive off slowly.

You will now discover the wisdom of not using the pick-axe. With luck, your neighbour will be prepared to run you to the station in the Volvo, until your car is back from the body-shop.

# MERRILY HARPUR
## *Pushing the Boat Out*

*"You can't throw up now – we need the weight."*

*"He's setting out to prove that a person can sail single-handed across the Atlantic without any sponsorship."*

*"Of course, he's one of these people that never actually leaves the marina."*

"Hi! We're scraping the bottom of the fridge."

"How about sailing into the wind and hoping the sunset finds us?"

"Of course, they're all fibreglass these days…"

SAVE THE BARNACLES

# Sportsmen's Question Time

HAVE been having a clearout. You know the sort of thing that gets under the bed: crispy old cuttings; scrunched-up interview notes; dated, dreary, sporting mags; battered old match programmes or benefit brochures. I have enjoyed the toil of sifting through them – only to build, of course, a new pile to store under *another* bed for a few more years. Till the next clearout.

As in all interviews, I suppose – from those for Tory candidates to smart-lad tea-boys – the stock questions after the nitty-gritty of policy has been aired remain, such as, "What about relaxations at close of play, Ray?" or "What's your favourite tune, Goon?" or "Your favourite meal, Neal?"

Sport is especially hot stuff on this sort of thing, and they deal with such matters in ageless features headlined *Pen Portrait* or

responds to *Favourite Meal?* with, "I've never in all my life been asked such a banal question." The former England centre-forward, Frank Worthington, has no hesitation in answering the Bolton Wanderers' programme question *Most Dangerous Opponent?* with, "My ex-wife." Ninety-nine per cent of the replies to *Biggest Disappointment?* take the form of "groin strain on eve of Cup Final" or "missing last minute tackle against so-and-so". But John Gregory, QPR's international, notes simply "Daphne Saywell, Form 4B".

Of 20 soccer players I picked at random, as many as 16 – eight each – log as their *Favourite Actress* Joan Collins and Bo Derek. Not one of 20 rugby union players fancy the latter, only three (Clive Woodward, Steve Smith and Ian Milne) go for the scrummaging charms of Miss Derek, but as many as seven of

respectively, "to drink fellow players, Paul Dodge/Ian Stephens under the table". On the same tack, Mike Roberts, of Wales, logs *Biggest Influence on Career* as, simply, "alcohol".

England's county cricketers are a more pleasantly abstemious and singular lot, judging by Mr Sproat's fascinating new annual. A game of rugger lasts only 80 minutes, soccer ten minutes longer. With the new "rain-proof" regulations, our cricketers can be on the job or hanging about the pavilion for, often times, an eight-hour day. But, when it comes to *Hobbies,* they can run through the card – and *Who's Who* is dotted with original stuff and not only of the bridge, chess, backgammon, crossword puzzle variety.

Of the 250-odd first-class cricketers in England, many love gardening, real ale and stamp collecting – Derek Underwood listing all

---

## "The centre-forward, Frank Worthington, has no hesitation in answering the Bolton Wanderers' question, *Most Dangerous Opponent?*, with 'My ex-wife'."

---

*Spotlight On . . .*, in which a player fills in a questionnaire with an invitation to flesh out his life. The timeless, tired old formula, I fancy, found a new zip after Hunter Davies's appendix to his riveting, revealing book on Tottenham Hotspur a dozen years ago (*"I can cook a steak and am learning to do omelettes"* – Alan Mullery. *"I only read the sports pages, I have never read a book in my life"* – Martin Chivers).

Sitting, cross-legged, on the floor this morning, re-piling the dusty hoarder's scraps, I got to cross-reffing these self-projecting lists and life-styles of British footballers and rugby players – and comparing them with cricketers culled from Iain Sproat's essentially cheerful new edition of *The Cricketers' Who's Who.*

Mostly, the hardy old questions are met, dead bat, with the hardy old, expected, answers. *Favourite Meal* is always "steak"; *Most Respected Captain/Coach* is invariably and diplomatically the current one; *Most Cherished Memory,* unfailingly the first cap/goal/ try for either club or country; *Favourite Music* is heavily in favour of middle-road pop like Elton John and Neil Diamond. I'm not criticising the lads, by the way, just reporting what seems to make them tick, fly the moon or vomit, parrotwise.

Not many original asterisks wink out of the humdrum lists. In the Chelsea FC programme, the radical Scottish left-winger, Pat Nevin,

the 20 (Mike Slemen, Andy Irvine, John Horton, Keith Robertson, Nick Stringer, Fran Cotton and Serge Blanco) drool over Barbra Streisand. John Cleese and *Fawlty Towers* are runaway favourites for all sporty TV viewers, with *MASH* a distant runner-up – though both Ollie Campbell and Andy Irvine apparently rush home faithfully for Nigel Starmer-Smith's *Rugby Special.*

*Person you'd Most Like to Meet?* has seven rugby players queuing up to shake Muhammad Ali's hand, but the remainder make some odd dates – with Steve Smith again unable to leave Bo Derek alone. Fran Cotton goes a bundle on Margaret Trudeau; both John Carleton and Bruce Hay are, for some reason, anxious to have words with Lord Gormley, of all people; Terry Holmes would like to meet the Pope; Jean-Pierre Rives plumps for "God, but not quite yet"; Colin Smart would be delighted to make the acquaintance of "the fellow who stole my wallet in Fiji", Mark Ella of "just one unbiased Welsh supporter", and Maurice Colclough is intent on a meeting with the players' unanimous critical hobgoblin, John Reason of the *Sunday Telegraph* – "preferably on a very dark night".

What do you want to do when you grow up? Almost to a man, both soccer and rugby players reckon *Ambition in Life* is "happiness and success in business", though for the England rugger men, Carleton and Colclough, it is,

three, by the way. J. K. Lever adores "cooking", Keith Pont *"watching* skiing", David Gower "vintage port", and Les Taylor "riding to hounds with the Atherstone". Graham Johnson's hobbies are "current affairs and ecology", likewise Stephen Henderson, whose speciality is "the conservation of hedgehogs". Too many to mention, but starting with Younis Ahmed and Javed Miandad, a great many cricketers are seeped in "a library of cricket books". Jonathan Agnew plays the piano and tuba, Simon Hughes the piano and organ (and is passionate about travelling by train). Graham Cowdrey is "a world authority on Van Morrison, the Irish musician", Mike Gatting on "the works of Tolkien", and the musical tastes of his county colleague, Graham Barlow, "range from Beethoven and, especially, Sibelius to Yes on the heavier side".

Geoff Boycott adores TV's *Rockford Files,* classical ballet, and reading wildlife magazines; Roland Butcher is "a devout member of the Anglican church"; Imran Khan also says his prayers every night, and wears "a verse from the Koran in gold around my neck". The one and only Vivian Richards also prays just before he sleeps: "To the delight of my parents I remain a religious person . . . and, yes, occasionally I pray for success on the field." Phil Edmonds lists his hobby as, simply, "reading the *Financial Times* at breakfast". He and Viv should go into partnership one day.

## The Manners of a Dancing-Master

THERE ONCE TRIPPED A TARANTULA WHOSE TERPSICHOREAN TALENT WAS TRULY TERRIFIC.

I don't care if you do fill Mr Astaire with fear and vexation, my good arthropod, this is a royal party and your persona is definitely non grata.

Ah, well, as I always told Robert Bruce...

...Try, try again!

Hold on — oh, to hell with it — one spider.

May I bite in?

No! You may **cut** in.

This is a tarantella, named after me.

Have compassion! Some of us are equipped with only two legs.

LITTLE DID THE HOOFER SUSPECT THAT HE HAD PARTNERED NONE OTHER THAN THE BRIDE OF THE HEIR APPARENT!

Now, darling, you mustn't be jealous! **You** are going to be king, but **he** will only ever be the most attractive, exciting, marvellous—

Oh, that's all right then.

But it **isn't** all right, is it, mum? An arachnid of no particular lineage, prancing about with one's good lady spouse?

I can give his descendants a bit of lineage, but not him.

Bah! Let him suffer. Give him a lousy knighthood.

THE HONOURS-LIST CANDIDATE WAS SUMMONED TO THE DUBBING ROOM.

What is your Christian name? I am a heathen, but knock knock.

Who's there?

Spider.

Spider who?

Spider Webb.

Very well, Mr Webb, if you will just—

Gotcha, ma'am! Spider is my surname.

Knock knock.

Who's there?

Spider.

Spider who?

Spider your insolence, I am going to knight you.

Drop to one knee — any knee, as long as it's yours.

Arise Sir Spider Spider, now back the hell out of here and refrain from prancing with my daughter-in-law.

Hurrah! Benighted at last.

Make that at **long** last.

I said **back** out, you slob.

Dance with me — I want my legs about you — the eggs about you will carry me through... ♪

Bring on Ginger.

BUT ALAS! SPIDERS ARE DEEPLY CANNIBALISTIC. WHEN UNUSUALLY HUNGRY OR SUSPICIOUS, THE FEMALE EATS THE MALE.

And some have black-widowhood thrust upon them.

Caught in my own web, how humiliating.

MORAL: Let Joy be unconfined, but no one else.

# Silly Old Daddy Goes House-hunting

"GRACIOUS, it's snowing!" cried Mother, pulling open the curtains.

"And it's only November!"

"Look on it as a practice run for the nuclear winter," said Daddy, and snuggled down under the bedclothes.

"Hurray!" shouted Nicholas, running into the room and across to the window, catching his father a sharp one across the top of the head with the butt of his A-Team UZ1 de-luxe submachine gun. "We can build a snowman!"

"Yes!" shouted his younger brother William, jumping on to the bed and driving his knee hard into his father's kidneys. "And we can use Daddy's watch for his mouth like we did last time!"

Mother smiled. She loved to see the boys so happy and excited.

"You *will* drive carefully, won't you, darling?" she said to Daddy as she did up her dressing-gown. "NICHOLAS, WILL YOU GET OFF WILLIAM'S HEAD IMMEDIATELY!"

Nicholas pricked up his ears.

"Where's Daddy going, Mummy?" he asked. "Is it a secret?"

"Oh no – it's no secret," said his mother. "Daddy's going off to the Cotswolds to look at houses."

"DADDY!" shouted Nicholas. "Are we going to move?"

Mother laughed. "Not for us, darling. For *Punch*."

"And Judy?" said William.

"I expect so," said Mother.

"And the crocodile?" said Nicholas.

"Yes, yes," said Mother.

"And the sausages?" said William.

"Go away!" shouted Daddy from under the bedclothes.

Nicholas emptied a couple of dozen rounds into his father's chest.

"I can't remember now why you're going to the Cotswolds," said Mother.

Daddy explained, yet again, that this was for the Christmas number, and how there was this picture on the cover of one of his old *Daily Mail* Annuals showing a snowy Victorian street scene with some children peering into a brightly-lit toyshop window, and how it looked just like Stow-on-the-Wold and that for as long as he could remember he had associated Christmas with the Cotswolds.

"Silly old Daddy!" shouted Nicholas and ran from the room, firing from the hip.

Although Daddy hadn't said so, he had often thought about moving to a country house, with a large garden and a paddock where the children could keep their ponies – preferably on the outskirts of a village, so they could run to the shops and back without fear of being molested – and generally be brought up in beautiful and healthy surroundings. The Cotswolds had always seemed to him the nicest place to live.

"There's good hunting with the Heythrop," he told himself, as he sped down the M40, "and plenty of good shooting." (He didn't actually do either, but he was keen to take up a hobby before it was too late.) "The children couldn't hope to mix with a nicer class of people, and of course it is only an hour and a half to Paddington!"

He also had a special fondness for oolitic limestone and wondered if his friend Peter Brit-

ton might know of a nice, unmodernised manor house or rectory in somewhere like Lower Swell, or Upper Slaughter, or Moreton-in-Marsh, which he could buy cheaply and do up. After all, Jackson-Stops and Staff are very well-known agents in the area.

It was snowing quite hard as he drove down the hill into Burford and parked outside the Priory Tea Rooms. He walked up and down the main street, looking at the home-made cakes and preserves in Huffkins's window and peering into the many lovely antique shops. He was sorry they didn't have a single copy of any of his books in the Red Lion Bookshop – not even under "Light Reading" – but even so, he felt very much at home – almost as though he had lived there for years. He was pleased to see so many distinguished-looking men in Barbours and green wellies with shopping-baskets and golden labradors, and ladies in woolly hats and sheepskin coats getting out of Rover 3000s, and, while sitting in The Lamb with Peter, eating steak pie and toasting his feet in front of a roaring log-fire, he had the feeling he was dreaming and had been carried back thirty years in time.

He pointed towards a grey-haired lady who was eating a salad on the other side of the room underneath a stuffed fish.

"She could easily be Miss Marple," said Daddy under his breath.

"I suppose so," said Peter, sipping his beer. "But then of course the Cotswolds *are* one of the last bastions of Empire!"

Daddy was feeling rather cheerful when they walked out of the warm pub into the wintry air. He was glad he had brought his scarf and his thick overcoat. Luckily, Peter's Volvo Estate had a very good heater, and soon they were driv-

*"Do you mind! That one's mine!"*

ing through the hilly countryside feeling as warm as toast!

Daddy loved the pretty little villages, with their smart beige cottages, their neatly-kept grass-verges and their gaily coloured burglar-alarms. His favourite was Stanway, all of which is owned by someone called Lord Neidpath, who lives in a huge house called Stanway House which has a lodge-gate designed by Inigo Jones. Daddy said he couldn't imagine how a man could find the time to do that and run a restaurant, too. Peter gave him a funny look but didn't say anything. He explained that, like Great Barrington, it was one of the last of the old estate villages and that it would be quite impossible to buy anything, only rent.

However, it might be possible to buy some-thing in the pretty, neighbouring village of Stanton – if there was anything for sale, which there almost never is, even though no one appears to live there. In fact, there didn't seem to be anyone anywhere much, except in bigger places like Chipping Campden and Broadway and Stow-in-the-Wold.

"Did you go to Bourton-on-the-Water?" Mother asked him at tea-time.

Daddy had been stuck in a traffic jam on Western Avenue for forty minutes, so he wasn't feeling in his usual jolly mood, but everyone seemed so glad to see him again and the boys

were bursting with so much school news that he couldn't stay grumpy for long!

"Yes," he said.

"What was it like?" asked Mother.

"All right, I suppose, if you like coach-loads of trippers in anoraks milling around in tea-rooms with names like Small Talk, and shops selling Scottish woollens, and motor museums and model railway exhibitions," he said.

"Model railways! Great!" shouted Nicholas, spitting soggy fragments of peanut-butter sand-wich all over his father's recently cleaned sports jacket. "Golly. Are we going to live there?"

"Do you really want to live in a two-bedroom, £60,000 bungalow with a name like Copperbeech, surrounded by retired Lancas-trians?" Daddy asked him.

"Yes, please!" shouted Nicholas, jumping down from his chair and rushing round the room making train noises.

"It sounds an expensive part of the world," said Mother, putting away the wooden spoon.

"That's nothing," said Daddy above Nicho-las's cries. "Jackson-Stops recently sold a three bedroom semi-detached cottage in Broadwell for £82,000! Mind you, Peter did say it was par-ticularly nicely done up."

"It sounds to me as though the whole of the Cotswolds has been done up!" said Mother.

"I'm afraid it has," said Daddy. "A lot of the cottages are owned by weekenders, and most of the big village houses have been bought for huge sums of money by people who work in London and only come down at weekends. Peter sold one old rectory in a village near Burford to a young banker for over £350,000 and it didn't even have a paddock for a pony!"

"Daddy, Daddy," shouted Nicholas, kneeing his father lightly in the groin. "I want a pony!"

"I want a cow!" shouted William.

"I'm afraid the days when Cotswold houses were full of faded chintz and walking-sticks in the hall are almost gone," said Daddy. "These days they're all ruched blinds and Osborne and Little."

"How lovely!" said Mother, smiling. "I love Osborne and Little!"

"Of course," said Daddy, "if people like us do decide to move down there, they almost cer-tainly have to send their children off to boarding-school."

William forced Teddy's head into his milk so that most of it squeezed out on to the table.

"What a good idea!" said Mother cheerfully.

Daddy went to his brief case and got out a Jackson-Stops brochure.

"What do you think of this?" he said. "Broad Campden. Seventeenth-century. Half-thatched, mullioned windows, ingle-nook fireplace. Three reception rooms, six bedrooms, two bathrooms. Lovely garden with stream. Unin-terrupted views. Only six miles from main line station at Moreton-in-Marsh. Needs a little work. £170,000. It's made for Osborne and Little."

Mother looked at the picture and sighed.

"It's lovely," she said.

"Look, boys," said Daddy. "Isn't that lovely? How would you like to live there?"

Nicholas stared at his father as if he couldn't believe his eyes.

"DADDY!" he said. "Don't be silly. We've got a house already!"

"Silly Daddy," said William.

"Yes," said Mother. "Silly old Daddy!" ❧

*"It's either Matins or Evensong but who cares?"*

# CAPTION COMPETITION
## WINNERS

I DON'T TASTE ANY FALLOUT IN MINE.
A. Gordon
of Glasgow

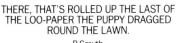

THERE, THAT'S ROLLED UP THE LAST OF THE LOO-PAPER THE PUPPY DRAGGED ROUND THE LAWN.
P. Smyth
of Crediton, Devon

**1861 caption** – *IGNORANCE NOT BLISS. LOOK AT THESE TWO FOREIGNERS IN AT MCBANNOCK'S IN REGENT STREET, WITH SCOTCH BREAD, AND BATH BUNS, AND CHEESECAKES, AND RASPBERRY THREE CORNERS: OH, AND LOTS OF OTHER JOLLY THINGS ON THE COUNTER, TO THINK OF THEIR CHOOSING CRUMPETS – COLD CRUMPETS! HA! HA!*

**1928 caption** – *EXASPERATED NEIGHBOUR. "CAN'T YOU DO SOMETHING TO STOP YOUR INFERNAL ROLLER SQUEAKING, SIR?" MODERNIST. "POSSIBLY I COULD, SIR, BUT I FIND ITS CHAOTIC DISSONANCE RATHER PLEASES ME."*

BUT DO BUCKS FIZZ ACTUALLY NEED A LATIN AMERICAN PERCUSSIONIST?
R. Bremner
of Carlisle

MR MENGELE, SIR, YOU'VE FORGOTTEN YOUR DEATH CERTIFICATE.
K. Timothy
of Tickhill, Yorks

**1862 caption**—FIRST HOUSEMAID. *"JANE, DID YOU EVER BRUSH YOUR HAIR WITH TWO BRUSHES?"* SECOND HOUSEMAID. *"NEVER TILL THE CAPTAIN COME AND LEFT HIS'N OUT. MY! ISN'T IT DELIGHTFUL?"*

**1927 caption**—HOUSEHOLDER (STARTING ON ANNUAL HOLIDAYS). *"WHY, ELLEN! WHAT –"* FAITHFUL MAID (JUST IN TIME). *"CAME – JUST AFTER – YOU STARTED – THINK – SOMETHIN' DO WITH – YOUR – INCOME-TAX, SIR!"*

# Death Warmed Up

"Wow!"

"Granny says he's an old friend of hers."

"I've been on the go all day!"

"He wasn't a bit like the characters he played in the movies – he was a really nice bloke."

"The only drawback is that we don't get holidays."

"A couple of famines and he thinks he's God Almighty."